UNDERSTANDING DEPRESSION

Is depression in women a psychological, social or medical problem?

Understanding Depression provides an in-depth critical examination of mainstream approaches to understanding depression and its treatment from a feminist and social constructionist perspective.

Janet Stoppard argues that current approaches provide only partial accounts. A greater understanding is possible when women's experiences and lived realities across the lifespan are considered in relation to the material and social conditions in which their everyday lives are embedded. The implications of this change in approach for modes of treatment are discussed and some solutions are suggested.

Understanding Depression will be useful to those with an interest in depression and gender, as well as mental health practitioners.

Janet M. Stoppard is a Professor in Psychology at the University of New Brunswick, Canada. She has worked as a clinical psychologist and has published widely on women, mental health and depression.

WOMEN AND PSYCHOLOGY
Series Editor: Jane Ussher
Department of Psychology, University College London

This series brings together current theory and research on women and psychology. Drawing on scholarship from a number of different areas of psychology, it bridges the gap between abstract research and the reality of women's lives by integrating theory and practice, research and policy.

Each book addresses a "cutting edge" issue of research, covering such topics as post-natal depression, eating disorders, theories and methodologies.

The series provides accessible and concise accounts of key issues in the study of women and psychology, and clearly demonstrates the centrality of psychology to debates within women's studies or feminism.

The Series Editor would be pleased to discuss proposals for new books in the series.

Other titles in this series:

THIN WOMAN
Helen Malson

THE MENSTRUAL CYCLE
Anne E. Walker

POST-NATAL DEPRESSION
Paula Nicolson

RE-THINKING ABORTION
Mary Boyle

WOMEN AND AGING
Linda R. Gannon

BEING MARRIED, DOING GENDER
Caroline Dryden

UNDERSTANDING DEPRESSION

Feminist Social Constructionist Approaches

Janet M. Stoppard

London and New York

First published 2000
by Routledge
11 New Fetter Lane, London EC4P 4EE

Simultaneously published in the USA and Canada
by Routledge
29 West 35th Street, New York, NY 10001

Routledge is an imprint of the Taylor & Francis Group

© 2000 Janet M. Stoppard

Typeset in Baskerville by
M Rules
Printed and bound in Great Britain by
Clays Ltd, St Ives plc

British Library Cataloguing in Publication Data
A catalogue record for this book is available from the British Library

Library of Congress Cataloguing in Publication Data
A catalogue record for this book has been requested

ISBN 0 415 16562-8 (hbk)
ISBN 0 415 16563-6 (pbk)

CONTENTS

ACKNOWLEDGEMENTS

While writing this book, I have benefited from the help and support of a number of people whose assistance I would like to acknowledge here. At various times, Sîan Lewis, Joan McFarland, Marianne Skarborn, Debbie van den Hoonaard, and Lucy Yardley read chapters, provided feedback on my ideas, or passed on useful reference sources. Deanna Gammell, Joan Hanley, Michelle Lafrance, and Yvette Scattolon, doctoral students in psychology at the University of New Brunswick, read several chapters in draft form and provided helpful feedback on their clarity and readability.

In the chapters which follow, I draw upon my research on depression in women and gratefully acknowledge the support provided by a grant awarded by the Social Sciences and Humanities Research Council of Canada (1997–2000) to carry out this research. My thanks go to the women who participated in these studies for their generosity in sharing their depressive experiences. I am also grateful to Dr. Richard Nicki, chair of my department at UNB, who responded to my need for extra time to write by adjusting my teaching load for the Fall term in 1998. I also thank the American Psychiatric Association for giving me permission to reprint the diagnostic criteria for Major Depressive Episode, originally published as p.327 in the *Diagnostic Statistical Manual of Mental Disorders, Fourth edition* (1994).

Many of the ideas developed in this book initially were formulated during a sabbatical year (1994–95) spent as a visiting academic affiliated with the Women's Health Research Unit at University College London. I am indebted to Jane Ussher for facilitating my sabbatical arrangements and for encouraging me to embark on this writing project.

Writing this book would have been immeasurably more difficult without the support of my longtime friend and scholarly companion Alan Miller, whose wise counsel and material help sustained me when energies flagged and spirits sank. As well, my sister Judy Long and her family have been a constant source of support, including me in their life and offering a "home away from home" in England, for which I am immensely grateful.

Part I

INTRODUCTION

1

DEPRESSION

A gendered problem

The aim of this book is to explore feminist social constructionist approaches to understanding depression in women. A central reason for focusing on depression is that, for several decades, both researchers and mental health professionals have repeatedly identified depression as being a problem that particularly afflicts women (McGrath *et al.* 1990, Nolen-Hoeksema 1987, Ussher 1991, Weissman and Klerman 1977, Weissman and Olfson 1995). In drawing this conclusion, experts in mental health and related fields point to evidence that depression is probably the most common mental health problem among women and that depressed individuals are predominantly female (Bebbington 1996, Nolen-Hoeksema 1990, Weissman *et al.* 1993). A proviso which should be attached to this statement is that the bulk of the research on depression in women has been conducted in western, industrialized regions of the world, particularly in the United States of America, Britain, Canada, and Australia.[1] This limitation is also reflected in the current work, which focuses primarily on depression in women in western countries. With this caveat in mind, to the extent that depression can be said to be a woman's "problem", it is one that falls within the domain of mental health professionals (e.g. counsellors, nurses, psychiatrists, psychologists, psychotherapists, social workers). This means that a substantial part of the work of many of those engaged in the mental health professions is likely to involve contact with depressed women. Thus, responding to the problem of depression in women comprises a major component of the work of many of those involved in the "helping professions" and accounts, in turn, for a sizeable proportion of resources allocated in society for responding to the mental health problems of individuals (e.g. treatment services of various kinds located in the community and within hospitals). These, then, are some reasons why the topic of depression in women would seem to me to be an important one to address.

What is the basis of the claim that depression is a problem which particularly afflicts women?

In reaching the conclusion that depression is a particular problem among women, several sources of evidence have been drawn upon by researchers and mental health professionals who work in this field. One type of evidence is based on statistics maintained by hospitals providing treatment services for people diagnosed with mental, disorders. These statistics provide a count of the number of people who receive such services (based on records of individuals admitted to and subsequently discharged from hospital), categorized according to diagnosis and other characteristics including gender. Findings from analyses of such statistics derived from mental health systems in various countries (e.g. Busfield 1996, McGrath *et al.* 1990, Stark-Adamec *et al.* 1986) converge on the conclusion that the most common diagnosis among women hospitalized for treatment of a mental health problem is some form of depressive disorder. Women are also disproportionately represented among those diagnosed with depression, usually outnumbering men to a large extent (Bebbington 1996, Culbertson 1997, Nolen-Hoeksema 1990).

Although statistics based on people's actual admissions to hospital inpatient services provide one kind of information suggesting that depression is a problem particularly experienced by women, interpretation of such information is not a straightforward matter. A serious limitation of hospital-based statistics is that someone has first to be admitted to a hospital in order to be counted and admission to a hospital usually requires referral by a physician. Perhaps depressed women, for some reason, are more likely than depressed men to be admitted to hospital. Another suggestion has been that women may be more likely than men to seek professional help for their mental health problems and are therefore more likely to be admitted to a hospital. Clearly, then, hospital statistics do not provide a direct index of the prevalence of mental health problems, such as depression, among those living in the community. Indeed, the argument has been made that hospital statistics may tell us more about the diagnostic practises of mental health professionals than about the problems experienced by women (Smith 1990). Nevertheless, such statistics do indicate that when women are hospitalized for treatment of a mental health problem, the problem is often diagnosed as depression.

Because of the limitations of statistics derived from hospital admissions as a basis for estimating how many people in a given population are likely to have various types of mental health problems, researchers have utilized other methods, which are considered more appropriate for this purpose. The methods most commonly employed are those developed within the field of epidemiology.[2] In this epidemiological approach, a large sample of individuals is selected randomly from a population of interest (e.g. people living in a particular city, region or "catchment area"). Individuals in this sample are then contacted by researchers and asked to complete a structured survey instrument designed to assess their mental health status. Two broad strategies have been followed in epidemiological research on depression.

In the first, referred to as a community mental health survey, people comprising the selected sample are asked to complete a structured questionnaire. An example of this kind of questionnaire, one used widely in the US, is the Center for Epidemiological Studies Depression Scale (Radloff 1977). People's answers on questionnaires like the CES-D yield information about their experiences of depressive symptoms. Findings with this research strategy indicate that fairly high levels of depressive symptomatology are reported by women in the general population and that overall levels for women are higher than those for men (Nolen-Hoeksema 1990). Moreover, this gendered pattern in the level of reported depressive symptoms is present among adolescents as well as in older age groups (Nolen-Hoeksema and Girgus 1994). Recent evidence from the US suggests that the gender gap in level of reported depressive symptoms may actually increase with age throughout adulthood (Mirowsky 1996).

Although people's answers on symptom questionnaires provide some information about their mental health status, findings from community surveys are considered to have limited utility for understanding depression diagnosed as a mental disorder. This concern arises because the questionnaires used are thought to measure nonspecific psychological distress rather than a specific disorder that would be diagnosed as depression. In response to this criticism, a second method has been employed in epidemiological research. In this approach, people in a selected sample are asked a series of structured questions by a trained interviewer. People's answers to these questions then provide the basis for determining whether their experiences meet the diagnostic criteria for various mental disorders, including depression. Thus, one aim of this research strategy is to determine the proportion of people in a given population whose symptoms fit the diagnostic criteria for depression.

Results derived from several large-scale epidemiological studies conducted within the last decade or so have consistently revealed that depression is one of the more common mental disorders diagnosed among women and also that women predominate among those who meet diagnostic criteria for this disorder (Weissman *et al.* 1993). When studies of this kind have been conducted in western countries, sex ratios (female:male) in the range 2 or 3 to 1 are typically reported (Culbertson 1997, Nolen-Hoeksema 1990, Weissman and Olfson 1995). There is now a consensus among epidemiological researchers that depression is one of the more prevalent mental health problems among women and also one that is more prevalent among women than men (Bebbington 1996).

A similarity of the research approaches described so far is that each depends on someone other than a woman herself to determine whether she is depressed. When hospital statistics are used, a diagnosis is provided by a mental health professional; in community mental health surveys using depressive symptom questionnaires, items are devised by researchers; and, in the case of epidemiological studies using structured diagnostic interviews, diagnosis is determined by researchers. A less frequently used approach has been to inquire from women themselves about the health and mental health problems which concern them. In a study conducted by Walters (1993) in which this strategy was employed with a large sample of women living in an urban area in central Canada, depression was one of the problems most frequently reported by women. About a third of the women in Walters' study reported that they had experienced depression. Among other problems reported by a sizeable proportion of women were stress, anxiety, tiredness and disturbed sleep. This study did not focus specifically on women's depressive experiences, so it is not known what the word "depression" meant to the women who reported it as a problem. Nevertheless, it would appear that the term "depression" is meaningful to women, one that many draw on when asked about the health problems which concern them.

A less direct source of information about the gender–depression link is provided by information on prescription of antidepressant drugs, the most common form of medical treatment for depression. Available evidence indicates that women are the major recipients of antidepressant medications (Ashton 1991, Hamilton and Jensvold 1995, Olfson and Klerman 1993). For instance, Baum *et al.* (1988) reported that about two-thirds of all prescriptions for antidepressant drugs in the US went to women, "a finding that appears to be in keeping with the sex ratio for depressive illness" (Hamilton and Jensvold 1995: 11). Issues concerning the safety of antidepressant drugs when used by adolescent and older women, particularly women of child-bearing age, have also been identified as important topics in need of research (Antonuccio *et al.* 1995, Weissman and Olfson 1995).

Thus, information from a range of sources, based on various ways of defining depression, seems to converge on the conclusion that depression indeed is a problem that particularly afflicts women. An important implication of this conclusion, one acknowledged by researchers and mental health professionals whose work focuses on depression, is that an adequate explanation of this problem must also involve an understanding of its gendered dimensions (Bebbington 1996, Coyne and Downey 1991). Any theory proposed to explain depression, the nature of the problem and why particular people experience this problem, must therefore be able to accommodate findings indicating that depression is a common problem among women and that women predominate among the depressed.

What does the term "depression" mean?

Before going any further, the meaning of the term depression needs to be considered, not least because how this term is defined has important implications for the way depression in women is explained and understood. This topic, explored in greater detail in Chapter 2, is one that has been, and continues to be, a source of considerable debate among researchers and professionals interested in depression. At this point, issues central to this debate will be outlined, in order to clarify the terminology used in the rest of this book.

The meaning of the word depression (and other words derived from it, such as depressive, depressed) depends to a large extent on the context in which it is used. A significant aspect of this context is who is using the word. One distinction is between the way the word depression is used by researchers and mental health professionals in their work, and how it is used by ordinary people in their everyday lives. When mental health professionals and researchers use the term depression, typically it is used in a technical sense, as a kind of shorthand to refer to a condition within an individual. This condition is further defined by a particular set of features which are reported by the individual or can be observed by others (such as a mental health professional or a relative of the individual). Thus, the term depression refers to a condition characterizing an individual that encompasses a set of experiences which include "symptoms" such as the following: feelings of sadness, dejection, hopelessness or despair, coupled with extremely pessimistic thoughts about one's self, situation and future prospects; lack of interest or pleasure in activities usually engaged in, along with social withdrawal; various bodily complaints including aches and pains, difficulty sleeping, fatigue, loss of appetite (or sometimes overeating); and in some cases suicidal thoughts or actions. Some of these features might be reported by a depressed individual herself whereas others may be inferred by a mental health professional based on observing, for instance, that a woman has a sad facial expression, slumped body posture, or lethargic demeanor.

A complicating factor in understanding the meaning of the term depression is that when this word is used by professionals and researchers, it also carries with it certain implications about how the condition referred to is best explained or understood. Thus, implicit in much use of the word depression is the assumption that the features (experiences, thoughts, feelings, behavior) subsumed under this label are manifestations of an underlying "illness" or "disorder", a form of "psychopathology". Because the features of depression tend to have some coherence, typically occurring in the same person at the same time, they are presumed to have the same source, some kind of disorder or dysfunction within the individual. In medically-oriented theoretical approaches, the origins of this disorder are generally located within the biochemistry of the brain. Although researchers and professionals who work from a non-medical perspective (e.g. psychologists, social workers, counsellors) may not attribute depressive symptoms to a biological disorder, the cause of such symptoms is still likely to be attributed to something called depression, a condition that lies within the individual.

Thus, depression has been considered a form of mental disorder or a mental illness, terms having similar meanings within the technical vocabulary of researchers and mental health professionals. As a mental disorder or illness, depression is diagnosed when a recognizable constellation of symptoms is present and the symptoms are reported by the person experiencing them to have been present for an extended period of time (usually at least two weeks). The symptoms used to diagnose depression are those listed already as the particular features that individuals report experiencing or things that others may observe about them. An added implication when the word depression is used in this diagnostic sense is that the disorder is presumed to be either present or absent. That is, a person either does or does not have the disorder of depression. From this diagnostic perspective, to say that a person's problem is depression is analogous to the situation when a person is diagnosed with a medical disorder such as diabetes or cancer. The person may have the disorder to a mild or more severe degree, but it is still present. When the word depression is used as a diagnostic label, it refers to a type or category of disorder, which also may be present in mild to more severe forms.

One area of debate concerns the particular features of a person's experiences that should be specified as symptoms of the disorder of depression. At the present time, among both mental health professionals and researchers, particularly in North America, the symptoms considered diagnostic for depression are those listed in the volume published by the American Psychiatric Association (APA), entitled the *Diagnostic and Statistical Manual of Mental Disorders* (DSM) (APA 1994).[3] Whether a person has a depressive disorder usually would be determined by a mental health professional, most often a psychiatrist (a medical doctor who specializes in psychiatric medicine), based on a series of structured questions asked in a clinical interview.

This categorical meaning of the word depression can be contrasted with another way in which this term is used by mental health professionals and researchers. Depression has also been conceptualized as a dimension or continuum. In this second usage, a person is considered to be more or less depressed. In this case, relatively greater emphasis is placed on a person's subjective experiences, particularly depressed mood or feelings of sadness, although attention is given to other depressive symptoms as well. When use of the word depression refers to a continuum, it is usually based on the experiences a person reports on a structured questionnaire or checklist devised specifically for this purpose by researchers who study depression. Such questionnaires are also widely used by mental health professionals. A well-known example of this kind of questionnaire is the Beck Depression Inventory (BDI) (Beck and Steer 1987). On such questionnaires, the more depressive symptoms a person indicates she is experiencing and the more severely each symptom is experienced, the higher the overall score and the more depressed she is said to be.

An issue that has been the focus of considerable debate in the academic and professional literature on depression is the relationship between depression defined as a category of mental disorder and depression defined as a continuum. Are these two ways of defining depression addressing the same phenomenon? Can a cut-off point be identified using the continuum approach, so that scores above that point indicate that a person would be diagnosed with a depressive disorder? Currently, there is some consensus among experts who specialize in depression (at least in North America) that depressive disorder is most appropriately defined by the diagnostic criteria listed in the DSM and the self-report questionnaires are measuring something different and should not be used to diagnose depression (Coyne 1994). Instead, questionnaires like the BDI, are generally considered to provide an assessment of something called "dysphoria". The term "dysphoria" (which might be thought of as the opposite of euphoria) refers to a subjective experience characterized by a sense of psychological distress or discomfort. Although a predominant character of psychological distress may be depressed mood, it is believed by those who work in the depression field that dysphoria is not a unique feature of depression, but overlaps with other negative mood states, like anxiety, and also with feelings associated with demoralization (Link and Dohrenwend 1980). One implication of this distinction between psychological distress characterized by dysphoria, on the one hand, and depressive disorder, on the other, is that the former may be considered a less serious mental health problem than the latter.

Such debates among mental health professionals and researchers are difficult, however, to resolve. Unlike other health conditions thought to originate within a biological disorder within the body, there is no procedure (analogous to a blood test or brain scan) independent of subjective (or "clinical") judgments made by clinicians to determine whether or not someone should be diagnosed with depression (Ross and Pam 1995) . Thus, knowledge about depression rests ultimately on what people tell mental health professionals or researchers about how they are feeling and acting, and on how they are observed to act by others. Recognition of the critical role that clinical judgment plays in the diagnostic process leads into another set of issues regarding the process of deciding which experiences are important in determining whether a person is depressed. These issues, discussed in more detail in Chapter 2, have particular implications for understanding depression in women. Specifically, how are women's accounts of their experiences to be interpreted? How are the relevance and meaning of women's experiences determined in relation to the diagnostic process?

As used by both mental health professionals and researchers, the term depression, in either its category or continuum sense, is grounded in the medical notion of the patient as someone who is lacking in expertise on the meaning of her own symptoms. The patient is merely the reporter of her own experiences and complaints and only a professionally-trained person can properly understand their significance for diagnosis and treatment. At the same time, the word depression is part of the vocabulary of ordinary women as a way of describing their experiences. Thus, a woman may say she "feels depressed" and others will have some understanding of what she means by this. The way the word depression is used by women in their everyday lives, what it means to them, has not been studied a great deal by researchers, although surveys with women indicate that many do identify depression as a problem they experience (Walters 1993). The issue of how women's understanding of their experiences is related to the meaning the term depression has for them will be explored in more detail in Chapter 2. At this point, the particular significance of this issue lies in noting that a woman's account of her experiences forms the basis of judgments made by mental health professionals and researchers about whether she is depressed.

A terminological note

The word "depression" appears to have a variety of meanings, both technical-professional and everyday. This state of affairs creates a problem for someone writing (and reading what is written) about depression, because of the varied ways in which the term has been used and interpreted. The approach I have decided to adopt is as follows. When I am discussing depression defined as a disorder by mental health professionals and researchers, the term *depressive disorder* will be used. When the meaning of the term depression is anchored in a person's responses on a questionnaire designed to assess experiences considered by clinical researchers to be symptoms of depression (or dysphoria), I shall employ the term *depressive symptoms*. When discussing the way women describe experiences that they call depression, as subjectively experienced in the context of their everyday lives, the term *depressive experiences* will be used. This leaves the word *depression* itself, which I shall use in a nonspecific way to refer to the general topic of depression. This more generic use of the term is not intended to presuppose or imply any particular way of understanding or explaining phenomena that mental health professionals, researchers or ordinary women might use the word depression to denote. With this attempt to offer a reasonably systematic set of terms for referring to the different meanings associated with the word depression, I turn next to consider issues that arise in explaining why depression is a problem that particularly afflicts women.

How has depression among women been explained?

How depression in women has been explained, along with exploration of the various theoretical approaches proposed to account for the predominance of women among the depressed, is the main topic of Part II in this book. The strategy followed in much of the research in this area has involved applying existing theories of depression to the problem of explaining why women predominate among the depressed. Such theories have focused primarily upon the etiological question of explaining what causes depression. The type of question such theories attempt to answer is "Why do particular individuals become depressed at a certain point in their lives?" Various mechanisms and processes, proposed as causal factors in depression, are then assumed to apply to all people, regardless of gender. If depression is particularly common among women, this is likely to be because these causal factors are more characteristic of women, or women are especially affected by them, or they arise more frequently in women's lives.

Theories proposed to explain depression have covered a wide spectrum, and include biological, psychological and social formulations. Theoretical approaches tend to emphasize one set of presumed causal influences over others, although explanations based on a single factor (whether social, psychological or biological) have now generally been discarded in favor of more complex multifactorial approaches (McGrath *et al.* 1990). This shift to a multifactorial approach reflects the assumption, held by most of those working in this field, that ultimately depression is likely to be explained as arising from some combination of individual biological make-up (genes, biochemistry), psychological characteristics (personality traits), and social conditions (circumstances of everyday life). The promise of this more multifactorial perspective continues to be explored, with various approaches to explaining depression emerging within different disciplinary fields. In psychology, for instance, psychosocial models have developed in recent years as one of the predominant approaches. At the same time, another set of psychological approaches draws on knowledge about the "psychology of women" to explain depression in women. From a more sociological perspective, various social models have been proposed to account for depression in women. Biological explanations for women's depression have also been proposed, particularly within psychiatric medicine. These theoretical approaches, which are discussed in more detail in Part II, are summarized briefly here.

Psychosocial models of depression

The form of psychosocial model that has received most attention recently is one referred to as "diathesis–stress". According to the diathesis–stress approach, if an individual with certain psychological characteristics (traits, attitudes), conceptualized as the "diathesis", experiences a stressful life event (the "stress" component) which in some way matches or is congruent with the psychological diathesis, then that individual is especially likely to become depressed. Such models could account for women's increased susceptibility to depression, if women are more likely than men to possess the psychological characteristics (diatheses) hypothesized to increase an individual's vulnerability to depression. Parallels have been drawn between the psychological characteristics posited as vulnerability factors for depression and personality qualities associated with traditional notions of "femininity". Thus, female socialization has been identified as a possible source of women's increased susceptibility to depression (Champion and Power 1995, McGrath *et al.* 1990, Nolen-Hoeksema 1990).

The social ("stress") component of these psychosocial models has its origins in formulations linking onset of depression to exposure to events with unfavorable or undesirable consequences for an individual, particularly events involving loss or failure. Such events, because of their negative implications for an individual's adaptation, have been termed "stressful life events". Attempts to account for depression in terms of exposure to stressful life events alone generally have been unsuccessful, however. Many people exposed to stressful events do not become depressed and some people who become depressed do not appear to have been exposed to events defined as stressful. The inability of stressful events, on their own, to predict whether someone becomes depressed has stimulated the development of diathesis–stress models. How depression in women is explained by this psychosocial approach is the topic of Chapter 3.

Woman-centered approaches to explaining depression

While explanations for depression in women have been derived from diathesis–stress models, such formulations have not focused primarily on the goal of understanding depression in women. The explanations proposed are not intended to be specific to women and the hypothesized causal factors are presumed to have relevance for explaining depression in all people, regardless of gender. Thus, in a fundamental sense, psychosocial theories of depression are gender-blind. A different theoretical strategy is one that focuses on women, with the aim of identifying causes of depression that are specific or unique to women.

Approaches of this kind have drawn on two main sources of information. One consists of evidence for personality differences between women and men, particularly with respect to psychological aspects of "femininity" and "masculinity". Having feminine personality traits is thought to increase susceptibility to depression in women. The other source of information is derived from research based in theories of women's psychological development which are grounded in explorations of women's lived experiences (Gilligan 1982, Jordan *et al.* 1991, Miller 1986).

From the more women-centered orientation of this theoretical perspective, the significance of relationships with others to women's development of a sense of self is emphasized. According to such formulations, relationality or connectedness with others is central to a woman's identity. Within these theoretical approaches, a positive emphasis is placed on such qualities as nurturance and caring for others, which stereotypically are associated with women and femininity. These qualities also tend to be devalued in a cultural climate dominated by the masculine values of competitive striving and self-assertion. At the same time, the centrality to women's psychological development of a "self-in-relation" also has been identified as a potential source of depression in women (Jack 1991). When opportunities for relational intimacy are blocked or thwarted, especially in a core relationship (such as marriage), women may experience a "loss of self", which may itself be part of depression. The process of loss or "silencing" of the self (ibid.) is exacerbated when a woman believes that her own needs should take second place to those of her relational partner in order to maintain harmony in the relationship (Jack and Dill 1992). The contributions to explaining depression in women of theoretical approaches that emphasize women's psychology are explored further in Chapter 4.

Social models of depression

Although the contribution of social influences to explaining why women become depressed is not entirely neglected in woman-centered approaches, such formulations have not focused systematically on the social environment. In contrast, social models directly address those features of the social environment that may render some individuals more susceptible to depression. Advocates of social models have pointed to the etiological importance in depression of social structural factors (such as poverty, living conditions, employment status), interpersonal relationships (for "social support"), and other sources of adversity arising within the fabric of people's everyday lives. Two broad streams can be discerned in attempts to develop social models of depression. The first, illustrated by the work of Brown and Harris (1978), has focused on women, with an expectation that the causal processes identified will have general applicability. The causal model developed by Brown and Harris overlaps to some extent with psychosocial models, in the emphasis placed on the role of stressful life events in explaining depression. Brown and Harris, however, have attempted to overcome the perceived limitations of the life stress approach by considering the meaning of events in the context of people's lives. By addressing the meaning of events, not merely their occurrence, the social model developed by Brown and Harris offers one avenue for explaining depression in women.

The second social approach has developed from feminist analyses of sources of disadvantage in women's lives (McGrath *et al.* 1990). These efforts have drawn attention to social factors that are specific to women's lives and which may explain the preponderance of women among the depressed. Among these gender-specific social influences are structural factors (e.g. women's "double day" of work inside and outside the home, gender inequities in paid employment), relationships with men (e.g. emotional and physical abuse) and other sources of adversity in women's lives (e.g. childhood sexual abuse, poverty associated with being a single parent). The contributions of social approaches to understanding depression in women and why women predominate among the depressed are evaluated in Chapter 5.

Biological approaches to explaining depression in women

In biological approaches to explaining depression in women, particularly those developed within a biomedical framework, emphasis is placed on genetics and biochemistry as causal factors (Paykel 1991). Biological formulations of women's vulnerability to depression have also focused on the hormonal status of women (Bebbington 1996, Gallant and Derry 1995). Evidence that biochemical processes may be associated with experiences defined as depressive symptoms is not the same, however, as concluding that depression is *caused* by biochemistry. Purely biological explanations for depression have been criticized on a number of grounds, not least their inability to explain women's apparent vulnerability to depression (Bebbington 1996, Weissman and Klerman 1987). There is also a consensus among researchers that genetic factors alone cannot explain the greater suscepti- bility to depression among women than men, implying that nongenetic factors must be taken into account in any explanations proposed (Bebbington 1996, Weissman and Olfson 1995). Moreover, findings on the role of the menstrual cycle, pregnancy, childbirth and menopause in depression in women, which I review in Chapter 6, have been less than conclusive.

Although evidence in support of purely biological explanations for depression in women has not been forthcoming, this does not remove the female body from fur- ther consideration. Indeed, none of the approaches to explaining depression in women outlined so far have addressed female embodiment, except as a biological entity. Part of the reason for this neglect may lie in a desire among nonmedical researchers and professionals to highlight the importance of social and psycholog- ical influences in explaining depression. Another reason may be more theoretical, rooted in traditions of thought that shape the work of both researchers and pro- fessionals. This concerns the difficulty of integrating knowledge about the body with knowledge about subjective, psychological experiences and social context. Nevertheless, the body is clearly implicated in depression, because however depression is defined, it is an embodied experience, one that is both physical and psychological.

Biological theories of depression have often been characterized as "dualist" and "reductionist" because explanatory priority is assigned to biological influences, while nonbiological influences (psychological and social) are viewed as ancillary to biochemical mechanisms, which are considered more fundamental. But theories which focus on psychological and social influences to the neglect of physical embodiment are equally limited in their explanatory potential. Attempts to understand depression in women from a perspective that can encompass the body, as well as nonbiological influences, present certain theoretical problems, however, which I explore further in Chapter 6. Recognition of the need for nondualist approaches to understanding depression also has occurred in response to critical analyses revealing theoretical shortcomings of the other models (psychosocial, women's psychological specificity, social) discussed already. The limitations of these models also are apparent in the inconsistent empirical findings yielded by research testing the causal hypotheses posited in each approach. These limitations will be discussed in more detail in the relevant chapters of Part II. In order to set the stage for this later discussion, a digression into the topics of epistemology and research methodology is necessary for the purpose of clarifying key issues which arise in evaluating the various approaches proposed for explaining depression in women.

Doing research on depression in women: epistemological and methodological issues

Research on depression has been conducted by investigators from various disciplinary backgrounds. For instance, clinical psychologists have carried out research to test hypotheses derived from psychosocial models. Social models have been explored by researchers whose disciplinary affiliation is with sociology or social psychology. Medically-trained investigators have carried out research on biological models. Despite the wide range of disciplinary fields represented among researchers whose work has focused on depression, a certain homogeneity is apparent in the research methodologies employed. The methodological commonalities shared by these research approaches are captured by the term "the scientific method" (also sometimes labelled "mainstream").

Key features defining the scientific method have been articulated in accounts of research methodology in the human and social sciences (cf. Harding 1986, Woolgar 1988). A paramount requirement is "objectivity", something which in part is accomplished by use of "objective" forms of measurement, so as to rule out the influence of the researcher on any results obtained. Thus, in mainstream approaches to research on depression, an issue that must be addressed before any information, or "data", can be collected is how depression will be defined and measured. In the vast majority of studies, this issue has been resolved by defining and measuring depression in terms of either depressive disorder or depressive symptoms (these terms were defined in the section on terminological issues earlier in the chapter). Use of standard ways of defining and measuring depression, which have wide agreement among researchers, is recognized as a prerequisite for attaining objectivity. One consequence of this methodological stance, however, is that the phenomenon being studied, in this case depression, is assumed to be adequately represented by the way it is measured. In a sense, the measure itself becomes the phenomenon. A further consequence is that aspects of experience which cannot easily be measured in a quantitative, numerical form, such as what it feels like subjectively to be depressed, tend to be ignored. Also underpinning objectivity is the assumption that the object of study (depression) is something that exists, i.e. has a reality in the world, separate from the researcher. Therefore, in following this methodological strategy, research on depression is viewed as being akin to research on other phenomena in the world, such as those studied by physical and natural scientists.

A further characteristic, integral to this form of scientific method, is that the ultimate goal of all research is to establish causal relationships. The main criterion for claiming to understand a phenomenon is that it can be predicted and, therefore, potentially is capable of being controlled. Causal relationships are established by changing one variable and observing the effect on another. The overarching goal of scientific research employing these mainstream methods is to identify causal relationships which have general applicability. When the scientific method is employed within research on depression, this usually translates into a requirement for large samples of "subjects", as a basis for generalizing the causal relationships discovered.

The approach to research referred to as the scientific method or mainstream is grounded in an epistemology (or philosophy of knowledge) that has been termed "positivist" (Banister et al. 1994, Harding 1986). As such, it reflects one perspective on what should be studied, how research should proceed, and what constitutes "knowledge", although often depicted as the only valid route to "truth" about the nature of things (Slife and Williams 1997). This positivist version of the scientific method has been the subject of extensive critiques by researchers and scholars in a variety of fields, including those in which research on depression is conducted. Feminist researchers, in particular, have been critical of research employing the positivist scientific method because the knowledge it produces is structured in ways that frequently distort or neglect aspects of experience central to women's lives (Harding 1986, Hollway 1989, Nicolson 1995).

According to feminist critiques of this positivist form of scientific method, women's experiences become invisible as a consequence of researchers' insistence on objectivity and the associated claim that the knowledge produced is therefore "value-free". Feminists and others have taken issue with this position, arguing that all knowledge incorporates and reflects the values and implicit assumptions of researchers (Harding 1995, Kimball 1995, Ussher 1992). The claim that research can ever yield "objective facts" is viewed by these critics as a myth. In contrast, feminist analyses of the knowledge generated by application of the positivist scientific method have characterized it as reflecting a conception of the world from the standpoint of male experience, a viewpoint that poorly represents women's lives (Harding 1986, Smith 1987). A rather different philosophy of knowledge, termed "social constructionist", is one that acknowledges the role of human values and particularly sociocultural influences in prestructuring and shaping all knowledge (Burr 1995, Hollway 1989, Kimball 1995).

The philosophical presupposition that all knowledge is socially constructed underpins the recognition among researchers who take a feminist and/or social constructionist perspective in their work that "reflexivity" is an important component of all such endeavors. The word reflexivity refers to an "awareness of what one is doing and why" (Ristock and Pennell 1996: 5) and, in the context of research, involves the explication and critical analysis of assumptions made at all stages of the process, from problem formulation to interpretation and dissemination of findings (Banister *et al.* 1994). Also, because the researcher is part of the research process, the researcher's own values and preconceptions, which inevitably color and form the background to decisions made in conducting research, need to be acknowledged in a reflexive way (Wilkinson 1988). From a feminist perspective, therefore, an important implication of this social constructionist epistemology is that knowledge is likely to be more valid, and useful for women, if it is generated from the standpoint of women.[4]

As feminists have pointed out, much social policy based on findings derived from application of the positivist version of the scientific method have had less than beneficial consequences for women's well-being. For example, when depression is defined as depressive disorder, a form of mental illness best treated by the medically-informed methods of hospitalization and antidepressant drugs, the result is that women's problems are medicalized and pathologized (Oakley 1986, Ussher 1991). And women's bodies are more likely to be exposed to psychotropic drugs, many effects of which are either unknown or relegated to the category of "side-effects" (Antonuccio *et al.* 1995, McGrath *et al.* 1990).

In raising these concerns about approaches to research employing mainstream, positivist methods, I am not suggesting that all knowledge about women and depression generated in this way should be discounted or rejected. Instead, my intention is to foster a critical, reflexive stance with respect to such knowledge, how it should be interpreted, and its implications for action. An alternative position, one compatible with a social constructionist epistemology, is to view all knowledge claims as being partial and contingent, rather than having the status of timeless truths that can be detached from the particular social context in which they are produced. Knowledge claims are always partial and contingent, because they are produced from a particular perspective and, therefore, considerations which might be judged as significant from a different vantage point or standpoint tend to be perceived as less important and are left out. In the next section, I consider some of the things which are left out when research on depression is conducted within the framework of the positivist version of the scientific method and how the knowledge produced by such research provides a partial and therefore limited understanding of depression in women.

What is left out when research on depression is conducted according to the positivist scientific method?

When research on depression is carried out according to the positivist scientific method, the resulting knowledge is shaped by the manner in which key aspects of both the topic being investigated and those who participate in a study are conceptualized and operationalized. The requirement that "variables" are defined operationally so as to permit their observation and measurement serves to produce particular ways of explaining depression. Central to an understanding of depression in women are gender, subjective experience or "subjectivity", and embodiment. When research is conducted according to the tenets of the positivist scientific method, these topics are defined and operationalized in ways that leave out important aspects of women's lived experience.

Gender

Although women participate, as gendered "subjects", in research on depression, the way gender is conceptualized precludes investigation of dimensions considered important from a feminist perspective. In research designed in accord with requirements of the scientific method, gender is treated primarily as a characteristic of the embodied individual. The boundaries of the individual are taken, in an unquestioned, common sense way, as the surface skin of the physical body and gender is defined almost exclusively in terms of a person's sex of assignment, as either female or male. When gender is treated for research purposes as an individual's "sex" and defined narrowly as a characteristic of the bounded individual, other components of gender are excluded from consideration.

Gender can also be conceptualized in terms of the division of labor in society, where women do most of the work involved in the home, caring for family members. A central aspect of this unpaid "reproductive" labor is caring for children. Not only do women bear children, but women bear most of the responsibility for childcare (Graham 1993, Lorber 1994). Although paid work (usually outside but sometimes inside the home) is now part of most women's lives, in western countries the majority of women who work for pay are employed in low-paid (and low-prestige) sales, service and clerical occupations (United Nations Development Program [UNDP] 1995). For instance, recent figures on paid employment among women in Britain indicate that while women now make up nearly 50 percent of the workforce, almost half of all female employees work in part-time jobs (Raston 1998) and the majority (81 percent) of women workers are employed in the service sector (Graham 1993). As Graham points out, when they have children, women in Britain are more likely to engage in part-time work, a type of employment that is associated with lower pay and lower occupational status.

The lives of women who combine marriage and motherhood with paid work have been depicted as involving a "double day" or "second shift" (Lorber 1994).

17

When gender is conceptualized only as a characteristic of the individual, the substantial ways in which the everyday experiences of women and men are likely to differ may be ignored altogether or, at best, are taken for granted. Even when an attempt is made to take the gendered division of labor into account, for example by including variables such as marital, parental and employment status, the effect is to oversimplify, by taking out of context, activities that consume the time and energy of many women on a daily basis.

Also unaddressed when gender is defined solely as an individual characteristic are symbolic aspects of gender within the language (or discursive) domain. As a part of cultural meaning systems, a central element of symbolic gender is the widely shared, but often implicit, set of beliefs about the nature of "femininity" and "masculinity" and their respective links with the individual component of gender (i.e. female, male). Symbolic aspects of gender not only infuse and permeate the experiences of women and men, they also pervade many areas of culture in western industrialized countries. For instance, the masculine–feminine duality maps on to other cultural dualisms, such as reason–emotion, aggressivity–passivity, competition–cooperation, science–art. In cultural contexts dominated by masculine values, the pole of each dualism associated with femininity is devalued, compared to the pole associated with masculinity. Cultural "discourses of femininity", moreover, portray the "good" woman as someone whose activities ideally are oriented around relationships and caring for others (especially family members) (Bordo 1993, Jack 1991, Ussher 1991).[5] Such discourses both dovetail with and support family and societal arrangements in which women perform most of the work of caring, and at the same time place the needs of others ahead of their own.

As a consequence of defining gender as an individual characteristic, while ignoring the gendered division of labor and symbolic aspects of gender, the social-cultural context of people's lives is rendered invisible. With regard to research on depression, this way of defining gender has the unfortunate effect of removing from consideration structural conditions that operate to maintain the gendered division of labor in society (e.g. availability of childcare services, parental leave policies, maternity benefits, pay and employment equity programs and so on). Also, by ignoring symbolic aspects of gender, the ways in which the lives and experiences of women are shaped and regulated by discourses of femininity remain unexamined, submerged in such individualizing notions as gender roles and personality.

Subjectivity[6]

An aspect of human existence that poses particular problems in application of positivist research methods is subjective experience. Subjective experiences are inherently unobservable and therefore present difficulties for objective forms of measurement. Within psychological research employing the positivist form of scientific method, a set of procedures has evolved to circumvent this problem. The strategy typically employed in psychological research on personality, and also in investigations of psychosocial models of depression, is to treat a person's verbal accounts as a form of self-observation, one in which the person observes and reports on her subjective experiences. Such self-reports form the basis for assessment of the psychological diatheses posited in psychosocial approaches to explaining depression (see earlier section in this chapter and Chapter 3 for discussion of psychosocial models).

The psychological diatheses proposed in psychosocial models have been formulated in terms of personality dimensions or traits. In order to assess a person's status on a personality dimension, the primary strategy has been for researchers to devise a series of statements which are considered to reflect the personality construct of interest. These statements, typically formatted as questionnaire items, are then presented to individuals who are asked to indicate on a numerical scale the degree to which each item reflects their subjective experiences. People's questionnaire responses then yield a summary score capable of analysis using statistical procedures.

The process of generating items for inclusion on a personality questionnaire draws on several sources of information, particularly the views of researchers with expertise in the area and past research findings bearing on the topic. While the content and wording of questionnaire items are selected by researchers, determination of the relevance and utility of items chosen to assess a specific personality construct relies on statistical procedures for item analysis and scale construction. Once developed, a questionnaire typically undergoes further refinement in order to establish its psychometric adequacy (reliability and validity) as a measurement scale. At this point, individuals' scores are interpreted directly as indicators of their standing on the personality construct of interest. As currently employed within research on depression, the subjective experiences assessed by personality questionnaires are most likely to be referred to as "cognitions". In this sense, personality is conceptualized in terms of individuals' habitual ways of thinking about and interpreting their experiences, their beliefs, attitudes and attributional styles (cf. Stoppard 1989).

Within mainstream research, the approach used to define and measure personality, while formally adhering to the requirements for "objective" measurement, has several consequences which serve to restrict possibilities for understanding individual subjectivity. First, once a questionnaire is created, individuals' experiences are constrained to fit the items it contains. Experiences lying outside the range of items included on a questionnaire essentially are deemed irrelevant and remain unexplored. Second, the nomothetic assumptions on which personality questionnaires are built bring with them the additional constraint that the meaning inherent in a particular item is interpreted and understood in the same way by all individuals.[7] Moreover, the meaning tapped by items is presumed to fit a pre-established conceptual scheme formulated by researchers. Third, when employed in constructing theoretical models, the terminology used to label personality dimensions is devised by researchers and inevitably incorporates implicit value judgments. For instance, terms used to refer to the psychological diatheses in psychosocial models of depression quite often have derogatory connotations. Some examples of such terms are "dysfunctional attitudes" (Beck *et al.* 1979), "dependent personality type" (Blatt *et al.* 1982), and "ruminative response style" (Nolen-Hoeksema 1987). Finally, and most critically from feminist and social constructionist perspectives, women's accounts of their subjective experiences are not treated as having validity in their own right. Instead, after being transformed into responses on standardized questionnaire items, women's reports of their experiences are reinterpreted by researchers as signifying their standing on various personality dimensions. The result is that women's accounts are treated as a resource for evaluating the validity of researchers' constructions, rather than having meaning in their own right.

Application of the positivist scientific method in research on subjective aspects of experience is accomplished by treating people's experiences as being separate and apart from the sociocultural context of their daily lives. At the same time, such experiences (in the form of responses on questionnaires) are interpreted by researchers according to their own implicit meaning systems, which are then treated for research purposes as objective accounts. Thus, much psychological research based on people's subjective experiences probably reveals more about the meaning systems of researchers than about how people make sense of their own experiences. The substitution of researcher-based meaning systems for those of participants in research studies designed to meet requirements of the scientific method also occurs with procedures used to assess depression. Routine use of standardized measures of depression (structured diagnostic interviews and symptom questionnaires) also relies on a process in which individuals' experiences are reinterpreted according to researchers' preconceived notions of what constitutes depression. The meaning of such experiences, as understood from the standpoint of the person reporting them, is discounted in favor of the (standardized) interpretations of researchers and mental health professionals.

Moreover, when a person's subjective experiences are reframed for research purposes as "cognitions", as phenomena that are both detached and different from the physical body, this way of doing research presupposes a separation between "body" and "mind". This body–mind form of dualism also is reflected in the disciplinary split between researchers in psychology and sociology, on the one hand, and those in medicine, on the other. A further consequence of this disciplinary divide is that psychosocial and social models of depression, as currently formulated, preclude any consideration of the physical body.

Female embodiment

In psychosocial, psychological specificity and social models of depression, female embodiment – a woman's physical body – is virtually ignored. At the same time, from a biomedical perspective, depression is explained in biological terms, the result of disordered brain biochemistry or hormonal influences within women's bodies. In contrast, when research on depression is conducted in fields outside biomedicine, female embodiment is hardly considered. To the extent that women's accounts of bodily experiences are acknowledged, they usually are subsumed under the heading of somatic symptoms and then set aside as more relevant to the domain of medicine.

In this way of thinking about female embodiment, the physical body has tended to be conceptualized as an entity which is both neutral and natural, governed only by biological mechanisms and so distinct from sociocultural processes. This view of the body poses certain difficulties for attempts to understand depression in terms of links between women's bodies and women's lives. At the same time, how-ever it is defined, depression is an embodied experience, one that is experienced subjectively and enacted physically by means of the material body.

Depression in women in context

One strategy for developing a way of thinking about depression in women as gen-dered subjects which allows consideration of female embodiment, along with subjectivity and social context, has been termed "material–discursive" (Ussher 1997a, Yardley 1997c). Theorizing about depression from a material–discursive perspective begins with the recognition that, like all human experiences, it is an integrated biopsychosocial phenomenon (Yardley 1996). Thus, depression involves experiences grounded in the materiality of the body which continually, and recip-rocally, feed back into people's experiences in the social context of their everyday lives. Developing a material–discursive understanding of depression also involves reconceptualizing in nondualist and nonreductionist ways the psychological and social influences which have been posited as causal factors in depression. In Chapter 6, the implications of material–discursive approaches for understanding depression in women are explored in more detail.

A material–discursive approach also is more compatible with methodological strategies for doing research which are informed by feminist and social construc-tionist epistemological perspectives (Stoppard 1997). Such research strategies offer possibilities for generating knowledge about depression in women that can encom-pass gender, subjectivity, and embodiment. The chapters in Part III provide examples of alternative ways of understanding depression in women that emerge when research begins from women's standpoint and is informed by a social con-structionist epistemological perspective. These examples, drawn from different phases or stages of women's lives, include depression in adolescent girls and their search for a viable identity (Chapter 7), links between marriage, motherhood and depression in women (Chapter 8), and depression in older women within a mate-rial and cultural context that depletes opportunities for self-affirmation (Chapter 9).

The book concludes, in Part IV, with an exploration of the implications for theory and action of the feminist social constructionist perspectives on depression in women developed in the earlier chapters. Many depressed women neither seek nor receive any form of professional help, so an important topic to be addressed in Chapter 10 is how women cope with depression in the context of their everyday lives. The aim here is to illustrate the range of strengths and resources drawn on by women, in contrast to some depictions of women's coping skills as "dysfunctional". Also considered are the options available to depressed women who seek help from mental health professionals. Discussed here are the advantages and drawbacks of forms of treatment provided by psychiatrists and medically-trained professionals (e.g. drugs, ECT) and those offered by psychologists and other nonmedical professionals (e.g. cognitive therapy, feminist therapy). Also considered are implications for action of feminist analyses linking the personal problem of depression in individual women to more political dimensions in the public sphere shaping the lives of women in general. Thus, from this feminist perspective, addressing the problems of depressed women now, as well as preventing depression among women in the future, requires collective forms of social-political action.

In the concluding chapter, key points from the preceding chapters are highlighted and an integrative feminist social constructionist perspective on depression in women is articulated. The main conclusion reached is that understanding and explaining depression in women means understanding women's lived experiences in the discursive and material contexts in which their daily lives are embedded.

Notes

1 In her overview of cross-cultural findings on gender and depression, Culbertson (1997) notes that, to date, research conducted in non-western, less-developed regions of the world has rarely considered gender. When gender has been addressed, however, rates of depression do not consistently reveal the predominance of women found in western countries.

2 Epidemiology, as a discipline, focuses on the study of disease occurrence in human populations and is concerned with the distribution and causes of disease.

3 In the DSM (APA 1994), the terms Major Depressive Episode and Major Depression are used to refer to depressive disorder, defined according to specified diagnostic criteria. In countries outside North America, the DSM has less influence on professional practise. For instance, the ICD (International Classification of Diseases) system is more likely to be used in the UK and Europe, where responsibility for diagnosing depression lies primarily with medical professionals. As Culbertson (1997) notes, efforts are underway by the World Health Organization to produce a diagnostic system integrating the ICD criteria for depression with those listed in the DSM.

4 It has become usual to identify three distinct approaches to feminist research – feminist empiricism, feminist standpoint, and feminist postmodernism (Harding 1986, Riger 1992). In pointing to the importance of research from the standpoint of women for understanding "depression" in women, while also emphasizing the need for a reflexive research process, the position I take is clearly more compatible with feminist standpoint and postmodernist approaches than with feminist empiricism. In addition, because of its emphasis on women's experiences, a feminist standpoint approach is also in keeping with a social constructionist epistemology and a nonpositivist, qualitative research methodology (Henwood and Pidgeon 1995). At the same time, I agree with Ristock and Pennell (1996: 5) that all three approaches to feminist research share in common a concern "to counter the androcentrism of the intellectual tradition out of which [each] emerged".

5 As used here, the term "discourse" refers to sets of shared cultural beliefs and practises that are drawn on by people in their everyday lives in order to construct meaning, identity, and subjectivity. As discursive resources, discourses are expressed and mani-

fested in the sociolinguistic domain and so language and social interaction are a particular focus of the form of inquiry called discourse analysis. "Discourses of femininity" are sets of shared cultural beliefs and practises that construct the meaning of "woman", what it is to be a woman, and experiences of subjectivity in women.

6 The term "subjectivity" is used by those working from a social constructionist perspective to refer to the state of personhood or selfhood. It addresses a range of subjective experiences, including identity, feelings and beliefs (cf. Burr 1995).

7 A nomothetic approach to the study of people attempts to establish general laws about human behavior. Thus, exploration of relationships among traits or behaviors requires the assumption that such characteristics are applicable to all individuals studied. A nomothetic approach is often contrasted with an idiographic approach in which individuals and their particular and unique characteristics are the focus of study.

2

WHAT IS DEPRESSION?

Definitional debates

In the previous chapter, I discussed different meanings of the term depression and drew a distinction between the way mental health professionals and researchers use this word and how it is used by ordinary people. When used by professionals and researchers, the word depression normally means *depressive disorder* or *depressive symptoms* (these terms were defined in Chapter 1). In this chapter, I discuss these two ways of conceptualizing depression in more detail, considering how they are employed in practise and also examining the assumptions on which they are based. An issue of particular interest to researchers and professionals (especially those in North America) is the need to distinguish between depressive disorder and depressive symptoms. Although these two ways of conceptualizing depression can be differentiated, they also have features in common which distinguish them from a third way of understanding depression, *depressive experiences*. When depression is understood in this way, the perspective shifts from that of researchers and professionals to that of women who are depressed, with a focus on subjective experiences.

In the theoretical approaches to explaining depression in women discussed in Part II, depression has been conceptualized as either depressive disorder or depressive symptoms. If considered at all, women's depressive experiences serve mainly as a resource used by researchers and professionals for diagnosing depressive disorder or for establishing the presence of depressive symptoms. Thus women's depressive experiences are not of direct interest in most positivist approaches to research and professional practise. From a feminist perspective, in contrast, women's reports of their depressive experiences are viewed as having meaning in their own right. Such accounts provide a basis for exploring subjectivity, specifically women's depressive experiences and their understandings of depression, and how both are shaped by discursive conditions within the sociocultural context of their everyday lives.[1]

For discussion purposes, I draw a distinction here between experts' (researchers and professionals) use of the term depression and how this word is understood by ordinary (lay) people. These two modes of understanding are not entirely separate, however. Experts are presumed to have specialized knowledge about depression, a form of expertise not readily available to lay people. Over time, however, the

24

terms and theories developed by experts become part of "lay" knowledge because of media influences (books, magazines, TV, the "internet", etc.) and through contacts between patients and professionals. Experts also may attempt to increase awareness about their specialized form of discourse around depression by means of public information campaigns.[2] This means that people's everyday or "common sense" understandings of depression will come to reflect a mixture of information from various sources, including their own subjective experiences, conversations with family members and friends, and versions of expert knowledge derived from the media and professionals. Lay knowledge about depression is also part of a broader set of beliefs within a particular sociocultural context about what constitutes normal or abnormal experiences and how such experiences should be explained and managed.

Although expert knowledge about depression draws on specialized terminology, concepts and theories, it is neither detached from, nor uninfluenced by, the broader sociocultural context within which it is generated and used. Instead lay knowledge and expert knowledge about depression represent interconnecting sets of ideas which influence each other, rather than being entirely separate with the latter considered more "valid" than the former. This interweaving is particularly visible in the interaction that takes place between a mental health professional and a patient for the purpose of the former determining the latter's diagnosis. In the next section, I focus on the process of making a diagnosis of depressive disorder, the methods and procedures employed, and the assumptions involved.

Diagnosing depressive disorder

While a woman may wonder if she is depressed, only a professionally-trained expert can determine whether her experiences (or "symptoms") would fit the criteria for a diagnosis of depressive disorder. Thus, it is quite possible for a woman to say that she feels depressed but for her not to be given a diagnosis of depressive disorder by a professional. The reverse situation can also occur where a woman does not use the word depressed to describe how she feels, although a professional may interpret her experiences are symptoms of a depressive disorder. An understanding of how a professional and a patient may arrive at different interpretations of the latter's experiences requires a closer examination of the diagnostic process and what it involves.

The diagnostic process

The information on which a diagnosis is based is usually gathered from a patient by a mental health professional in a particular form of interview called a "clinical interview". Although the specific format of a clinical interview will vary depending on the background of the professional involved typically a woman will be asked about her subjective experiences (feelings, thoughts etc), everyday activities and physical health (sleep, appetite, etc). This information is likely to be supplemented with observations made by the professional about the woman's behavior during the interview and perhaps with input from members of the woman's family and the person who made the referral (e.g. a family doctor).

A diagnosis of depressive disorder would be made if, in the professional's judgment, the experiences a woman describes are consistent with the criteria for this disorder. During training, professionals learn to do clinical interviews and to make diagnoses based on diagnostic criteria which are established by professional bodies. For instance, the diagnostic criteria for depressive disorder ("Major Depressive Disorder") used by professionals in North America, and increasingly in many other parts of the world (cf. Culbertson 1997), were developed by the American Psychiatric Association (APA). These criteria are published in the *Diagnostic and Statistical Manual of Mental Disorders* [DSM] (APA 1994), and those listed in the recent (fourth) edition of the DSM for the main type of depressive disorder are shown in Table 1.

In essence, the diagnostic criteria for depressive disorder consist of a list of subjective and bodily experiences. These experiences, termed symptoms, need to have been "present during the same two-week period" and to "represent a change from previous functioning" (see Table 1) to make a diagnosis of depressive disorder. An individual's symptoms can meet the DSM criteria in a variety of ways, provided that at least one of the first two in the list (see Table 1) is present. These two symptoms are "depressed mood most of the day, nearly every day" and, "markedly diminished interest or pleasure in all, or almost all, activities most of the day, nearly every day". There are seven additional symptoms (see Table 1), with at least four needing to be present before a diagnosis of depressive disorder is made.

Diagnostic criteria for depressive disorder: format and content

Several observations can be made about the format and content of the diagnostic criteria for depressive disorder given in the DSM. First, the criteria are formatted in a precise way, with clear directions for diagnostic decision-making (e.g. "Five [or more] of the following symptoms have been present"). Also, the form in which the criteria are presented, and their impersonal phrasing (there is no mention of the person being assessed), help to create an impression of detached scientific objectivity. The message which seems to be implied by this format is that the criteria have been established through impartial inquiry by those with expertise in the field of depression. This issue of the scientific basis for the diagnostic criteria for depressive disorder is addressed again later in the chapter. Another aspect of the formatting of the criteria, which enhances the impression of scientific rigor, is their presentation as a numbered list and the specification of an exact number of criteria required for a diagnosis to be made. The apparent preciseness of this numerical requirement is undermined however when it is realized that there are up to 70 different combinations of criteria (i.e. "symptoms") which would meet the minimum number required for a diagnosis of depressive disorder.[3]

A second feature to note is the wording of the criteria. The criteria include terms

Table 1 Criteria for major depressive episode

A. Five (or more) of the following symptoms have been present during the same 2-week period and represent a change from previous functioning; at least one of the symptoms is either (1) depressed mood or (2) loss of interest or pleasure.

Note: Do not include symptoms that are clearly due to a general medical condition, or mood-incongruent delusions or hallucinations.

(1) depressed mood most of the day, nearly every day, as indicated by either subjective report (e.g., feels sad or empty) or observation made by others (e.g., appears tearful). Note: In children and adolescents, can be irritable mood.
(2) markedly diminished interest or pleasure in all, or almost all, activities most of the day, nearly every day (as indicated by either subjective account or observation made by others)
(3) significant weight loss when not dieting or weight gain (e.g., a change of more than 5 percent of body weight in a month), or decrease or increase in appetite nearly every day. Note: In children, consider failure to make expected weight gains.
(4) insomnia or hypersomnia nearly every day
(5) psychomotor agitation or retardation nearly every day (observable by others, not merely subjective feelings of restlessness or being slowed down)
(6) fatigue or loss of energy nearly every day
(7) feelings of worthlessness or excessive or inappropriate guilt (which may be delusional) nearly every day (not merely self-reproach or guilt about being sick)
(8) diminished ability to think or concentrate, or indecisiveness, nearly every day (either by subjective account or as observed by others)
(9) recurrent thoughts of death (not just fear of dying), recurrent suicidal ideation without a specific plan, or a suicide attempt or a specific plan for committing suicide

B. The symptoms do not meet criteria for Mixed Episode.

C. The symptoms cause clinically significant distress or impairment in social, occupational, or other important areas of functioning.

D. The symptoms are not due to the direct physiological effects of a substance (e.g., a drug of abuse, a medication) or a general medical condition (e.g., hypothyroidism).

E. The symptoms are not better accounted for by Bereavement, i.e., after the loss of a loved one, the symptoms persist for longer than 2 months or are characterized by marked functional impairment, morbid preoccupation with worthlessness, suicidal ideation, psychotic symptoms, or psychomotor retardation.

Reprinted with permission from the Diagnostic and Statistical Manual of Mental Disorders, Fourth Edition. Copyright 1994 American Psychiatric Association.

(e.g. "insomnia or hypersomnia", "psychomotor agitation or retardation") unlikely to be familiar to people without medical training. At the same time, although the tone of the wording is objective and scientific, the criteria themselves are still somewhat vague. For instance, the qualifier "markedly" in Criterion 2 (see Table 1) gives professionals little help in deciding whether a woman's "diminished interest or pleasure in all, or almost all, activities most of the day, nearly every day" is sufficient to meet this criterion. How is "markedly" defined? How much of a diminution in interest or pleasure does there need to be? Another example is the wording of Criterion 7, where the qualifier "excessive" is used in conjunction with "guilt". How is the excessiveness of guilt evaluated? Without belaboring the point, it should be clear that the process of arriving at a diagnosis of depressive disorder is not a straightforward matter; considerable professional judgment is involved. The importance of professional judgment in determining a patient's diagnosis is explicitly indicated in the DSM.

> In some cases, sadness may be denied at first, but may subsequently be elicited by interview (e.g. by pointing out that the individual looks as if he or she is about to cry). In some individuals who complain of feeling "blah", having no feelings, or feeling anxious, the presence of a depressed mood can be inferred from the person's facial expression and demeanor.
>
> (APA 1994: 320–21)

The role of clinical judgment in the diagnostic process

Communication between a patient and a professional, so that the professional can collect information about the patient's symptoms, is a prerequisite for clinical decision-making in the diagnostic process. To communicate with a patient, a professional has to translate technical terms into language that the patient will find understandable. Thus, inquiries about insomnia or hypersomnia are likely to be rephrased in terms of "sleeping problems" or "difficulty getting to sleep". As Coyne points out, a degree of probing of a patient's answers to interview questions may be necessary in order to establish the presence of a symptom.

> Mental health professionals evaluating a patient also depend on the subject's self-report, but they are free to decide how to probe, and they can draw on their experience observing signs and symptoms. Thus, a depressed man might deny a loss of the ability to experience pleasure, but on probing disclose that golf is simply boring rather than the passion it once was for him, that he is no longer following what had been his favorite baseball team, and that for the first time in 20 years he has renewed neither his fishing nor his hunting license. With this information having been elicited, he might be more able to recognize that what is meant by *loss of pleasure* applies to him. (emphasis in original)
>
> (Coyne 1994: 32)

As this quote illustrates, arriving at a diagnosis of depressive disorder is a process which requires a professional to make a series of judgments about the meaning of a patient's responses.

Apart from eliciting information about specific symptoms, a professional also determines whether the experiences represent a "change from previous functioning". Although the patient may describe her experiences as being different from usual, this may not always be the case (as suggested in the quote above from Coyne). Thus, a professional also has to decide whether the experiences a patient reports reflect a change from her previous functioning. The DSM criteria are somewhat silent on this aspect of diagnostic decision-making. How much change is required? The phrasing of the criteria for Major Depressive Episode (see section A in Table 1) implies that "previous functioning" represents a baseline against which current functioning is compared. Presumably, information given by the patient provides an indication of her previous functioning which is assumed to be her usual functioning. This strategy, of course, requires additional judgments on the part of the professional about how the woman functioned previously.

The DSM criteria also direct professionals to consider other explanations for individuals' symptoms before arriving at a diagnosis of depressive disorder. Alternative explanations for a woman's symptoms, which would rule out a depressive disorder diagnosis, include grief following bereavement, substance abuse, and organic medical conditions (see Table 1). Thus, the process of clinical diagnosis extends well beyond merely determining whether the symptoms listed as criteria for depressive disorder are present. Although the scope of diagnostic assessment is quite broad, little attention is given to either the context of a woman's everyday life or more subjective aspects of her experiences. To the extent that these areas are considered, they would be used primarily to determine the presence of symptoms rather than being explored in their own right. For instance, although a woman's account of her experiences is a critical element in establishing Criterion 1, "depressed mood most of the day, nearly every day", once a professional decides that this symptom is present, a woman's account may hold little further interest. In this diagnostic process, how a woman understands her experiences and the meaning they have for her are not the main focus of professional attention.

Diagnosis as a social construction

This analysis of the role of clinical judgment in the diagnostic process is intended neither as a criticism of professional practise nor as implying that the symptoms women report should be discounted as unproblematic, imagined or unreal, or as not warranting attention. Instead, my purpose here is to illustrate the process whereby the experiences a woman might report to a mental health professional become *constructed* as *symptoms* in the context of the special form of social interaction called a clinical interview. By saying that experiences are constructed, I mean that symptoms do not have an objective reality independent of the interpretative processes involved in making clinical judgments. In this interpretative process, moreover, although both a professional and a patient are participants, the perceptions and judgments of the professional take priority in determining a diagnosis.

At the same time, the suggestion that a woman's experiences are socially constructed as symptoms of depressive disorder does not imply that they have no physical basis. Nevertheless, when someone describes their experiences to another person, inevitably language is involved. Interviews between patients and professionals rely almost totally on a shared use of language. This communicative process also extends beyond spoken language to include non-verbal behavior, such as facial expression and bodily posture. These non-verbal forms of communication have meaning for an observer and provide a context for interpreting what is said verbally. Another way of describing the processes involved in arriving at a diagnosis is to say that depression is discursively constructed as an entity in the course of a particular kind of interpersonal interaction called the clinical interview.

A professional's interpretation of the content of a clinical interview also occurs in relation to the social and cultural context forming a background to the interaction which takes place during an interview. Professionals could not make judgments about the experiences reported to them by patients without drawing on this sociocultural knowledge. This more contextual form of knowledge is not, however, an explicit part of the diagnostic process. And this lack of explicitness means that such knowledge creates an invisible backdrop to diagnostic decision-making. For instance, although a professional will record whether a patient is female or male (individual gender), other aspects of gender are likely to be taken for granted. If a woman is married and has children, her work in the home, taking care of her family (an aspect of the gendered division of labor) would probably be assumed as a given and not explored further. Similarly, a professional might expect a woman to place more emphasis on her marital relationship than pursuit of a career, a belief reflecting discourses shaping cultural conceptions of femininity. In the clinical interview, therefore, gender is likely to be considered solely as an individual characteristic, while the gendered division of social labor and symbolic aspects of gender are ignored.

Both professionals and patients are likely to take women's caring work for granted because of widely shared beliefs about women's nature and the centrality of interpersonal relationships to femininity. Such beliefs, or discourses of femininity, are also part of the discursive conditions which operate in maintaining and regulating gendered social arrangements within a particular sociocultural context. With respect to the diagnostic process, these social arrangements and the beliefs supporting them are largely invisible and the potential relevance of women's everyday lives for understanding their experiences is hardly considered at all.

The mental disorder concept: experiences taken out of context

Lack of attention to the social context forming the background to women's lives is also an inherent aspect of the diagnostic criteria for depressive disorder. The criteria focus primarily on an individual's subjective and bodily experiences. This decontextualized way of thinking about individuals and their experiences is entirely consistent with the definition of "mental disorder" which guides the DSM approach to diagnosis. In the DSM, the concept of mental disorder is defined as follows:

> [E]ach of the mental disorders is conceptualized as a clinically significant behavioral or psychological syndrome or pattern that occurs *in an individual* and that is associated with present distress (e.g., a painful symptom) or disability (i.e., impairment in one or more important areas of functioning) or with a significantly increased risk of suffering death, pain, disability, or an important loss of freedom. In addition, this syndrome or pattern must not be merely an expectable and culturally sanctioned response to a particular event, for example, the death of a loved one. Whatever its original cause, it must currently be considered a manifestation of a behavioral, psychological, or biological dysfunction *in the individual*. Neither deviant behavior (e.g., political, religious, or sexual) nor conflicts that are primarily between the individual and society are mental disorders unless the deviance or conflict is a symptom of a dysfunction *in the individual*, as described above. (emphases added)
>
> (APA 1994: xxi–xxii)

According to this definition, a mental disorder is something which resides within the individual. This way of conceptualizing mental disorders has obvious parallels with medical definitions of diseases, conditions affecting the biological body. The authors of the DSM state that the purpose of this manual is primarily descriptive, serving to identify disorders, with a neutral position taken with respect to etiology. Nevertheless, the definition shown above clearly implies that the causes of mental disorders are located within the individual.

Thus, the diagnostic criteria for depressive disorder (and for the other disorders listed in the DSM) are primarily descriptive, intended to facilitate identification of the disorder by professionals, rather than promoting a particular theory of depression. The claim is made, therefore, that the DSM is atheoretical, a repository of accumulated empirical-clinical knowledge about the symptoms of specific disorders (APA 1994: xviii). Because of its descriptive character and apparent lack of commitment to a specific explanatory framework, the DSM is presumed to be compatible with a wide range of theoretical perspectives employed within mental health fields. Indeed, the DSM framework has been adopted by mental health professionals and researchers around the world and is considered to be an important tool in the scientific study of mental disorders and in particular for research on depression (APA 1994: xxiv, Coyne 1994, Culbertson 1997, Weissman and Olfson 1995).

As outlined in Chapter 1, the first step in application of the positivist scientific method is development of an objective measure of the phenomenon to be studied.

In research on depression, this purpose is often served by use of the DSM diagnostic criteria for depressive disorder. If depression is socially constructed as an entity through the conceptual work of professionals and researchers, an issue that arises is how the diagnostic criteria (symptoms) for depressive disorder listed in the DSM were determined in the first place. More generally, what is the basis of the claim that disorders and their diagnostic criteria are the product of scientific research?

Science and the DSM

In contrast to notions of scientific research as involving an objective and rational form of inquiry, accounts of the procedures used to determine which disorders and diagnostic criteria should be included within the DSM depict them as having more in common with political debates than with scientific deliberations. It may come as a surprise to learn that decisions regarding the specific disorders and diagnostic criteria to be included in the DSM are made on the basis of committee consensus and votes (Caplan 1995, Kitzinger and Perkins 1993). Although these decisions purportedly are based on findings from empirical studies, critics of the DSM point to the inadequacies of the evidence used to support inclusion of specific disorder categories (Caplan 1995, Parker *et al.* 1995). Criticisms of the DSM as lacking a firm grounding in scientific research, raise the further issue of what would constitute adequate empirical evidence. What kind of evidence would provide empirical support for inclusion of a category of disorder within the DSM?

An answer to this question requires some consideration of links between the concept of mental disorder and ideas about what is abnormal (McReynolds 1989, Parker *et al.* 1995, Ussher 1991). In biomedicine, a disease or disorder is usually detected on the basis of tests (blood analyses, X-rays, biopsies, etc.) conducted on a relevant organ or system of the body. Attempts to identify similar biological markers for categories of mental disorder, such as depressive disorder, or for specific depressive symptoms, generally have failed (Ross and Pam 1995). Instead, in the absence of independent markers, individuals' behaviors and experiences are judged to be abnormal if they violate in some way culturally shared (and largely implicit) notions of what constitutes normality (McReynolds 1989). Some examples of culturally-defined standards for distinguishing abnormal from normal behaviors and experiences include severe levels of subjective distress (such as extreme sadness, dejection, or despair), inability to meet basic self-care needs (such as a prolonged lapse in daily routines and activities), and self-damaging or destructive behavior (such as refusal to eat or suicidal actions). These standards, although largely implicit within a particular sociocultural context, also are incorporated within the diagnostic criteria for depressive disorder (see Table 1). Depression is sometimes referred to as a "functional" disorder, because it is manifested primarily in terms of people's inability to function in their everyday lives in a manner that is considered normal (and, therefore, socially acceptable) and this impaired functioning cannot be explained by physical illness.

Thus, at root the form of abnormality called depression is defined by judgments made by a person or those around them that they are not functioning normally. Persistent feelings of sadness or hopelessness, which some consider a hallmark of depression, may be the experience that triggers this recognition. At this point, a person may label themselves as depressed, an awareness which may by followed by seeking professional help. However, the ideas shared by ordinary people about what is abnormal do not overlap completely with experts' criteria for diagnosing mental disorders (Parker *et al.* 1995). Conceptions of mental disorders and their symptoms evolve through the work of professionals and researchers and in this process become more formal and explicit than common sense understandings of abnormality among lay people. In some respects, therefore, mental disorders are produced by the conceptual practises of experts rather than already existing as phenomena in the world awaiting discovery by researchers and mental health professionals (Smith 1990).

The diagnostic categories within the DSM and their associated criteria are claimed by those who developed them to be the product of "rigorous scientific research" (APA 1994: xv-xvi). At the same time, the DSM has been criticized, especially by those who work from a feminist perspective, as being unscientific (Caplan 1995, Russell 1995, Ussher 1991). The main target of these criticisms has been the inclusion within the DSM of diagnostic categories which can be applied only to women (e.g. Premenstrual Dysphoric Disorder), whilst no categories apply solely to men, and these female-specific categories are not adequately supported by empirical evidence (Caplan 1995, Figert 1996). These feminist critiques, along with other critical analyses, reveal the socially constructed character of conceptions of mental disorders and their diagnostic criteria (e.g. Caplan 1995, Smith 1990) and also challenge the claims of scientific validity made by the DSM's proponents (Parker *et al.* 1995). Can these conflicting positions on the scientific status of the DSM be reconciled so that women's mental health concerns can also be acknowledged?

In debates on the scientific merits of the DSM, discussion often seems to hinge on a rather narrow interpretation of the term "scientific". Although scientific forms of inquiry are usually taken to mean research conducted according to the positivist version of the scientific method, this is not the only source of knowledge available to mental health professionals. As Polkinghorne (1992) has pointed out, professionals also derive knowledge through their contacts with patients. Rather than limiting the basis of clinical decisions to findings from scientific research, professionals' actions are also guided by pragmatic concerns to help those who seek their services. Polkinghorne argues that the knowledge base informing the work of mental health professionals is more compatible with an "epistemology of practise" than with the positivist epistemology underpinning research conducted according to the scientific method.

An epistemology of practise has some affinities with a social constructionist epistemology, particularly in the awareness among practitioners that clinical knowledge is specific to the particular time and place in which it is generated. According to Polkinghorne (ibid.: 158), rather than viewing mental disorders as "natural categories of psychological reality", practitioners have an appreciation of their arbitrary character. This awareness of the socially constructed nature of the DSM's categories, as Polkinghorne points out, is indicated by the following disclaimer included in the DSM.

> [T]here is no assumption that each category of mental disorder is a completely discrete entity with absolute boundaries dividing it from other mental disorders or from no mental disorder.
>
> (APA 1994: xxii)

The various changes to specific diagnostic categories and their associated criteria which have taken place over the course of successive editions of the DSM (there have been four, to date) also are in line with Polkinghorne's social constructionist reinterpretation of the diagnostic endeavor.

If the diagnostic categories in the DSM are recognized as being social constructions formulated in the context of knowledge derived from accumulated clinical experience, how can their validity (or accuracy) be determined? Critics of the DSM process have taken particular issue with the use of clinical opinion and committee consensus as the basis for decision-making, contrasting it unfavorably with more rigorous procedures implied by use of the positivist scientific method. To be considered scientific, these critics claim, decisions should be informed by available empirical evidence. Consideration of the decision-making procedures used more generally by researchers, however, reveals a somewhat different situation. Research findings are subjected to a stringent "peer-review" process in which dissemination (e.g. through publication) depends on other researchers being satisfied that the research meets appropriate methodological standards and the findings make sense in the context of the existing knowledge. The peer-review process employed in scientific research (e.g. in decisions on publication and awarding of grants to support research) typically involves at the most three or four people who are experts in the particular research area. By comparison, development of the DSM has involved literally hundreds of experts, the equivalent of an extensive "peer-review panel". Thus, there are clear parallels between the validational processes used in construction of the DSM and those employed in "scientific" research (cf. Yardley 1997a: 36). Although the role of peer-review is often obscured in the reporting of research findings, acceptance within the scientific community is a key prerequisite for endorsement of new findings as valid forms of knowledge.

When reinterpreted from a social constructionist perspective, therefore, the "scientific validity" of the DSM would seem less of an issue than its critics contend. Other features of the DSM, however, are more legitimate targets of criticism. Of particular concern to feminist researchers and practitioners is that the diagnostic process encourages a tendency to "reify" the notion of mental disorder. The term "reification" refers to a way of thinking in which concepts (such as mental disorder) are treated as labels for real entities which are presumed to have a material existence independent of the terms used to denote them. In the case of the DSM, this reification is fostered by the assumption that mental disorders lie within individuals, implying that physiological processes within the body are involved. An added concern is that individuals diagnosed with a mental disorder such as depression are considered to be patients within the medical domain. As a consequence of their contact with professionals, women and their problems often become medicalized and their experiences viewed as signs of internal, individual problems, or "psychopathology" (Oakley 1986, Russell 1995, Ussher 1991).

An alternative to conceptualizing depression as a mental disorder is to focus on those experiences and behaviors considered depressive symptoms (i.e. the diagnostic criteria), without assuming that such symptoms necessarily signify a depressive disorder. In the next section, this way of defining depression and the procedures involved in assessing depressive symptoms are considered in more detail.

Assessing depressive symptoms

The main method used to assess depressive symptoms is self-report questionnaires or checklists. Not only are such paper-and-pencil measures cost-efficient, they also provide a rapid means of gathering information about the severity of individuals' depressive experiences. Typically, symptom questionnaires yield a total score calculated by summing scores across individual items, with higher overall scores indicating a more severe level of depression.[4]

Although much of the research on depression in women has involved use of symptom questionnaires, this method has been criticized as assessing dysphoria rather than depressive disorder defined according to diagnostic criteria (Coyne 1994). In support of this position, researchers point to evidence that a person may have a high score on a symptom questionnaire but not be diagnosed with depressive disorder, whereas someone whose score on a questionnaire is low may be diagnosed in this way. It appears that many more people overall will have high scores on depression symptom questionnaires than would be diagnosed with depressive disorder. This means that a woman may not be diagnosed as depressed even though she reports a fairly high level of depressive symptoms on a questionnaire. Thus, research findings based on symptom questionnaires may be misleading if interpreted as though they apply to depression defined as depressive disorder. For instance, although a positive relationship has often been found between women's scores on depressive symptom questionnaires and indices of social adversity in their lives (e.g. poverty, unemployment, single parenthood), adverse social conditions alone do not predict depressive disorder in women (Coyne and Downey 1991, Stoppard 1993).

Because of findings such as these, a consensus has emerged among researchers that depressive symptom questionnaires should not be used for diagnostic purposes (Coyne 1994, Link and Dohrenwend 1980). If a woman's score on a symptom questionnaire is not relevant for determining whether she would be diagnosed with a depressive disorder, how should her questionnaire responses be interpreted? Among those employing positivist research approaches, there is agreement that people with high scores on depressive symptom questionnaires are more appropriately described as "distressed", "dysphoric" or "demoralized" than depressed. Although depressed mood may characterize people who report high levels of subjective distress, such feelings are likely to be more transient than would be experienced by individuals who are diagnosed with a depressive disorder (APA 1994: 320, Coyne 1994).

A distinction between depressive symptom questionnaires and diagnostic criteria for depressive disorder follows fairly directly from the positivist epistemology which underpins much contemporary research on depression (see Chapter 1). In research based on this epistemological perspective, the measures used are treated as representing the phenomena being investigated, which in turn are presumed to exist independently of the measurement procedures used by researchers. Thus, depressive disorder and depressive symptoms are conceptualized as separate entities, which require different assessment methods. Excluded from consideration, however, in research from this perspective are assessment methods themselves, and how the content of measures, and consequently the meaning of people's responses, are pre-structured by researchers' interpretations.

Earlier in the chapter, I discussed how patients' accounts of their experiences are socially constructed as symptoms of depressive disorder by professionals within the interaction which takes place during a clinical interview. When a self-report questionnaire is used to assess depressive symptoms, however, there is no interviewer. The interviewer's contribution to diagnostic assessment is highlighted by Coyne (1994) in his analysis of symptom questionnaires. The particular importance of the interviewer for distinguishing dysphoria from depressive disorder is emphasized by Coyne (1994: 33): ". . . endorsements of such [questionnaire] items may reflect negative affectivity or neuroticism . . . that would readily be distinguished from depressive symptomatology in an interview with a mental health professional". Thus, Coyne seems to suggest that the accuracy of people's responses on symptom questionnaires cannot be determined unless a professional serves as an intermediary. What is overlooked by Coyne, however, is that because questionnaire items are themselves devised by experts, they may only partially reflect the experiences of the people who answer them. In addition, the format of most questionnaires is standardized, which means that the specific circumstances of a person's life are not considered at all. Thus, neither questionnaires designed to assess depressive symptoms, nor clinical interviews to diagnose depressive disorder, can provide much information about women's depressive experiences from their own standpoint without first being filtered through the perspective of researchers and professionals.

Exploring women's depressive experiences

When depression is conceptualized as depressive disorder or depressive symptoms, the perspective taken is external to that of a woman who is depressed.

Although the diagnostic criteria for depressive disorder and the content of items on symptom questionnaires may have originated in experiences reported by patients to clinicians, these accounts become homogenized when reconstituted in the language of experts. The use of objective measurement procedures, required by the positivist scientific method, has the further effect of ruling out subjective aspects of experience as suitable topics for research. In a feminist approach to research, in contrast, women's accounts of their experiences become the focus of inquiry. This approach to research has been pursued in part as a strategy for ensuring that women's concerns are included in decision-making involving social policy in the public domain (cf. Doyal 1995, Lorber 1994). In feminist research on depression and other mental health problems in women, this approach has been adopted to develop knowledge from women's standpoint and also to address subjective aspects experiences, largely neglected in mainstream research (Henwood and Pidgeon 1995, Nicolson 1995). In particular, women's experiences have received little attention as a source of knowledge for understanding depression.

When research focuses on depression from the standpoint of women, qualitative approaches are most likely to be used. Although not unique to feminist research, qualitative methods are particularly useful for exploring subjective experiences (Henwood and Pidgeon 1995). Qualitative research relies on various methods, particularly interviews, to gather verbal accounts (cf. Banister *et al.* 1994, Richardson 1996). Of particular interest in qualitative research is the language used by those interviewed, how they talk about and make sense of their experiences. In exploring the meaning of experiences from the standpoint of women a qualitative approach also shifts the focus from the researcher to the research participant by acknowledging that women's accounts have validity in their own right, rather than validity being determined only from the perspective of researchers (Harding 1986, Smith 1987).

Interviews have been used in qualitative studies of depression in women to explore women's depressive experiences. For example, women who identify themselves as depressed have described their experiences as "like being in a black hole" (Gammell 1996) or "slipping into a deep, dark hole" (Schreiber 1996). According to women's accounts, these experiences are likely to be accompanied by feelings of sadness, thoughts of suicide, fatigue and a sense of being unwell (Gammell 1996, Schreiber 1996). Parallels are apparent, therefore, between women's accounts of their depressive experiences and the way depression has been conceptualized by experts. Not surprisingly, the women who were interviewed in the studies by Gammell and Schreiber were diagnosed as depressed when they sought professional help for their depressive experiences.

A focus on verbal accounts also provides an avenue for exploring subjectivity, which includes a woman's sense of self or identity and how she understands and explains depression and her depressive experiences. When approached from a social constructionist perspective, identity and the meaning of experiences are viewed as being constructed in language and through social interaction. Thus, a focus on women's accounts allows the discursive conditions shaping women's experiences within specific sociocultural contexts to be explored. Included here would be discourses about depression, the meaning of depressive experiences, and their causes and implications for women's lives. Such discourses represent resources drawn on by women in their attempts to understand and make sense of their depressive experiences. Findings from qualitative studies point to themes in these discursive resources which include ideas about "women's nature" along with assumptions about the activities that constitute "women's lives" and "womanly" ways of enacting them (Jack 1991, Lewis 1995, 1997, Nicolson 1992).

Qualitative exploration can also shed light on how women explain experiences of ill-health such as depression. These explanations, which focus on women's bodies and the stressful conditions of women's everyday lives, typically reflect prevailing theories about "depression" (Lewis 1995, Stoppard 1997, Walters 1993). As will be discussed in Chapter 6, women's understandings of depression tend to mirror experts' accounts. A focus on women's accounts, at the same time, offers possibilities for developing an understanding of depression which can avoid the limitations of mainstream theories. Directions such alternatives might take are explored in more detail in Chapter 6 and in the chapters in Part III. When women's accounts are treated as a source of knowledge in their own right some additional issues arise and these are discussed next.

Women's ways of understanding their depressive experiences and theories of depression proposed by experts are intersecting forms of knowledge, rather than being distinct from each other. Nevertheless, experts' accounts are legitimized as scientific knowledge and so generally are viewed as having greater validity that lay accounts. However, the intertwining of expert and lay knowledge about depression is apparent in women's use of popularized versions of experts' formulations in understanding their own depressive experiences. For instance, some women attribute depressive experiences to aspects of female reproductive biology, such as menstruation or menopause (Lewis 1995, Walters 1993). In this way of thinking, the body is assumed to be a natural biological organism quite separate from sociocultural influences. As will be discussed in Chapter 6, however, women's accounts of their depressive experiences also point to alternative ways of conceptualizing the role of the body in relation to depression. Instead of viewing the body as solely a biological organism, women's accounts suggest that their embodiment is integral to their depressive experiences, which in turn are closely tied to the context of their everyday lives. This way of understanding depression is one which can encompass both material and discursive aspects of women's lived experiences.

Findings from qualitative studies also reveal a tendency among women to "normalize" their life experiences, to see their everyday lives as having little relevance for explaining their experiences of distress (Blaxter 1993, Walters 1993). This tendency among women to normalize and downplay the contribution of mundane social circumstances to their depressive experiences also is reflected in the virtual neglect of women's lives in experts' theories of depression. As a consequence of these normalizing tendencies, which are present in women's accounts as well as experts' theories, the biological body usually emerges as the only reality with the potential to explain depression in women. Although women may draw connections between their lives and their depressive experiences, understanding based on experiential (or subjective) knowledge is likely to be discounted by experts as anecdotal, or reinterpreted as signs of a woman's mental illness or psychopathology. Because the social conditions of women's lives are largely neglected within mainstream theories, depressive experiences among women can be validated only when attributed to an internal disorder. Depressive experiences arising in the context of situations which occur routinely in women's lives (e.g. fatigue because of sleep deprivation in new mothers or the "double day" combination of work inside and outside the home) typically are interpreted by ordinary women and experts alike as normal forms of distress. More particularly, from the vantage point of experts", women's depressive experiences are likely to be discounted unless they can be defined as symptoms of depressive disorder.

Some may consider women's accounts of their experiences to offer a limited perspective on depression because attention is restricted to the discursive arena. Also, more active and direct efforts to address depression in women may appear to be precluded when the focus is on language. A counter argument to this view is that exploration of women's accounts involves taking women's experiences seriously so that they become the center of investigation. Beginning inquiry from the standpoint of women offers possibilities for developing ways of understanding depression which have more emancipatory prospects than available formulations. At the same time, generating new discourses around depression can provide new resources for women struggling with their own depressive experiences, as well as for researchers and professionals in mental health fields who work with women clients.

Can definitional debates be resolved?

In the search for a resolution of the definitional debates outlined in this chapter, it is tempting to conclude by recommending that depression be defined with greater emphasis on women's experiences. From a feminist perspective, one strategy might be to argue that more attention be given to women's accounts of their depressive experiences. Whatever the choices made about how to define and conceptualize depression, they will have important implications for how depression is understood and explained. Rather than succumbing to pressures to resolve definitional issues, the position which currently makes most sense to me is to accept that there are various ways of conceptualizing depression, and that each has a contribution to make in understanding depression in women. Instead of striving for a definitional consensus (which in any case is unattainable), all definitional approaches should be viewed as *partial*. Each approach emphasizes some aspects of experience, while omitting others, and each necessarily reflects different standpoints. Recognition of the partial character of any attempt to define "depression" also means that when discussing research findings it is important to consider not only what is given weight but also what is left out or excluded. From a social constructionist perspective, knowledge is viewed as local and situated, rather than being timeless and general in its applicability. A final consideration, therefore, is to avoid overgeneralizing knowledge claims to all women, but instead to recognize the importance of attending to the specific circumstances of particular women's lived experiences.

Notes

1 The term "discursive conditions" is defined by Ristock and Pennell (1996: 114) as "non-material conditions relating to language and ideologies".

2 During the mid-1990s within Canada, a public awareness campaign about depression was mounted by the Canadian Psychiatric Association, with public service announcements on both TV and radio. The televised version depicted a "depressed" person, accompanied by the message that "depression can be treated". As well, a toll-free telephone service (partly funded by pharmaceutical companies), introduced in Canada and the United States, offers people information on symptoms of depression for self-diagnostic purposes. As Allwood (1996) notes, in recent years a similar information campaign, directed toward general practitioners, has been mounted in Britain.

3 In the DSM, the sets of diagnostic criteria presented for many of the disorders are "polythetic". This means that "the individual need only present with a subset of items from a longer list" (APA 1994: xxii). With respect to Major Depressive Episode, nine criteria are listed, but only five need be present to make a diagnosis (see Table 1). With the restriction that one of the first two symptoms listed must be included, there are 35 different sets of symptoms which include the first symptom (but not the second symptom) and four of the remaining seven. Similarly, there are 35 different symptom sets including the second symptom (but not the first) and four of the remaining seven. When the first two symptoms are considered along with the other seven, there are 122 additional symptom sets that would meet the criteria for depressive disorder, for an overall total of 192 different combinations of symptoms.

4 A widely used questionnaire to assess depressive symptoms is the Beck Depression Inventory (BDI) (Beck and Steer 1987). Items on the BDI are formatted in the following way:

    A   I do not feel sad.
    B   I feel sad.
    C   I am sad all the time and I can't snap out of it.
    D   I am so sad or unhappy that I can't stand it.

The person answering the questionnaire circles the option that best describes their experiences. If option A is selected, it receives a score of 0, B receives a score of 1; C a score of 2; and D a score of 3. A total BDI score is computed by summing scores across the 21 items making up the scale.

Part II

EXPLAINING DEPRESSION IN WOMEN

Mainstream frameworks

3

LOOKING FOR SOURCES OF DEPRESSION WITHIN PERSON–ENVIRONMENT INTERACTIONS

Diathesis–stress models

As was outlined in Chapter 1, within psychology interest in development of psychosocial approaches to explaining depression has focused on diathesis–stress models. The origins of diathesis–stress models as explanations for depression can be traced to both psychoanalytic approaches to personality (Coyne and Whiffen 1995) and behavioral approaches to altering maladaptive behavior (Kantrowitz and Ballou 1992). Diathesis–stress models are part of a broader psychological perspective in which behavior is understood as resulting from the joint effects of personality and environment influences (Mischel 1973). The basic assumption of diathesis–stress approaches to explaining depression is that individuals with certain personality characteristics (the "diathesis" component) are particularly vulnerable to becoming depressed when negative events occurring in their lives (the "stress" component) mesh with or "match" their particular personality orientation or style.

In the first part of this chapter, I outline how the main components of contemporary diathesis–stress models of depression have been conceptualized and measured for the purpose of testing hypotheses derived from these models. Following this, I discuss the implications of these models for explaining depression in women. Next, the adequacy of diathesis–stress models is assessed with respect to attempts to evaluate them empirically. Finally, the assumptions on which these models are based are analyzed from feminist and social constructionist perspectives to reveal their conceptual limitations when applied to the problem of explaining depression in women.

Diathesis–stress models: key concepts and measures

Conceptions of personality diatheses

An important forerunner of contemporary diathesis–stress models is the cognitive approach to explaining depression. The work of Beck (1991) is most closely associated with this approach. According to the cognitive model proposed by Beck and his collaborators (Beck *et al.* 1979), individuals who become depressed are characterized by a distinctive cognitive style (or way of thinking) in which negative interpretations of their experiences tend to predominate. This tendency toward cognitive negativity encompasses individuals' interpretations of their past and current experiences as well as their expectations for the future. According to this cognitive formulation, depressed individuals are characterized by a style of information processing which leads to a negative, pessimistic outlook. Cognitive therapy is an approach to treatment of depressed individuals based on this cognitive theory of depression.

Cognitive theory of depression has undergone further refinements in recent years to address the issue of why some people but not others become depressed. There is abundant evidence that when individuals are depressed, their thinking is dominated by negative, pessimistic thoughts (Coyne 1994). However, evidence has not been forthcoming that this distinctive thinking style is also present when these same individuals are not depressed (Clark and Steer 1996). Cognitive theorists now postulate instead that individuals prone to depression are characterized by personality traits which predispose them to becoming depressed (Beck 1996, Clark and Steer 1996). These personality "orientations" or "modes" are not simply triggered by a depressive state, but are presumed to exist before a person becomes depressed. In recent reformulations of Beck's theory, two broad personality orientations have been proposed as constituting predispositions for depression (Clark and Steer 1996, Coyne and Whiffen 1995). These personality orientations are labelled "sociotropy" and "autonomy".

Individuals with a *sociotropic* personality are said to place a high value on having close interpersonal relationships and being loved and accepted by others. Thus, sociotropic or "socially dependent" individuals "satisfy their needs for security and self-worth by pleasing others and avoiding others' disapproval through maintenance of close interpersonal attachments" (Clark and Steer 1996: 81). Individuals with an *autonomous* personality orientation are said to be characterized by a high investment in personal independence, achievement and freedom of choice. The highly autonomous individual "derives self-worth from mastery and achievement, which may lead to excessive personal demands for self-control and accomplishment" (ibid.). Such individuals also are thought to be less sensitive to the needs of others, preferring solitude and privacy to the company of other people.

For individuals characterized by one or the other of these personality predispositions, one effect is to sensitize them to certain kinds of experiences. A "sociotropic" personality orientation involves a particular sensitivity to experiences involving relationship loss or threat of such loss. The personality orientation of "autonomy" sensitizes individuals to experiences involving failure in achievement of personal goals. When "vulnerable" people become depressed, they interpret their experiences as supporting negative beliefs about the self in a direction which reflects their preexisting personality orientation. For instance, a person whose personality orientation is "sociotropic" is likely to interpret a relationship loss in terms of personal abandonment. A person with an "autonomous" personality orientation is likely to interpret an achievement set-back as signifying personal failure. Thus, central to the cognitive perspective on depression is the idea that individuals actively construct their "reality" through the particular way in which they interpret the meaning of events in their lives. Although this active construction or cognitive representation of reality is a general feature of human information processing systems, individuals with heightened vulnerability to depression are more likely to construct a negative view of their own "reality". From this cognitive perspective, therefore, individuals who have a personality orientation which increases their proneness to depression when certain kinds of negative events are experienced are especially likely to interpret their experiences negatively.

Within Beck's theory of depression, the personality orientations of sociotropy and autonomy represent the "diathesis" component of the diathesis–stress model. The term "diathesis" has medical roots and is used within medicine to refer to a constitutional (or inborn) predisposition to a disease. Adoption of the term diathesis within Beck's theory implies that some individuals are inherently depression-prone, because of their personality. Use of the term diathesis, then, implies that personality is inborn. Indeed, in a recent statement of his theory, Beck suggests that the personality diatheses for psychological disorders such as depression, have their origins in "primal modes [that] evolved in ancient environments" (Beck 1996: 12). Such primal modes, according to Beck (1996: 12–13), "were better adapted to solving the crude primeval problems than the more complex problems of contemporary life".

Notions of personality diatheses for depression have also been formulated within psychoanalytic theories. According to psychoanalytic theory, an individual's personality develops early in childhood, particularly in the context of interactions with the primary care-giver, usually the mother (Chodorow 1978). The personality types of "dependency" and "self-criticism" have been proposed by researchers who work within a psychoanalytic framework as predisposing individuals to depression (Blatt *et al.* 1982, Coyne and Whiffen 1995). These personality types are presumed to be distinct, to occur in different people, and to involve enduring, stable clusters of traits. According to this formulation, individuals with *dependent* personality traits derive self-esteem from having secure interpersonal relations and have strong needs for acceptance and support from others. The *self-critical* personality type is characterized by strong concerns with personal achievement and individuals with this type of personality set high standards for accomplishing personal goals and are likely to evaluate their own performance harshly (Blatt and Zuroff 1992).

There are clear parallels between the personality type of dependency and the personality orientation of sociotropy and between the self-critical personality type and the personality orientation of autonomy (Coyne and Whiffen 1995). Indeed, the marked similarities between these two formulations of personality diatheses for depression have prompted suggestions of a convergence between cognitive and psychoanalytic perspectives at the theoretical level (ibid., Epstein 1994). The stress component of the diathesis–stress interaction also has been conceptualized in similar ways in cognitive and psychoanalytic formulations.

Conceptualizing the stress component

Within both cognitive and psychoanalytic versions of diathesis–stress model, the stress component is conceptualized in terms of the occurrence of "negative events". A negative event is one which potentially is "stressful" for the person who experiences it. To date, conceptualization of the stress component of diathesis–stress models is relatively under-developed, a situation which probably reflects the more established tradition within psychology of a focus on intrapsychic influences on behavior, particularly in research informed by psychoanalytic theories.

According to cognitive theory, events occurring in people's lives do not have an objective reality which can be defined separately from the meaning such events have for the person who experiences them. Thus, whether a specific event is likely to trigger a depressive reaction depends on how it is interpreted. According to Beck's theory, people's interpretations of events are shaped by their personality mode or orientation. Individuals with a sociotropic personality orientation are considered more likely to become depressed if they experience an event which they interpret as involving a loss of social resources (acceptance, support, love). Individuals having an autonomous personality orientation are likely to become depressed if they experience an event that they interpret as involving a personal failure or loss of independence or control (Clark and Steer 1996). In research investigating Beck's cognitive diathesis–stress model, negative events have been classified as either interpersonal- or achievement-related (Clark and Steer ibid.). An example of a negative interpersonal event would be the breakup of a romantic relationship or an interpersonal rejection. A negative achievement event might involve failure on an examination or loss of a job.

The stress component also has been conceptualized in terms of negative events when the diathesis component is defined as dependency and self-criticism (Coyne and Whiffen 1995). From this theoretical perspective, individuals with a dependent personality are likely to become depressed when an interpersonal relationship fails, while individuals having a self-critical personality type become depressed when they fail to achieve a personally significant goal (Blatt et al. 1982). Thus, according to both the psychoanalytic form of diathesis–stress model and that based in Beck's cognitive theory, individuals have an increased vulnerability to depression when they experience a negative event which "matches", or is congruent with, their particular personality type (Coyne and Whiffen 1995).

Assessing the diathesis–stress components

In order to test the hypothesized interaction between personality diatheses and negative events, a requirement of positivist research methods is that each component of the diathesis–stress model can be measured. Thus, following the measurement strategy used in research on personality (described in Chapter 1), various self-report questionnaires have been devised to assess the personality diatheses. The Sociotropy and Autonomy Scale (SAS) (Beck et al. 1983) has been developed to assess the diathesis component proposed in Beck's theory. The Depressive Experiences Questionnaire (DEQ) has been developed to assess dependency and self-criticism (Blatt *et al.* 1976). These two questionnaires contain items derived from theoretical accounts of the relevant personality orientations or types and the item content has been refined through the application of psychometric procedures. The SAS and DEQ continue to undergo revision and new questionnaires for assessing the personality diatheses are being developed (Clark *et al.* 1995, Robins *et al.* 1994).

The following are examples of items contained in the SAS: "Being able to share experiences with other people makes them much more enjoyable for me" (Sociotropy item), "It is more important to be active and doing things than having close relations with other people" (Autonomy item). The following items are taken from the DEQ: "I am very sensitive to others for signs of rejection" (Dependency item), "I often feel that I don't live up to my own standards or ideals" (Self-critical item). A person's total score on each personality scale is used to determine her or his predominant personality orientation or type.

A similar methodology has been used to devise questionnaires for assessing the "stress" component of diathesis–stress models. The strategy typically followed in development of these questionnaires is that researchers first generate a list of negative events, such as the break-up of a romantic relationship or failure on an exam, which are then classified as either interpersonal- or achievement-related events. The stress component is assessed by asking individuals to indicate which of the events they have experienced during a specified time frame (e.g. the last month). The events indicated by an individual can then be assigned to the appropriate category (i.e. either negative interpersonal or negative achievement) based on the predetermined classification developed by researchers.

Testing diathesis–stress explanations for depression

The hypothesis that individuals are likely to become depressed when they experience a negative event matching their personality is usually tested with a research design in which data are produced which can be analyzed by means of statistical procedures to evaluate interactions between variables. The term interaction has a specific technical meaning when data are analyzed using statistics. If an interaction is found to be "statistically significant", this would indicate that the effect of one variable (e.g. stress) on a second variable (e.g. depression) is moderated, or influenced, by a third variable (e.g. personality).

According to proponents of diathesis–stress models, a particular form of interaction is predicted to occur (Clark and Steer 1996, Coyne and Whiffen 1995). Individuals having a sociotropic or dependent personality should become depressed when they experience a negative interpersonal event, but not when they experience a negative achievement event. In contrast, individuals characterized by an autonomous or self-critical personality should become depressed when they experience a negative achievement event, but not when they experience a negative interpersonal event. Thus, neither personality diatheses nor stressful events alone are expected to have an effect on level of depression. If either of these variables on its own were found to predict depression, *and the hypothesized interaction was not present*, such findings would contradict the diathesis–stress approach to explaining depression.

How diathesis–stress models explain depression in women

Two of the approaches to defining and assessing depression which I discussed in Chapter 2 have predominated in research on diathesis–stress models. Depression has been defined as either depressive disorder or depressive symptoms and researchers have argued in favor of each of these approaches (Clark and Steer 1996, Coyne and Whiffen 1995). The third approach discussed in Chapter 2, in which depression is conceptualized as depressive experiences, has not been used in research on diathesis–stress models.

As Coyne and Whiffen (1995) have noted, virtually no attempt has been made in the research on diathesis–stress models to explain women's apparent susceptibility to depression. This neglect is somewhat curious, given consistent findings (reviewed in Chapter 1) of higher rates of depressive disorder and higher levels of depressive symptoms among women than men. The ability of diathesis–stress models to account for these gender-related differences would provide one avenue for evaluating their validity. How might diathesis–stress models account for these gendered patterns?

One possibility is that the proposed personality diatheses may be more characteristic of women than men. For instance, both interpersonal dependency and an affiliative orientation have been considered aspects of "femininity", part of a feminine gender identity (Kantrowitz and Ballou 1992, Miller 1986). And attempts have been made to explain women's greater vulnerability to depression in terms of their feminine personality traits (Whitley 1985). When formulations of diatheses are derived from psychoanalytic theory, characteristics associated with femininity are considered to predispose women to depression. Experiences in early childhood are thought to create psychological conditions which render girls and women more likely than boys and men to develop a "dependent" (or "sociotropic") personality type (Coyne and Whiffen 1995). According to psychoanalytic theory, gender identity has its roots in the dynamics of the mother–child relationship. As a result of continuous contact with the mother in early childhood, both girls and boys develop an identification with, and emotional attachment to, their mother. For girls, this early source of identity is consistent with a subsequent female gender identity. For boys, however, development of a male gender identity requires a switch or separation from the mother as the primary identification figure to that of the father. Thus, male gender identity develops in a context of separation from the mother, rather than an uninterrupted connection with the maternal figure. Also, development of a male gender identity involves identification with the father, who may be an emotionally distant figure in the life of a male child. Such experiences in childhood are theorized to foster greater independence in boys than in girls, whereas, for girls, continuous identification with the maternal figure encourages an interest in interpersonal relationships. According to psychoanalytic theory, therefore, gender differences in vulnerability to depression are established in personality during early childhood (Chodorow 1978).

Is there any evidence that women are more likely than men to have the personality characteristics proposed as diatheses for depression? Some evidence has been reported that on average women do score higher than men on questionnaires designed to assess the personality diatheses of sociotropy and dependency (Clark *et al.* 1995, Rude and Burnham 1995). At the same time, other findings indicate that scores on the SAS and the DEQ measures of personality diatheses correlate less strongly with depressive symptom scores than they do with gender (Coyne and Whiffen 1995). This pattern of findings would not be expected if sociotropy and dependency played the role attributed to them in diathesis–stress models of depression. Such findings suggest instead that the personality orientations of sociotropy/dependency and autonomy/self-criticism may reflect normative conceptions of femininity and masculinity. The suggestion that measures of diatheses for depression may simply be alternate ways of assessing femininity and masculinity seems plausible, given the lack of attention by researchers to symbolic and sociocultural aspects of gender in the development of personality questionnaires. Thus, researchers' conceptions of personality diatheses for depression may incorporate implicit (and therefore unacknowledged) assumptions reflecting a femininity–masculinity form of dualism.

An alternative explanation for women's greater susceptibility to depression is that women are more likely than men to be exposed to stressful events. The stress component of diathesis–stress models typically is assessed using checklists consisting of negative events which are categorized by researchers as involving interpersonal loss or achievement failure. As will be discussed later in this chapter, a limitation of the use of checklists in assessment of stressful events is that they define the social environment in a narrow way so that the perspective they provide on women's lives is rather restricted. The issue of whether women's susceptibility to depression can be explained in terms of their greater exposure than men to negative events is considered in more detail in Chapter 5 when social models are discussed.

Another way in which diathesis–stress models could explain gender-related patterns in rates of depression would be if women are both more likely than men to be characterized by the personality types posited as diatheses *and* more likely to experience negative events that match their personality. This possibility, like the other diathesis–stress explanations for women's increased vulnerability to depression discussed already, would pose difficulties with regard to assessment of personality diatheses and stressful events. Limitations in the conceptualization and measurement of these key components probably underlie the somewhat inconsistent findings of research to date on diathesis–stress models (Coyne and Whiffen 1995).

Empirical evaluations of diathesis–stress models

Both cross-sectional and prospective designs have been employed by researchers in studies evaluating diathesis–stress models. The key hypothesis tested in these studies is that individuals will become depressed when they experience a negative event which matches or is congruent with their personality. Thus, the personality diatheses are expected to interact with exposure to specific types of negative events to predict whether someone will be or become depressed. In cross-sectional studies, the three elements of the hypothesized interaction (personality, negative events, depression) are assessed at the same point in time within a sample of individuals. In such studies, depression typically has been defined as depressive symptoms and assessed via a self-report questionnaire (e.g. the BDI). A prospective design involves first assessing personality diatheses and depression level in a sample of individuals. At a later point (usually several weeks or months after the first assessment) the depression level of the same individuals is assessed a second time and they are asked to report any negative events they may have experienced in the time since the initial assessment.

In a recent review of research on diathesis–stress models of depression by Coyne and Whiffen (1995), five studies were identified in which a cross-sectional design was employed. The most consistent finding across these five studies was a significant interaction between sociotropy or dependency and negative interpersonal events in predicting depression scores. In none of these studies, however, was depression found to be predicted by the interaction between an autonomous or self-critical personality orientation and negative achievement events. Although finding an interaction involving sociotropy (or dependency) would be in line with predictions from diathesis–stress models, Coyne and Whiffen suggest an alternative interpretation. A high score on sociotropy (or dependency) which occurs in conjunction with both the experience of a negative interpersonal event and a high level of depressive symptoms may reflect the effect on a person's interpersonal functioning of a pre-existing state of depression. Thus, high scores on a measure of sociotropy (or dependency) are as likely to be associated with current psychological distress as they are to reflect a stable, enduring personality orientation. In sum, it would appear that findings of cross-sectional studies have not been especially supportive of diathesis–stress explanations for depression.

Studies in which a prospective design has been employed to test the congruency hypothesis also have not yielded particularly encouraging findings. Coyne and Whiffen (1995) included nine prospective studies in their review. In some studies, the interaction between sociotropy (or dependency) and negative interpersonal events was significant, and in others the interaction between autonomy (or self-criticism) and negative achievement events was significant. However, when the predicted interactions were statistically significant, their explanatory power was usually quite modest (i.e. only a relatively small proportion of the "variance" in depression was accounted for). Clark and Steer (1996) describe a more recent prospective study in which the personality diatheses were defined in terms of sociotropy and autonomy and once again the congruency hypothesis received only partial support. The interaction between sociotropy and negative interpersonal events predicted depression (scores on the BDI), whereas the interaction between autonomy and negative achievement events was not significant.

Coyne and Whiffen point out that even when a diathesis–stress interaction is statistically significant, its meaning may be ambiguous. Individuals' responses on personality diathesis measures may reflect reactions to their ongoing life circumstances (e.g. living in an abusive relationship or in poverty), rather than indicating a stable personality trait. Overall, Coyne and Whiffen evaluated the research findings on diathesis–stress models in the following way: "This review does not conclude that personality can be ruled out as a vulnerability factor in depression, but it does suggest that it may be more difficult to establish its role that was first apparent" (1995: 373). Clark and Steer (1996: 91) echoed this conclusion in their analysis of research on Beck's diathesis–stress model of depression: "Until the next generation of cognitive vulnerability studies are completed, the empirical evidence for cognitive diathesis–stress will be at best inconclusive." Nevertheless, the tone of these recent appraisals implies that with some refinements of the theory and adjustments to the research methods, in due course more supportive findings on diathesis–stress models will be forthcoming.

As currently conceptualized, diathesis–stress models are assumed to apply equally well to women and men. One implication of this assumption is that gender does not especially matter in explaining why someone becomes depressed. Is gender as irrelevant to these psychosocial models as their proponents seem to suggest? Coyne and Whiffen (1995) note an apparent "indifference to the question of gender differences in depression" (p. 368) and a lack of exploration of "the relationship of gender to other variables of interest" (p. 368) on the part of those investigating diathesis–stress models. If gender were to be addressed more explicitly in research on diathesis–stress models, would this lead to better understanding of depression in women? Greater recognition among researchers of the need to consider gender in studies on depression might be viewed in a positive light. Such a move would fail, however, to address more fundamental problems in the formulation of diathesis–stress models and the research approaches used to evaluate them.

A feminist and social constructionist analysis of diathesis–stress models

Research on diathesis–stress models of depression generally has been conducted within the framework of the positivist scientific method, which means that particular emphasis is placed on the "objective" measurement of "variables" as a prerequisite for testing causal relationships between variables. This methodological strategy is based on the assumption that observations, interpretations and decisions by researchers can be made in a non-biased, value-free manner to produce "truths" (empirical research findings) with general applicability across individuals, time periods and situations. As I discussed in Chapter 1, an alternative to this positivist perspective is one in which all knowledge (including that produced by the scientific method), is considered to be socially constructed and always partial. The theoretical and methodological assumptions embedded in diathesis–stress models are particularly critical for assessing the relevance of these approaches for understanding depression in women because of the narrow way in which gender (if addressed at all) has been conceptualized. Consequences of the failure to address gender become discernible, however, when the diathesis and stress components of these models are examined more closely, revealing ways in which these formulations are far from gender neutral in their implications.

Gender and diathesis–stress models of depression

To the extent that gender is considered in diathesis–stress models, it is addressed as "sex of subject". That is, research participants are grouped according to their biological sex of assignment as female or male. Thus, any exploration of gender is limited to analysis of sex differences on the variables of interest. Defining gender solely as an individual characteristic is a restriction which precludes consideration of the gendered division of labor in society or symbolic aspects of gender within the sociocultural domain (see Chapter 1 where the concept of gender is discussed). When gender is conceptualized only as a characteristic of the individual, the substantial ways in which the lived experiences of women and men are likely to differ are ignored entirely, or at best are taken for granted. For instance, many women's lives have been depicted as involving a "double day" or "second shift" (Lorber 1994), in which paid employment is added to family responsibilities. Whether women work outside the home or not, women bear children and also are primarily responsible for the care of their children. Although some men may "help" in the home and with childcare, few men experience either the unrelenting demands that caring for children involve or the "double day" constituting many women's lives.

Also unaddressed when gender is conceived as an individual characteristic is the symbolic component of gender. Central to symbolic gender are the widely shared, but largely implicit, beliefs about the nature of femininity and masculinity. Symbolic aspects of gender pervade the cultural domain in western societies and permeate people's lived experiences. For instance, cultural "discourses of femininity" portray the "good" woman as someone whose activities ideally are oriented around relationships with, and caring for, others (especially family members) (Jack 1991, Lorber 1994, Ussher 1991). When gender is defined as an individual characteristic, symbolic aspects of gender are ignored and the sociocultural context of people's lives is rendered invisible.

In research on diathesis–stress models of depression, one consequence of the lack of attention to gender (or a limited treatment of gender as sex of subject) is that social conditions maintaining the gendered division of labor (e.g. unavailability of childcare services, pay and employment inequities) are neither acknowledged nor addressed. Also, failure to consider symbolic aspects of gender means that ways in which the lives and experiences of women are shaped and regulated by cultural discourses of femininity remain unexamined.

Gender and conceptions of diatheses

Within diathesis–stress models, the diatheses are conceptualized as personality traits. These personality traits are presumed to be stable characteristics of an individual and use of the term diathesis implies a predisposition that is inborn. Although the origins of proposed diatheses are not the particular focus of diathesis–stress models, published statements by leading proponents of these models provide an indication of assumptions about their likely sources. Beck (1996: 2), for example, gives the following account of the origins of the personality diatheses (termed primal modes) he posits as underlying vulnerability to various forms of "psychopathology", including depression:

> The "primal modes" of most interest for the study of psychopathology include the derivatives of ancient organizations that evolved in prehistoric circumstances and are manifested in survival reactions, but also, in an exaggerated way, in psychiatric disorders.

In locating the source of diatheses within evolutionary influences, Beck appears to base his theoretical perspective on assumptions which not only set limits on possibilities for individual change, but also rule out any role for contemporary social and cultural influences in understanding why some people become depressed.

Where do diathesis–stress theories come from? In accounts written by researchers who work within a positivist research perspective, ideas typically are expressed in a somewhat detached way (note the third person phrasing in the quote from Beck in the previous paragraph), a style which helps to give the impression that researchers' suppositions are based on objective knowledge. What tends to be overlooked by researchers who take a positivist stance, however, is that whether something is construed as evidence is a matter of interpretation. These interpretational processes moreover are always expressed linguistically, using written or spoken language, and ideas expressed in language inevitably incorporate meaning. The words used to denote a concept or idea simultaneously connote a variety of possible interpretations which are embedded in cultural meaning systems. For instance, the terminology chosen by researchers to refer to personality diatheses carries implicit value assumptions about the characteristics denoted. The term "dependency", for example, not only has a specialized technical meaning with reference to a particular personality orientation, it also signifies a characteristic which is not particularly valued in western culture, in contrast to its obverse "independence", which is more culturally approved.

One strategy adopted by researchers to avoid confusion between technical and everyday meanings of words is to create new terminology to label personality constructs. Use of the term "sociotropy" is an example of this strategy, although the formal definition of sociotropy still refers to personal qualities (i.e. "placing a high value on having close interpersonal relationships and being loved and accepted by others") that do carry value associations. The notions of dependency and sociotropy both imply that being over-involved, or over-invested, in interpersonal relationships is undesirable for a person's psychological functioning and general mental health. Being over-involved in relationships with others, according to diathesis–stress models, is maladaptive because if a relationship breaks down or is otherwise no longer available the dependent or sociotropic person will have an increased risk of becoming depressed.

Personality diatheses are generally conceptualized as bipolar traits. The dimensional nature of diathesis constructs is reflected in the scales used in their assessment, with possible scores ranging from low to high. An interesting feature of these scales is that while the pole defining the diathesis is given a label, its opposite pole is usually left unlabeled and therefore implicit. The opposite of high dependency or high sociotropy for instance might be characterized as placing a low value on interpersonal relationships or having a weak need for support and acceptance from others. As a cluster, perhaps such traits might be labeled "emotional independence" or "relational detachment". If both poles of the dimension anchored at one end by sociotropy/dependency are considered together, it seems to me that they map quite closely onto a dimension defined in terms of cultural notions of femininity and masculinity.

A similar analogy may be drawn between cultural conceptions of masculinity and the personality diatheses of "autonomy" and "self-critical". The central point here is that regardless of empirical evidence marshalled in support of personality diatheses as vulnerability factors for depression, the way they are conceptualized also reflects cultural beliefs about the natures of women and men (i.e. femininity and masculinity). This should hardly be surprising as theorists' ideas are not generated in a vacuum but in a culturally specific context and so are likely to reflect the prevailing cultural beliefs. More generally, this means that standards of adjustment implied by the personality traits hypothesized to be diatheses for depression do not have an objective basis divorced from theorists' values, but are grounded in cultural conceptions of what is considered mentally healthy.

Although little explicit attention has been paid to gender in diathesis–stress models, a focus on the personality traits presumed to underlie vulnerability to depression does have implications which are related to gender. The diatheses of sociotropy and dependency for instance emphasize interpersonal relationships, an area of lived experience culturally associated more with women than men. Caring for others (especially family members) is something which women are expected to do, and many women do give priority in their lives to meeting the caring needs of family members. In conventional terms, developing and cementing a relationship with a man (dating and marriage) are expected to be central goals in young women's lives. Once married, "having a family" becomes the next step for most couples and following the birth of a child mothering becomes a major commitment of most women's lives. The choice to remain unmarried or childless is one that women are neither encouraged nor expected to make. Cultural discourses of femininity, as well as the reality of having children and family members to care for, combine to foster an orientation among women in which "a high value is placed on interpersonal relationships". According to diathesis–stress models, this kind of personality orientation increases the risk of depression. Another way of putting this might be to say that being a woman increases risk of depression. Thus, by ignoring gender, diathesis–stress models unwittingly incorporate assumptions which attribute the source of depression in women to women's feminine personality traits.

The primary purpose of theories of depression is to explain and understand why some people become depressed. When applied to women, diathesis–stress models have been characterized as "victim-blaming" (Lyddon 1995, Stoppard 1989); that is they promote an understanding of depression in which women may be blamed for becoming depressed because of their presumed personality traits. At the same time, a focus on personality serves to encourage the attribution of the causes of women's psychological distress to their personal characteristics, rather than their social circumstances.

Gender and conceptions of stress

Diathesis–stress models incorporate the social environment through use of the stress concept. The stress component of diathesis–stress models is conceptualized in terms of events experienced by a person which are judged to be negative. Typically, the negative quality of events in people's lives (such as the break-up of a close relationship or loss of a job) has been defined by researchers in terms of personal loss or failure (Coyne and Whiffen 1995). As discussed already, the development of measures to assess negative events reflects the assumption that there exists a shared social consensus on what constitutes such events. An issue arising here is the standpoint from which certain events are defined as negative. In research conducted according to the positivist scientific method, negative events are usually defined from the standpoint of researchers. Moreover, in studies testing diathesis–stress models, the categories of stressful events created are assumed to apply in the same way to all research participants, regardless of gender (or social class, age, ethnicity, sexual orientation, and so on).

Efforts by researchers to develop explanations for depression which attend to aspects of the social context of people's lives would appear to represent a promising extension of purely psychological models. As currently conceptualized, however, when the notion of stress is operationalized as "negative life events", it achieves this purpose in a very limited and often misleading way. Although the goal is to address features of the social environment constituting people's everyday lives, formulations of the stress component achieve this in a manner that also "decontextualizes" people's experiences. That is, people's experiences are taken out of context. This decontextualizing or "context-stripping" occurs in two main ways. The first concerns the assumption that events have a shared meaning as negative.

The second involves researchers' neglect of the broader social context beyond the immediate circumstances of people's lives. In each case, although gender has not been addressed explicitly, inclusion of gender would have a considerable impact on how the stress component of diathesis–stress models is conceptualized.

The meaning of an event, its interpretation as negative or otherwise, is likely to depend critically on the life circumstances of the individual to whom it happens. An event, such as the break-up of an intimate relationship or marriage breakdown (considered as a negative interpersonal event in diathesis–stress models), is likely to have rather different implications, and therefore meaning, for women and men. For example, the break-up of the marital relationship of a couple in their forties is unlikely to have a similar meaning for each partner. A woman may have been a housewife and mother for most of her married life and so have fairly limited employment experiences or prospects in terms of ensuring her future financial security. Also, as she ages, opportunities for developing another intimate relationship (marital or otherwise) are likely to be sparse in a cultural context in which women are often judged against standards of physical attractiveness emphasizing a youthful appearance. For a woman, therefore, the ending of a marital relationship is likely to mean more than loss of another's affections (and perhaps also freedom from an abusive partner). It may signify a financially uncertain future in a cultural context in which older women (especially the formerly married) lack both social status and access to economic resources.

For a man in his forties, marital breakdown is likely to have a rather different set of meanings. By the time many men reach middle-age, they have accumulated considerable employment experience as well as financial assets. While the break-up of a marriage may mean loss of a partner's affections and the accompanying life (and identity) as a married man, it is unlikely to have as much impact on other aspects of a man's life. And re-marriage is not ruled out as a possibility for most men. As this example illustrates, ostensibly similar events take on rather different meanings when viewed through the lens of gender.

The failure to take gender into account has additional consequences with regard to the relevance of current formulations of stress for understanding depression in women. People's life circumstances, although partly shaped by their own decisions and actions, also are regulated by conditions which lie beyond their control (and often outside their immediate awareness). These conditions are linked to the broader social, economic and political environment of the society in which they live. When viewed from a feminist perspective, policies and practises prevailing in most areas of the western world operate to create social systems which discriminate against women. This form of discrimination is not limited to situations in which someone behaves in a sexist way toward a woman (e.g. an employer refusing to hire a woman based on her sex). The term "systemic discrimination" refers to the pervasive effects of a system of social and economic conditions in which women face less favorable and more restrictive life options than do men. Women's life circumstances and options are shaped and channeled by political, economic and social conditions in the country where she lives. One consequence of systemic forms of discrimination against women is that many women lead their lives in conformity with prevailing cultural beliefs about what are appropriate life activities for women, while avoiding activities considered culturally inappropriate. Women who attempt to pursue nontraditional lifestyles (for members of their gender) are likely to face impediments which some may find too daunting or difficult to overcome.

The operation of systemic discrimination is well-illustrated in the case of childcare. Caring for children is generally believed to be a particularly appropriate activity for women, not only because women give birth to children but also because of the compatibility assumed between feminine personality traits and the nurturing activities presupposed by childcare. In practise, women are responsible for performing most of the work that mothering children entails and many women do gain considerable satisfaction from their work as mothers. The point here is that if a woman has a child, usually the main option available to her is to provide much of the daily childcare herself. Except for women with the financial resources to pay for childcare, this is likely to be a full-time responsibility (not just nine-to-five, Monday to Friday), at least until a child reaches school age. Women are not paid for the work they do in providing care for their children and, especially during the early years of a child's life, women's employment options are likely to be circumscribed by childcare considerations. Thus, the decision to have a child has implications for a woman's future possibilities which go well beyond the immediate circumstances of her life. If a woman pursues paid employment in conjunction with raising a family, the range and scope of the jobs she can contemplate doing are likely to be much more limited than those open to most men. Systemic gender discrimination also operates in the realm of paid work through the continued existence in most western countries of pay and other employment inequities (United Nations Development Program 1995). It remains the case that most work is structured so that women who are unable to work full-time or who are unavailable for work-related travel are disadvantaged in terms of salary levels, promotion opportunities, and pension provisions.

These are just a few examples of how systemic discrimination based on gender can compound the adverse consequences for women of events, such as marital breakdown, which already are likely to have a negative impact on their lives. When stress is conceptualized without regard to gender, diathesis–stress models seem to offer limited directions for increasing understanding of depression in women. More critically, from a feminist perspective, when formulations of stress ignore gender they serve only to reinforce the status quo of women's lives, because systemic forms of gender discrimination are taken for granted.

According to diathesis–stress models, depression occurs when a person with a particular personality orientation experiences a negative event which is congruent with her personality. Thus, personality is assumed to play an important role in explaining why someone becomes depressed. Diathesis–stress models imply therefore that if a woman only had a different personality, she would not become depressed. The potential for victim-blaming is likely to be exacerbated when pessimistic interpretations by women of negative events in their lives are attributed to their personality rather than to gendered aspects of a negative social reality (Lyddon 1995).

Concluding comments

As I hope the foregoing discussion has indicated, when the core concepts of diathesis–stress models are analyzed from feminist and social constructionist perspectives, consequences of the neglect of gender issues become apparent. However, these are not the only concerns which can be raised about these models. The main mechanism in causing depression postulated by proponents of these models is an interaction between the diathesis and stress components. How such interactions occur, the processes involved, has not been elaborated beyond pointing to such vague notions as "maladaptive appraisals of events". A further limitation of these models is that the focus of theoretical attention is restricted to psychological phenomena and negative events in the social environment. Beyond this, embodied aspects of experience are largely ignored. The physical body is clearly implicated in women's depressive experiences and failure to consider female embodiment would seem a notable omission in any model proposed to explain depression.

4

DEPRESSION AND WOMEN'S PSYCHOLOGY

Susceptibility or specificity?

In this chapter, I focus on explanations for depression in women which have drawn on ideas about women's psychological development. Central to these psychological approaches is the assumption that certain personality traits underlie or explain women's increased *susceptibility* to depression (Nolen-Hoeksema 1990). One version of this psychological approach is based on the assumption that development of a sense of self has different roots in women than men. In this case, an increased vulnerability to depression among women is presumed to lie in the *specific* or unique psychological characteristics which women develop by virtue of being female (Jack 1991, Kaplan 1991). The main way in which these psychological approaches differ from the diathesis–stress form of psychosocial model discussed in the previous chapter is that psychological approaches focus primarily on the personality characteristics of women *as women* to explain why women become depressed. In contrast, explaining depression in women has not been a particular concern of diathesis–stress models.

The chapter is organized as follows. First, I describe the psychological approaches in which certain personality traits are identified as increasing women's *susceptibility* to depression. Discussed next are *specificity* approaches in which women are presumed to develop a gender-specific personality orientation which, under certain circumstances, increases their vulnerability to depression. For each of these approaches, I outline the evidence drawn on to validate claims made by their proponents. Finally, I consider the usefulness of these psychological approaches for understanding depression in women by analyzing the assumptions on which they are based from feminist and social constructionist perspectives.

Female personality characteristics and women's susceptibility to depression

The main idea behind susceptibility formulations is that having certain personality characteristics leads to an increased vulnerability to depression and that women are more likely than men to develop such characteristics and so to be more "depression-prone" (Nolen-Hoeksema 1990). In susceptibility approaches, personality has usually been conceptualized as traits. Traits are conceived as consistent and enduring patterns of beliefs, attitudes and behavioral tendencies which are presumed to predict how someone will feel, think and behave across many situations and across time (Phares 1984).

Personality theorists have proposed that women are likely to develop a particular set of traits as a result of their experiences during development (see Nolen-Hoeksema 1990: Chapter 5). These traits are ones which overlap closely with characteristics considered to reflect psychological aspects of femininity. The notion of a feminine personality is one grounded in views shaped by psychoanalytic theories in which being biologically female is presumed to lead to development in women of feminine psychological characteristics. From this perspective, biological sex prefigures the psychological development of women and men along lines that are consistent with their reproductive functions and also in keeping with the social roles (patterns of daily activities) customarily engaged in by members of each sex.

Women are presumed, therefore, to develop a constellation of feminine personality traits which foster and complement their involvement in activities traditionally performed by women such as childcare and domestic pursuits in support of the needs of family members. Feminine traits emphasize "expressive" personal qualities and include expression of warm emotions, concern for others' feelings and needs, and lack of competitive striving or aggressiveness. From this theoretical vantage point, men are presumed to develop masculine personality traits more in keeping with their traditional role as family breadwinner and protector. Psychologically, masculinity includes traits generally conceived as emphasizing "instrumental" qualities such as competitive striving and self-assertion, lack of interest in relationships or feelings, and an independent stance toward others (Broverman *et al.* 1972). As I outlined in Chapter 3, one way in which these gendered patterns of personality development have been explained is in terms of identification by girls and boys with the mother during the early childhood years. These personality patterns also have been explained as resulting from differential socialization pressures in childhood which channel psychological development of girls and boys along gendered lines.

In theories of depression, parallels have also been drawn between conceptions of feminine personality traits and clinical observations of depressed patients. Accounts by clinicians who work with depressed patients have highlighted the tendency of some individuals to become depressed when a relationship providing emotional support is threatened or lost (e.g. through divorce or death). The personality traits of individuals prone to depression have been described as characterized by excessive needs for approval and support from other people. Thus, according to these clinically-based formulations, people who are likely to become depressed also tend to have difficulty functioning on their own without emotional support from others. In certain respects, these characteristics are similar to the personality orientations of "sociotropy" and "dependency" described in Chapter 3. The similarity between personality traits believed to underlie depression-proneness and those identified as characterizing femininity therefore provides the basis of one psychological formulation for explaining why women might be particularly vulnerable to depression. The source of women's vulnerability to depression resides in their propensity to develop personality traits which also underlie susceptibility to depression.

Conceptions of personality derived from cognitive theories also have been a source of hypotheses about women's susceptibility to depression. In the "learned helplessness" theory of depression, for example, having a cognitive style characterized by a tendency to attribute negative events to causes which cannot be controlled or changed (e.g. personal qualities or aspects of the external environment judged to be intractable) is postulated to increase an individual's vulnerability to depression (Abramson *et al.* 1978). In this case, a link between psychological femininity and a "helplessness" cognitive style has been drawn because this style implies a more passive, less instrumental orientation to the external environment than is associated with psychological masculinity (Nolen-Hoeksema 1990). If a cognitive style which fosters a pessimistic outlook when negative events occur is a feature of feminine psychology, then one outcome would be a heightened vulnerability to depression among women. According to this cognitive perspective, individuals with a helpless attributional style are likely to engage in self-blame and to feel hopeless, experiences which also are part of depression (McGrath *et al.* 1990). An undesirable side-effect of these psychological perspectives in my view is that they put forward ideas which might themselves engender a somewhat hopeless and fatalistic outlook in women who draw on them for understanding their depressive experiences. The message conveyed by these frameworks is that women are powerless to avoid depression because of their femaleness which renders them inherently vulnerable to becoming depressed.

Evaluating psychological susceptibility approaches to explaining depression in women

In research conducted to evaluate psychological susceptibility explanations for depression in women, studies generally have employed the positivist methodology described in Chapter 1. Assessment of personality traits and depression (usually defined as depressive symptoms) has relied mainly on self-report questionnaires. To be supported empirically, a susceptibility explanation for depression in women must meet two initial conditions. First, the personality traits hypothesized to increase vulnerability to depression should be more characteristic of women than men. Second, personality traits proposed as increasing depression-proneness should be more characteristic of depressed than nondepressed individuals.

Over the last few decades a large amount of research has been carried out to investigate whether personality characteristics are associated with gender in a systematic way. The strategy typically employed in these studies has been to compare the scores of females and males on questionnaires designed to assess feminine and masculine traits. A commonly used procedure has been to assess individuals' self-perceptions with regard to whether they possess personality traits categorized respectively as feminine or masculine. The Sex Role Inventory, developed by psychologist Sandra Bem, is an example of this type of measure (Bem 1974). In studies using the Bem Sex Role Inventory and other similar measures, women are generally found to rate themselves as having more feminine and less masculine personality characteristics than do men. Numerous studies also have been conducted to investigate the relationship between individuals' self-rated personality descriptions and their self-reported depressive symptoms. Based on these findings, reviewers have concluded that there is little or no empirical evidence of a relationship between femininity and depression (e.g. McGrath *et al.* 1990, Whitley 1985). At the same time, a consistent finding has been an inverse (i.e. negative) relationship between masculinity and depression. People whose self-descriptions include more masculine, instrumental traits tend to report lower levels of depressive symptoms than do people whose self-descriptions include fewer such traits (McGrath *et al.* 1990, Whitley 1985). This latter finding has been interpreted as indicating that instrumental traits (those stereotypically associated with men and masculinity) may offer some psychological protection against becoming depressed. An alternative interpretation of these findings is that a third personality attribute, self-esteem, may explain the negative relationship between depression and masculine instrumental characteristics, in which case low self-esteem rather than lack of instrumental traits would underlie women's vulnerability to depression (Whitley and Gridley 1993).

In research on susceptibility explanations for depression in women personality traits usually have been assessed at the same time as depressive symptoms. Even if level of depression was found to be related to specific personality characteristics, this cross-sectional research strategy cannot directly address the question of whether vulnerability to depression is greater in individuals with predominantly feminine personality traits than in those with a masculine personality orientation. Such questions can only be answered using a longitudinal research design. An additional limitation of this research is the method used to assess personality traits. When individuals are asked to characterize themselves on traits classified as feminine and masculine, their self-descriptions are likely to be influenced by culturally shared and stereotypical views of gender.

A slightly different research strategy has been to focus on single personality traits which are assumed to be feminine and also hypothesized to increase vulnerability to depression. Several overviews of the findings of this kind of study (e.g. Hamilton and Jensvold 1992, McGrath *et al.* 1990, Nolen-Hoeksema 1990) have arrived at similar conclusions. When such traits as unassertiveness, dependency, and a pessimistic attributional style have been considered, studies have failed to reveal clear-cut or consistent findings of differences between women and men on these personality characteristics. Moreover, as Nolen-Hoeksema (1990) noted, when sex-related differences have been found, their magnitude generally is insufficient to account for observations of higher rates and levels of depression among women than men. Nolen-Hoeksema (ibid.: 157) summarized the findings of these studies in the following way:

> The most salient feature of the literature reviewed here . . . is the absence
> of evidence of some of the most commonly held beliefs about sex differ-
> ences in personality: that women are less assertive, more dependent, and
> have worse attributional styles than men.

Nolen-Hoeksema's conclusion argues against the position that feminine personality characteristics underlie women's vulnerability to depression – at least when
personality is defined in terms of traits and measured using positivist methods.
Formulations based in the trait concept represent only one way in which personality aspects of femininity can be conceptualized. Psychological specificity
approaches offer a perspective based in a somewhat different conception of personality.

Women's psychological specificity and depression: the relational self

Specificity approaches to understanding depression in women are grounded in theories of women's psychological development in which a central concept is "the
relational self" (Chodorow 1978, Miller 1986). From this perspective, psychological development in women is understood as taking place within a gender-specific
interpersonal context which results in women developing a personality orientation
which also is gender-specific. Relationships with others lie at the core of this female
psychological specificity, shaping both women's lived experiences and their sense of
self. In contrast to susceptibility approaches, in which feminine personality traits
may be seen as a psychological liability (especially when coupled with lack of masculine traits), expressive aspects of femininity are viewed positively within specificity
approaches, marking an area of strength in female psychology. Thus, rather than
rejecting notions of inherent personality differences between women and men,
relational approaches both affirm such differences and place a positive value on
psychological femininity (Jordan et al. 1991).

According to relational theories, sense of self develops in women in the context
of their ongoing relationships with others, a process beginning with the
mother–daughter dyad (Chodorow 1978, Jordan et al. 1991). Relational theorists
also take issue with the assumption underpinning most mainstream personality
models that development of an autonomous, independent self-concept is the hallmark of a healthy, well-adjusted personality. Instead, relational theorists highlight
connection with others as the critical experience in psychological development in contrast to separation from others. Within this theoretical perspective, women's
relationships with others represent a critical context for psychological growth and
learning (Surrey 1991).

Depression is understood within relational accounts of women's development as
a set of experiences which are grounded in interpersonal processes. Thus, women
are likely to become depressed when their possibilities for relational intimacy with
another person are blocked or thwarted (Kaplan 1991). This assumption provides

63

the basis for the model of depression formulated by relational theorist Dana Jack (1991). According to Jack's model, depressive experiences in women are closely linked to a dynamic she calls "self-silencing", a process exacerbated by a relational context in which a woman fears being abandoned emotionally by a key relationship partner (typically a romantic partner or spouse). Within this framework, experiences which are part of depression are particularly likely to arise when a woman realizes the impossibility of developing an intimate connection with her relational partner. Self-silencing involves a woman's denial of her own needs and feelings as a way of maintaining the relationship while keeping open the possibility that a sense of connectedness with the partner may still be developed.

From this relational perspective, women's relationship orientation is seen as a gender-specific psychological strength involving qualities underpinning women's participation in nurturing activities, particularly within the family context. At the same time, these psychological assets may handicap woman's well-being. Through development of a self-identity grounded in relationships, a woman's nurturing activities are guided by an ethic in which meeting others' needs takes precedence over meeting her own needs. When a woman's core relationships (i.e. as a wife and a mother) provide opportunities to express and act upon her own needs in ways enabling her to maintain a relational sense of self, psychological well-being is not jeopardized. On the other hand, if key relationships are conflicted or fail to provide an interpersonal context in which her relational needs can be met, a woman's identity is also undermined. At the psychological level, if a woman's relational needs are disappointed, she may respond by silencing the self (Jack 1991), a process which also curtails her own development. For many women, the option of seeking new relational connections is not one pursued easily, especially when children are dependent on a mother's care and access to material resources is limited. According to Jack, risk of depression in women increases within relational contexts which foster self-silencing in women, conditions exacerbated by power inequalities in women's relationships with men. From this relational perspective, depressive experiences are the outcome of a woman's realization that she has "lost herself" in a failed effort to establish and maintain a connection with her relationship partner. The experiences called depression, therefore, are the psychological consequences of a woman's inability to develop her relational self (Jack 1991, Kaplan 1991).

Evaluating psychological specificity approaches to understanding depression in women

Specificity approaches to understanding depression in women are informed by analyses of women's experiences, particularly accounts gathered in the context of therapy (Jordan *et al.* 1991). Thus, researchers whose work is informed by a relational perspective generally rely upon the method of qualitative interviewing (Kimball 1994). An important example of this work is that by psychologist Dana Jack, who explored the implications of a relational perspective for understanding depression in women in her book *Silencing the self: Women and depression* (1991).

The analysis presented by Jack is based on material she collected in semi-structured interviews with twelve women who had been diagnosed by a physician as "clinically depressed" according to the diagnostic criteria for depression given in the third edition of the *Diagnostic and Statistical Manual of Mental Disorders* (DSM) (American Psychiatric Association 1980). The women ranged in age from 19 to 55 and were described as being "caucasian". All were currently or formerly married and eight had children. Each woman was interviewed on two occasions, once when she was actively depressed and again about two years later.

In analyzing themes in the women's accounts of their depressive experiences Jack paid particular attention to the moral content of their narratives. A dominant theme in these accounts was the importance for the women of living up to their conception of what it meant to be a "good woman". A good woman, according to these accounts, is one who places the goal of pleasing others (especially a husband) ahead of meeting her own needs. These depressed women viewed failure in the relationship domain as a negative indictment of their self-worth. For instance, one woman interviewed by Jack (1991: 99) is quoted as saying: "If you please, you're the kind of woman, the kind of wife you should be. And if you don't, then you're not". Another woman said "[t]his has always been my baseline, and that is, to please my husband" in describing her ideal of a "good wife" (Jack 1991: 75). For the women interviewed by Jack, being a good wife meant avoiding conflict with, and not expressing anger toward, the relational partner.

In the qualitative research approach used by Jack, evidence for themes revealed in her analysis of the women's accounts is presented in the form of excerpts selected from the interview transcripts. An evaluation of the validity of this evidence rests on somewhat different considerations than those involved when research is conducted according to the positivist scientific method. Stiles (1993) has identified two key issues which arise when judgments are made about the validity of findings from qualitative research. The first, termed "procedural trustworthiness", concerns the adequacy of a researcher's exposure to, or immersion in, the particular phenomenon which is the focus of inquiry (in this case women's depressive experiences). The second is referred to by Stiles as "interpretational trustworthiness" and concerns whether the analysis presented provides sufficient information for readers to form their own judgments independent of the researcher's interpretations. Also related to this last point is whether the formulation proposed offers useful (or "fruitful") directions for further understanding (Stiles ibid.). Usefulness in this case might be judged, for instance, with respect to whether the analysis presented by Jack is one that other women find meaningful. From a feminist perspective, additional considerations might include the impact of the analysis on actions intended to alleviate the distress experienced by individual women as well as its implications for improving the lives of women in general.

A more mainstream validational strategy is employed by Jack, involving use of a questionnaire, the *Silencing the Self Scale* (STSS) (Jack and Dill 1992), to assess self-silencing beliefs. According to Jack (1996: 12), "The STSS measures two things: first, a set of beliefs or images about *relatedness* . . . and second, the *experience of self* that occurs as one lives out the behaviors and judges the self according to these beliefs about how one 'should' relate intimately" (emphasis in original). The STSS consists of 31 items organized into four subscales which were rationally derived to represent separate dimensions reflecting the main themes in Jack's analysis of the accounts of depressed women. These four subscales are labeled: *Externalized Self-Perception* (judging the self by external standards); *Care as Self-Sacrifice* (securing attachments by putting the needs of others before the self); *Silencing the Self* (inhibiting one's self-expression and action to avoid conflict and possible loss of relationship); *Divided Self* (the experience of presenting an outer compliant self to live up to feminine role imperatives while the inner self grows angry and hostile) (Jack and Dill 1992). The STSS is completed by asking a person to rate each item on a five-point scale (from strongly agree to strongly disagree) and then subscale and total scale scores are generated by summing ratings across the relevant items.

The personality attributes assessed by the STSS are not conceptualized as stable traits by Jack (1991, 1996). Instead, self-silencing beliefs and the behaviors which stem from them are considered to be "reflexive" in that they are influenced or shaped, by a woman's social context and specific relationships. The source of self-silencing, according to Jack (1996: 15), lies in conditions characterized by "specific forms of unequal, negative intimate relationships as well as larger social structures that demean an individual's sense of self-worth".

Information bearing on the validity of the STSS has been provided by several studies (see Jack 1996, Jack and Dill, 1992). A consistent finding of these studies has been that higher STSS scores are associated with higher scores on depressive symptom measures, a relationship now replicated with various samples of women and men. A finding which cannot easily be explained in terms of Jack's self-silencing theory is that men's scores on the STSS have been found on average to be higher than women's (Gratch *et al.* 1995, Jack and Dill 1992, Thompson 1995). Jack (1996) has argued that although men may silence the self as much as, or more than, women, the *meaning* of self-silencing is different for each gender. In support of this proposition, Jack cites findings showing that relationship variables, such as attachment style, perceived power and use of direct power strategies in relationships, are correlated differently with the STSS in women and men. Nevertheless, these findings challenge the idea that self-silencing, at least as indexed by scores on the STSS, is a process unique to women. This is a particular problem for Jack's relational theory of depression because of the claim that self-silencing beliefs are reflexive with social context and specific relationships.

If self-silencing beliefs are reflexive attributes rather than stable personality traits, endorsement of such beliefs should vary across groups of women who differ in the degree to which their experiences occur in contexts shaped by social, economic and interpersonal inequalities. In support of this aspect of her theory, Jack points to evidence that women with a history of sexual and/or physical abuse have higher STSS scores than women who have not been victims of abuse (Jack 1996, Jack and Dill 1992). Moreover, women whose primary source of income is social assistance ("welfare") were found to have higher STSS scores than women whose financial support came from family sources (i.e. self-earned, jointly with husband/ partner or husband/partner alone) (Jack 1996). A similar pattern of findings on the STSS was reported by Belliveau (1998) based on a study of depression with women who were single-parents. Belliveau found that women with a history of sexual and/or physical abuse had higher STSS scores than women who did not report such a history and that women receiving social assistance had higher scores than women who were economically self-sufficient. In sum, when evaluated using main-stream research methods, this aspect of silencing the self theory has received some support from empirical findings.

A central assumption of self-silencing theory is that women's vulnerability to depression lies in their development of a self-identity which is grounded in inter-personal experiences. This relational self can be contrasted with a separated sense of self, which is depicted in relational theories as more characteristic of men's psy-chological development than women's. Silencing the self theory therefore rests on the assumption that women and men are essentially different in their personality development. Moreover, unlike susceptibility approaches which point to socializa-tion practises as a key source of psychological differences between females and males, specificity approaches imply that more fundamental psychological differ-ences exist between the sexes prior to the influence of socialization experiences. In specificity approaches, these psychological sex differences are presumed to have their origins in the mother–child relationship during infancy. For female children, a form of psychological identification based in biological similarity is posited to occur between a mother and her daughter. A relational orientation, the hallmark of feminine personality, is theorized therefore as the "natural" outcome of an identification process which is rooted in female biology. Thus, this psychological account implies that vulnerability to depression is an inherent feature of women's biological makeup, a predisposition which is reinforced when women mother children.

A feminist and social constructionist analysis of psychological accounts of depression in women

The susceptibility and specificity forms of psychological approach both draw on personality constructs to account for vulnerability to depression in women. Although personality is conceptualized in somewhat different ways within these two approaches, each is predicated on somewhat similar assumptions about per-sonality and also about depression and gender. Analysis of these approaches from feminist and social constructionist perspectives reveals that the conceptions of per-sonality, depression, and gender they incorporate limit the utility of these theories for understanding women's depressive experiences. In the following discussion, although these topics are addressed separately, this should not be taken to imply that the concerns I identify are distinct and unrelated. They have common roots in more overarching assumptions about what constitutes knowledge and the appro-priate methods for acquiring knowledge. These assumptions, which I discussed earlier (see Chapters 1 and 2), are those underpinning the positivist epistemology informing mainstream approaches to research on depression.

Conceptions of personality in susceptibility and specificity approaches

In both susceptibility and specificity approaches, personality generally is conceptualized as a set of relatively enduring psychological attributes which are manifested by individuals in a consistent way over time and situations. A woman's personality is seen therefore as an important determinant of her behavior. Although situational factors may be given some weight in explaining an individual's behavior, environmental influences are viewed as conditions external to the person which have an influence on behavior through their interactions with personality. This way of conceptualizing personality presupposes that individuals have an inherent personality, or psychological nature, discoverable by means of questionnaires or other objective procedures. Although this view of personality may have a common sense validity (we think of ourselves and others as having personalities), it reflects an assumption which has been termed "essentialist". Essentialism is defined as "the view that objects (including people) have an essential, inherent nature which can be discovered" (Burr 1995: 184)). An essentialist view of personality is apparent in both susceptibility and specificity approaches to explaining depression in women.

Within susceptibility approaches, personality traits characterizing psychological femininity are hypothesized to be a source of women's vulnerability to depression. The origin of these feminine traits has not been a particular concern in susceptibility accounts of depression in women, although usually assumed to be the result of socialization experiences. In this view, girls develop gender-typed personality characteristics through observing and interacting with adults. Once acquired, these feminine traits are assumed to be a stable feature of a woman's personality and to influence how she behaves.

The focus of specificity approaches is the relational self, a sense of self which women develop through forming intimate connections with others (Jordan et al. 1991, Miller 1986). The account of depression in women provided by Jack (1991) presupposes the relational self as the most authentic component of women's personality. It is this authentic relational self, according to Jack, which becomes silenced when women evaluate themselves against the values associated with the good woman. To consider herself "good", a woman must willingly sacrifice her own needs in service of those of husband and family and put the needs of these relational others ahead of her own. In this formulation, beliefs underlying the process of self-silencing reflect cultural discourses which construct nurturing activities as primarily a woman's responsibility, a reflection of social values based in patriarchal (male-centered) assumptions about women. In Jack's view, depression in women is an experience of self which arises from contradictions between the authentic, relational self and beliefs about the self reflected in patriarchal ideologies and dominant social discourses. In her self-silencing account of depression, Jack comes close to adopting a nonessentialist, social constructionist perspective on personality. Ultimately, however, an essentialist perspective is maintained when the notion of authentic self is invoked and a woman's relational self is taken as signifying her "true" self.

From a social constructionist perspective, the assumptions underlying conceptions of personality in susceptibility and specificity approaches are problematic because they ignore the contributions of language and social interaction in people's attempts to make sense of their experiences. Within a social constructionist approach, people's experiences of self – their sense of who they are – are understood as being formed (or constructed) in the course of their interactions (both interpersonal and symbolic) with the world around them. Much of this interaction takes place linguistically through expression of meaning in various forms of communication (e.g. talk, written and visual media, and nonverbal modes). Identity is part of "subjectivity" (see Chapter 1 where this term was discussed) which is understood within a social constructionist perspective as constituted by the discourses (or sets of cultural meanings) circulating within a particular societal context. Ideas circulating discursively around what it means to be a woman have cultural implications for conceptions of "woman's nature" which are varied and often conflicting. For example, contemporary discourses about the place of women in society include the following contradictory positions: "women are essentially maternal and having children represents the fulfilment of their natures" and "women have the same abilities as men and have as much right as men to pursue fulltime careers." The ideas people have about who they are (identity) and what actions they should pursue in their lives are shaped in relation to these discursive constructions. The "subject positions" which people take up are constituted within the discourses available to them. For instance, some of the subject positions discursively available to women in the current era are "mother", "wife", and "career woman". From a feminist perspective, many of the discourses circulating about women and their place in society are considered to promote patriarchal views and to construct subject positions for women which subordinate them to men. At the same time, an important issue from a social constructionist perspective is how women develop a coherent sense of self, given the conflicting and contradictory nature of the discursive resources available to them.

Attempts to explain depression in women relying on personality formulations submerge subjectivity and identity issues within such essentialist concepts as trait and relational self. The emphasis in positivist research on the need for researchers to be objective also serves to foster a view of knowledge as detached from the influence of prevailing cultural values. This objective stance obscures the role played by language in shaping the meaning of concepts. As I discussed in the previous chapter, the terms used to label personality constructs are never entirely value-neutral and inevitably reflect symbolic aspects of gender. Labels for concepts used in academic publications and in textbooks sooner or later are taken up in everyday (or "popular") discourses and in this way contribute to discursive constructions of the "psychology of women". Personality formulations of depression in women, whether the susceptibility or specificity variant, also can be used to support views in which women are blamed for their psychological distress. These approaches provide a context in which victim-blaming interpretations can flourish because they direct attention away from the broader social context and ways in which women's lives are regulated by systemic forms of discrimination within the social, economic and political domains.

Conceptions of depression in susceptibility and specificity approaches

In research on personality approaches, depression has most often been defined as depressive disorder or depressive symptoms. When these definitional approaches are used, depression is conceptualized as a condition which exists within a woman, something capable of being understood separately from her personality. The assumption that depression is a condition within the person is implicit in the use of diagnostic procedures and symptom questionnaires to assess depression. The widespread adoption of these measurement strategies reflects unquestioned acceptance of a conception of depression as a form of individual psychopathology, a mental disorder rooted within the body's biological processes. A consequence of this uncritical reliance on mainstream formulations is that it undermines the potential of accounts based in women's experiences for challenging prevailing assumptions about depression. As an example, in studies investigating depression in women from a relational perspective, researchers have often failed to distinguish between depression defined as a disorder and depression defined as symptoms. So long as this confusion exists, findings of studies are likely to be dismissed by mainstream researchers.[1]

When conceptions of depression are preset by the contents of diagnostic criteria and symptom questionnaires, as is the case in much of the research on susceptibility and specificity forms of psychological approach, possibilities for understanding women's experiences are foreclosed. Although an attempt is made in specificity formulations to develop an understanding of depression in terms of women's experiences of self, this effort falls short because depression is conceptualized as a condition apart from the relational self. This conceptual confusion is further confounded by reliance on assumptions derived from a psychoanalytic theoretical perspective. The account of depression offered by researchers who position their work in formulations of women's psychological specificity incorporates explanatory mechanisms couched in terms of "loss" (of "self") and "anger turned inward", ideas having psychoanalytic origins (Jack 1991, Kaplan 1991).

Conceptions of gender in susceptibility and specificity approaches

In both susceptibility and specificity approaches, gender has been conceptualized primarily in terms of individual gender, as characteristics of individuals who are either female or male. The gendered division of social labor, and the structural conditions maintaining this division along gendered lines, have not been considered as aspects of gender in susceptibility formulations. Within specificity approaches, the gendered character of work within the family (e.g. childcare is carried out mostly by women) is attributed to women's psychological orientation toward relationships and their development of a relational self. Structural conditions (economic and political) which operate to maintain existing gender arrangements are largely ignored in specificity approaches (although acknowledged in Jack's theory), so in general these formulations provide little support for feminist efforts to challenge systemic gender inequalities. From a feminist perspective, the compatibility of specificity approaches with the status quo of prevailing gender relations diminishes their potential for contesting either the continued dominance of men and male values in the public sphere or social conditions which relegate women to the private sphere of the home and family life.

Symbolic aspects of gender within the linguistic domain also are neglected in psychological approaches to depression in women. In susceptibility accounts, symbolic aspects of gender are most likely to be characterized as instances of gender stereotype beliefs. From a mainstream standpoint, gender stereotypes are widely shared, but largely erroneous, beliefs about the natures of women and men. The tendency of women to develop expressive rather than instrumental personality traits is attributed to the actions of parents who socialize their children in conformity with gender stereotypes. From this perspective, part of the solution to addressing the problem of depression is to refute gender stereotypes through empirical demonstration of the absence of sex differences on key personality variables (e.g. Nolen-Hoeksema 1990). When symbolic aspects of gender are interpreted as the vestiges of misplaced beliefs in gender stereotypes, susceptibility approaches provide a warrant for intervention strategies which have the aim of helping women to develop more masculine personality characteristics. The rationale for programs designed to increase women's self-confidence or assertiveness, for example, is that they offer women ways to offset or counteract the presumed debilitating consequences of their psychological femininity.

Symbolic aspects of gender receive more explicit acknowledgement in specificity approaches. Rather than disputing gender stereotypes, such beliefs are reinforced by placing a positive value on expressive traits and women's relational orientation in an effort to challenge the cultural denigration of feminine characteristics. This move by specificity theorists toward a re-valuing of traits culturally defined as feminine has not however been accompanied by a thorough-going exploration of symbolic aspects of gender. In Jack's (1991) self-silencing theory moral themes in depressed women's narratives are highlighted. These themes were reflected in the meanings associated with being a good woman. According to Jack, the source of depression in women lies in deep-rooted contradictions between cultural images of the good woman and an individual woman's ability to meet her own needs, defined in terms of her relational sense of self. In this formulation, women's experiences of depression are presumed to result from a loss of self or an inability to express the authentic self. Although some areas of women's experiences can be conceptualized as symbolic aspects of gender (e.g. discourses of the good woman), the relational self is viewed as a manifestation of personality, a characteristic of individual women. Measurement of self-silencing beliefs (e.g. with the STSS) further obscures symbolic aspects of gender in individualizing constructs. A finding which is particularly difficult for this specificity approach to explain is that men have been found to endorse self-silencing beliefs as much as, or more than, women do (Jack 1996). Such findings appear puzzling so long as symbolic aspects of gender are confounded with individual gender characteristics.[2]

A limitation of both susceptibility and specificity approaches is that they assume a conception of gender defined narrowly as an attribute of the individual. Neither approach addresses the gendered division of social labor or structural conditions which discriminate against women and channel their activities into the confines of the private, domestic arena. In susceptibility approaches, moreover, conflation of symbolic aspects of gender with gender stereotypes, precludes any consideration of gender within the cultural and linguistic domains. Although there is some acknowledgement of symbolic aspects of gender within specificity approaches, this is not well-developed and ultimately gender is conceptualized in individual terms.

Concluding comments

Unlike the diathesis–stress models discussed in Chapter 3, gender has been a central theme when explanations for depression have drawn on psychological constructs, although this attention has been restricted to a focus on individual gender. Structural and symbolic aspects of gender, on the other hand, have barely been recognized. The other two components of these psychological approaches – personality and depression – generally are conceptualized in ways which ground them firmly in mainstream formulations of these constructs.

From a social constructionist perspective, a limitation which pervades these psychological approaches is their inability to escape from positivist epistemological assumptions. Consequently, psychological explanations for depression in women do not address how subjectivity (sense of self) in women is socially constructed within the symbolic realm of language and meaning. Instead susceptibility approaches point to socialization experiences and specificity approaches focus on beliefs about self-in-relationships. Psychological formulations also pay little attention to women's bodies and their contribution to depression in women. In specificity approaches, although women's psychology is rooted in female biology, women virtually disappear as "embodied subjects" in relational accounts of depression.

As feminist psychotherapist Harriet Lerner concluded in discussing relational theories of women's psychology: "it is not women's 'affiliative needs' or 'relationship-orientation' that predisposes females to depression, for emotional connectedness is a basic human need as well as a strength. Rather, it is what *happens* to women in relationships that deserves our attention" (Lerner 1987: 218, emphasis in original). The things that happen to women in relationships have been the focus of attempts to link depression in women to their social situations. Social models of depression in women are considered in the next chapter.

Notes

1 The research conducted by Jack and her colleagues is a case in point. The women who participated in Jack's (1991) study were diagnosed as "clinically depressed" according to DSM criteria. In studies using the Silencing the Self Scale (Jack and Dill 1992), in contrast, depression usually has been assessed with self-report symptom questionnaires.
2 As Kimball (1994: 391) noted, failure to distinguish individual and symbolic conceptions of gender is an unrecognized source of confusion in debates between psychologists who work within a "gender similarities" perspective and those who take a "gender differences" position.

5

SOCIAL MODELS OF DEPRESSION

Sources of adversity and stress in women's lives

At the core of social models of depression is the idea that people become depressed because of things which happen to them. Social models locate the source of depression within a person's environment, whereas in the diathesis–stress and personality approaches discussed so far, the source of depression is located either partly or wholly within the individual. Researchers interested in social explanations for depression have focused on identifying those aspects of the environment in which people live which have a negative influence on their mental health and increase their risk of becoming depressed.

A central issue in social models is how best to define the environment and two main strategies have been followed. The first strategy has focused on particular events or circumstances in people's lives and how they should be conceptualized and measured. The types of events and circumstances most often investigated are those characterized by negative or unpleasant consequences for individuals who experience them. Collectively termed *adversity*, events and circumstances with negative consequences include such things as the death of a close relative, becoming unemployed, the break-up of a close relationship, or being the victim of a serious crime or accident. The mechanism most often proposed to explain the link between adversity and depression is *stress* (Kessler 1997).

In its focus on the negative events occurring in people's lives, this approach to conceptualizing the social environment has some similarities with the way stress has been defined in the diathesis–stress models I discussed in Chapter 3. Depression in women has not been a central concern of social models using this strategy for defining the environment, though the work of George Brown and Tirril Harris (1978, 1989), which has focused almost exclusively on women, has been particularly influential. Brown and Harris have developed a method for assessing life event stress in which special attention is paid to the contextual details of people's everyday lives. This "contextual" approach to assessment of the environmental influences in people's lives is considered by some researchers to be the most useful of the methods currently available (Coyne 1994, Kessler 1997). The implications of Brown and Harris' work for understanding depression in women is explored in greater detail in the next section, where I discuss the form of social model in which depression is explained in terms of adversity and stress in people's lives.

The second main strategy followed in the development of social explanations for depression has focused more directly on the lives of women and men with the goal of identifying how sources of stress arise in different ways in the lives of each gender. Underlying this strategy is the assumption that women are more likely than men to become depressed because of women's lower status in society and, more especially, women's roles within the family (McGrath *et al.* 1990, Nolen-Hoeksema 1990). These approaches, therefore, explain depression among women in terms of specific sources of adversity and stress which are likely to be present in their lives. Explanations for depression in women addressing the gendered character of adversity and stress are explored in a later section. I conclude the chapter with an evaluation of social models from feminist and social constructionist perspectives.

Life events and depression: adversity and stress

Attempts to explain why people become depressed in terms of the things which happen to them are certainly not new. Writing around the beginning of the twentieth century, Freud (1917) drew a connection between mourning and melancholia (an earlier term for depression) and clinicians have long noted the frequency of events involving loss in the lives of depressed patients. In more recent decades, interest in whether psychological distress is caused by events in people's lives has been stimulated by Selye's work on the role of psychosomatic processes within the human body in understanding how people adapt to environmental stressors (Selye 1956). Evidence that levels of depressive symptoms and rates of depressive disorder within a population are related systematically to such characteristics as socioeconomic, marital, and employment status also points to the potential importance of social influences in explaining depression. Levels and rates of depression have been found to be higher among those with lower levels of income and education and who are unemployed and lower among married people and those employed in more prestigious (and higher paying) occupations (Aneshensel 1992, Turner and Roszell 1994). Efforts to understand these associations between people's social characteristics and their risk of becoming depressed have motivated various attempts to identify the features of people's lives which could explain variation in risk of depression across individuals.

To test social models of depression, information about people's life experiences has been collected in two main ways. The first has involved the use of life event checklists like those described in Chapter 3 for assessment of the stress component of diathesis–stress models. The contextual method developed by Brown and Harris (1978, Brown 1989) is the other main approach used. Although various checklists have been devised to assess life events, there is currently some agreement among researchers in this field that the use of checklists alone is inadequate (Kessler 1997, Munroe and McQuaid 1994). The main limitation of checklists lies in their inflexibility and inability to capture the unique and idiosyncratic nature of events occurring in people's lives. Although the standardized format of checklists appears to be objective and provides an efficient way of collecting information, a drawback of this method is its lack of sensitivity to differences between individuals in the impact of apparently similar events (Kessler 1997). Checklists also have been criticized because of their limited coverage of events involving personal trauma (e.g. sexual and physical abuse) and other forms of victimization more commonly experienced by women than men (Koss *et al.* 1994, McGrath *et al.* 1990).

Proposals for overcoming the limitations of checklists include combining them with interviews and refining their design to allow more detailed information to be collected (Kessler 1997, Munroe and McQuaid 1994). The use of interviews to gather information about the events and circumstances of people's lives was pioneered by Brown and Harris (1978). A noteworthy feature of Brown and Harris' interview approach is the emphasis placed on gathering information about the specific circumstances of people's everyday lives to provide a background context for determining the impact of the events they experience. This contextual method of assessment is described next.

Contextual assessment of life event severity

The concept of "provoking agent" is central to Brown and Harris's (1978, 1989) social model of depression and assessment of life event severity is the primary means by which provoking agents are identified. In their concept of provoking agent, Brown and Harris include both fairly discrete life events as well as ongoing, chronic life difficulties. The severity of each type of experience is assessed using the same basic procedure and, for discussion purposes, I focus here on the method used to assess life events. The main tool developed by Brown and Harris for assessment of life events is the Life Events and Difficulties Schedule (LEDS) (Brown 1989, Brown and Harris 1978), which is a semi-structured interview designed to collect information from a person about a wide range of potential sources of stress. As mentioned already, the bulk of Brown and Harris' research on depression has focused on women and so in describing the LEDS I assume that the person being interviewed is a woman. Information collected in the LEDS interview covers both the life events a woman may have experienced and the background to these events with reference to the present and past circumstances of her life. This contextual form of assessment is therefore quite different from the checklist approach because the information gathered goes well beyond simply asking individuals to indicate which of the events on a predetermined list they have experienced.

A second distinctive feature of the LEDS is the procedure used to evaluate the severity of life events. Severity ratings are made by judges based on a woman's interview transcript, but without having any information about her diagnostic status with regard to depression or her reactions to the life events she reports. Judges rate an event's unpleasantness with respect to the threat it poses in the context of a woman's ongoing life. These ratings of contextual threat are anchored in relation to how an "average woman" or "most women" living in similar circumstances and having a similar biography would be expected to feel. Brown and Harris have consistently found that only "severe" events (i.e. those having "marked" or "moderate" long-term threat) focused either directly on a woman or jointly with someone else, predict depression.[1]

As Brown and Harris (1978: Chs. 4 and 5) explain, use of independent judges to assess event severity is necessary in order to control for possible sources of contamination or bias which could inflate an association between life events and depression. Without this precaution, they argue, it would not be possible to establish a causal link between life events and the subsequent onset of depression. In a similar vein, a woman's reported reaction to an event (e.g. her statement that she found an event unpleasant and upsetting) could not be used to provide an indication of event severity, because it might reflect her depressed state and for this reason would not be considered an objective source of information. According to Brown and Harris (1978: 273), independent ratings of severity also are needed, because "the world is capable of having an impact irrespective of the meanings a person brings [to] it." Thus, a woman might report that she did not experience an event as unpleasant or upsetting, while an independent observer might have a different view. If this were the case, basing an analysis of links between life events and depression on a woman's account would obscure a relationship which might actually exist. Regardless of the rationale given, Brown and Harris appear to have adopted the strategy of using independent judges as a way to maximize objectivity, a key requirement of research conducted according to the positivist scientific method.

One of the first studies to use the LEDS was reported by Brown and Harris in their 1978 book *The social origins of depression: A study of psychiatric disorder in women*. This study involved a large sample of women living in a south London community. Based on ratings of contextual threat to measure event severity, Brown and Harris found that more than two-thirds of the women diagnosed as depressed during the one-year study period had experienced a severe life event (or provoking agent). Among the women who did not become depressed, less than one third had experienced an event rated as having severe contextual threat. This basic finding has been replicated in several subsequent studies with other samples of women (Brown and Harris, 1989).[2]

Contextual threat and the meaning of events in women's lives

In Brown and Harris' social model, the depressive impact of provoking agents is attributed to the severity of events in women's lives. Severity is defined in terms of contextual threat, which in turn is based on ratings by independent judges whose judgments are intended to reflect the meaning of events reported by women in the LEDS interview. As indicated by Brown and Harris (1978: 91), "[w]e wished these contextual measures to retain an important, perhaps crucial, element of meaning while ignoring what we had obtained by way of self-reports of threat and unpleasantness." The importance placed on the meaning of events in this social approach is further underlined in the following excerpt from Brown and Harris' 1978 book:

> In depression the role of the provoking agents is more than that of mere triggers of a condition whose aetiology lies largely elsewhere and we attribute its onset . . . primarily to experiences of loss and disappointment, *particularly those involving the woman's view of her own identity* (emphasis added, pp. 285–6).

Despite this emphasis on the need to explore the meaning of women's experiences, use of the LEDS to assess life event severity depends on independent judges, rather than women themselves. When the LEDS is employed in this way, the meaning of women's experiences is addressed by proxy from the perspective of researchers. This position is explicitly acknowledged by Brown and Harris (1978: 273):

> The question therefore arises whose perspective do we take about life-events and the changes they entail? Is any perspective more true than another? Much will depend on what we are trying to do but it is difficult to contemplate any way of dealing with such multiple perspectives without the investigator at some stage imposing his [sic] *own* viewpoint on the world (emphasis in original).

Thus, although Brown and Harris claim to be interested in the *meaning* of women's experiences, to the extent that such meaning is considered it is from the vantage point of independent observers. The contextual assessment of life event stress undoubtedly identifies something of importance, but the potential of this measure for understanding depression in women is never fully realized because women's accounts of their experiences have not been the central focus of Brown and Harris' research.

Conceptual issues of a different kind, concerning how findings with contextual measures of life events should be interpreted, have also been raised. For instance, Kessler (1997) points out that in use of the contextual approach, factors which may act to modify the stressful effects of life events in causing depression are subsumed within, and so confounded with, ratings of event severity. According to Kessler (ibid.: 201), "information used by the Brown & Harris ratings panels can be seen as hypotheses concerning stress modifiers that never have a chance to be investigated because they are assumed in rating event severity." Kessler's concern arises from the requirements of positivist research approaches which emphasize objective measurement of "independent variables" and the need to maintain clear distinctions between variables to facilitate their "manipulation" and "control". The problem Kessler identifies with the LEDS procedure is that potentially important causal influences (as conceptualized by researchers) are likely to be confused and so the findings generated are difficult to interpret clearly.

Kessler's critique of the LEDS methodology shifts the focus of research on social models away from Brown and Harris' interest in addressing the meaning of events toward a greater concern with objective measurement procedures and the exclusion of subjective aspects of experience. In recent years, somewhat divergent positions have emerged among researchers on the utility of the LEDS approach for assessing stressful life events. For instance, Coyne (1994) has advocated use of the LEDS as the method of choice, whereas others (e.g. Kessler 1997, Munroe and McQuaid 1994) argue that the LEDS approach is in need of further refinement. Thus, Brown and Harris' original interest in the meaning of experiences in women's lives is in danger of being sidelined as their assessment method is modified to conform more closely with the precepts of the positivist scientific method.

As noted earlier, although women have been participants in much of the research conducted by Brown and Harris, their primary interest has been hypothesis testing and theory development, rather than understanding depression in women. Brown and Harris' decision to restrict their sample to women participants in the study described in their 1978 book was guided more by methodological and practical concerns, than by a specific interest in depression in women. They justified the decision to use an all-female sample in their 1978 study in the following way.

> Such an interviewing program is expensive and one way to reduce its cost was to study women only, as they probably suffer from depression more often than men. . . . If such findings were to be trusted, we would need to approach only half as many women as men to obtain the same number with depressive disorders.
>
> (Brown and Harris 1978: 22)

As a further reason for limiting their sample to women, Brown and Harris (ibid.) point out that "women, who are more often at home during the day, would be more willing to agree to see us for several hours, the time we needed to collect our material." Thus, understanding depression in women would not appear to have been the primary goal motivating Brown and Harris' research.

Adversity and stress in women's lives as a source of depression

Social explanations for depression in which women are the central focus also have been developed. These formulations have emphasized the activities and circumstances of women's everyday lives as sources of stress which can have an adverse impact upon women's mental health. According to these approaches, depression among women can be explained as something occurring in response to the stressful conditions characterizing the lives of many women. These stressful conditions, which are gender-specific, as well as being widespread among women, are considered to underlie the higher rates of depression in women than men (McGrath *et al.* 1990).

Women's roles as wives and mothers

As wives and mothers, women often are expected to take on the primary responsibility for care of children and family. While women's roles within the family undoubtedly are a source of satisfaction and well-being for many women, such activities also may be a source of stress. The burdensome nature of women's activities in the home, coupled with the low status, social isolation and lack of financial resources of women who are full-time housewives, have been well-documented by feminist researchers (e.g. Doyal 1995, Lorber 1994). And of course, many women now combine their family responsibilities with paid work outside the home, facing the demands of a "double day" which few men experience.

Although there is evidence that, like men, women reap the mental health advantages of involvement in paid employment, all too frequently, however, women gain such benefits at the cost of reduced leisure and relaxation time (McGrath *et al.* 1990, Walters 1993). The work done by women on behalf of family members also exacts its own "costs of caring" (Umberson *et al.* 1996). Typically women are the ones called upon to respond to the caring needs of others in the family's social network and being the recipient of such social support it is likely to be a mixed blessing because "caring debts" are accumulated when women receive help from others (Champion and Goodall 1994).

Childcare responsibilities

With few exceptions, once a woman has a child, childcare becomes her responsibility and the findings of numerous studies have pointed to an increase in risk of depression among women who are mothers of young children (Bebbington 1996, McGrath *et al.* 1990). Depression occurring during the period following childbirth is referred to as post-natal or post-partum depression, although efforts so far to identify a form of depression which is specific to childbirth have not received unqualified empirical support (Whiffen 1992). Instead, childbirth and the demands of infant care, often with little help or support from others, have been conceptualized as sources of stress in women's lives (Nicolson 1998, Taylor 1996).

The transition to motherhood may be a source of stress in other ways because of the changes in a woman's identity accompanying the process of becoming a mother (Nicolson 1998). A key feature of these changes in identity is a sense of loss, an experience which is compounded in a cultural context in which the identity of being a mother is not valued highly and the work of mothering is devalued (Lewis 1997). For mothers who also are employed outside the home, risk of depression is exacerbated when difficulties are encountered in arranging satisfactory childcare, especially when a spousal partner provides limited help (Ross and Mirowsky 1988). Not surprisingly, levels of depressive symptoms are reported to be particularly high among women who are single-parents (Bebbington 1996, Belle 1990).

Poverty and employment

Poverty is well-known to be associated with feelings of demoralization and depression within the general population and lack of money is an endemic problem among women who parent alone (Belle 1990, Graham 1993). Moreover, in western countries, women engaged in paid employment tend to be concentrated in low-paying (and low-prestige) work in clerical, sales and service sectors of the economy, a situation which contributes to the pervasive lack of access to financial resources among women (United Nations Development Program [UNDP] 1995). At the same time, gender-based inequalities in the employment sphere (e.g. pay inequities, inadequate provision of maternity leave and childcare services, lack of fringe benefits for part-time workers), ensure that relatively few women are in a financial position to support themselves and their children. The persistent belief that men should rightfully be family breadwinners, and therefore paid more than women, fosters women's economic dependence on men (or the state). Despite legislative efforts to redress gender-based pay inequalities, women's wages continue to lag significantly behind those of their male counterparts. In western countries, women's average earnings hover around 75 percent of men's, a statistic inspiring little hope that this income disparity will be eradicated in the foreseeable future (UNDP 1995).

Violence against women

The family can be a source of stress in other ways when girls and women suffer (often in silence) sexual and physical abuse in the privacy of the home. It is now well-documented that girls and women comprise the overwhelming majority of victims of interpersonal violence (Koss *et al.* 1994) and sexual abuse during childhood, in particular, has been linked to women's vulnerability to depression. For instance, based on an analysis of data on rates of depression in the general population of the USA, Cutler and Nolen-Hoeksema (1991) concluded that elevated rates of childhood sexual abuse among girls could explain women's preponderance among depressed adults. In support of Cutler and Nolen-Hoeksema's position, recent studies have reported findings of an association between sexual abuse in childhood and having a history of depression in adulthood (Beitchman *et al.* 1992, Whiffen and Clark 1997). This link between childhood sexual abuse and depression in adult women is not fully understood, although researchers have suggested that abuse trauma underlies the loss of a sense of trust and safety, self-blame, and somatic symptoms such as insomnia which characterize the experiences of those victimized by abuse (Koss *et al.* 1994). Parallels have also been noted between the signs of emotional distress reported by adult survivors of childhood abuse and those observed in individuals diagnosed with post-traumatic stress disorder (Kendall-Tackett and Marshall 1998).

Women also are much more likely than men to be victims of violence within intimate relationships (Koss *et al.* 1994). Increased levels of psychological distress, including symptoms of depression and anxiety are reported by women who have been physically abused by a male partner as well as among women who have been sexually assaulted (Hamilton and Jensvold 1995, McGrath *et al.* 1990). Emotional abuse of women in intimate relationships (e.g. belittling a woman's competence and appearance, controlling a woman's activities through threats of violence) also is associated with depression (Koss *et al.* 1994). Emotional forms of abuse and the feelings of depression associated with such victimization can undermine a woman's attempts to leave an abusive relationship (Merritt-Gray and Wuest 1995). For women trapped in abusive relationships, lack of financial resources is likely to contribute to the stressfulness of their living situation.

Depression and women's lives

Explanations for depression which focus on sources of stress in women's everyday lives have primarily been generated in response to findings I reviewed in Chapter 1 that depression is a more common problem among women than men. Thus, much of the research on depression conducted within this "women's lives" perspective also has the goal of explaining gender-related differences in depression (see McGrath *et al.* 1990 and Nolen-Hoeksema 1990 for reviews of this research). A difficulty arises for interpretation of findings from studies of this kind, however, if a study fails to yield evidence that women are more depressed than men. Would absence of a gender difference on a measure of depression imply that gender-based inequalities within society have been overcome and that systemic gender discrimination has been eradicated? Failure to find evidence of gender differences on depression measures is somewhat problematic for this social approach to explaining depression in women.

Although there is considerable evidence linking aspects of women's lives as mothers, wives and paid workers to their reports of depression, much of this research has been conducted within the framework of the positivist scientific method, a strategy also referred to as "feminist empiricism" (Harding 1986). This is an approach to research which tends to be followed by those who assume the existence of basic psychological similarities between women and men (Kimball 1994). Within a gender similarities framework, women and men are assumed to be essentially similar in their potential to become depressed and therefore the source of women's heightened vulnerability to depression is attributed to the social circumstances of their everyday lives. The primary goal of research from this feminist empiricist perspective is that of uncovering aspects of women's lives which can account for their higher rates of depression.

Because of its grounding in a positivist epistemology, research investigating "women's lives" explanations for depression in women generally is guided by a search for causal relations between various social parameters (e.g. marital, parental or employment status) and depression (assessed by diagnostic criteria and depressive symptom measures). In studies of this type, the usual benchmark for determining the meaning of findings is statistical significance, a criterion on which inferences about differences between groups can be based, but the goal of understanding women's experiences from their own standpoint is not addressed. The correlational nature of much of this research, however, rules out the possibility of establishing causal links between social influences and depression. Nevertheless, whichever type of research design is employed, findings of statistically significant associations between variables can never warrant the conclusion that *all* women whose lives are characterized by a particular combination of social circumstances will become depressed. For instance, by no means are all women who are full-time housewives and mothers depressed; the majority of women who combine the roles of mother and paid worker are not depressed; not all adult survivors of childhood sexual abuse become depressed; and not all women who are single-parents are depressed. Furthermore, not all depressed women have lives which would be characterized as stressful. Of course some might argue that merely being a woman in a patriarchal society is stressful in itself, but then why are all women not depressed? If followed to its logical conclusion, this line of argument stretches the notion of depression to the point where it loses all meaning. Pursuit of the women's lives approach therefore comes perilously close to an essentialist position in which women's increased vulnerability to depression is assumed to be the result of being members of the category "woman", one marked by female biology.

Attempts to develop explanations for depression in women which are framed in terms of sources of adversity and stress in their everyday lives therefore are short-circuited by positivist epistemological assumptions and methodological strategies, limitations also shared by the social models I discussed earlier in this chapter. These social models take for granted a conception of the social environment as something which is distinct from the individual, so that an "individual–society" form of dualism is assumed. The individual who becomes depressed is conceptualized apart from the influences causing her depression, which are located within the external social world. Thus, as currently formulated, social explanations for depression conceptualize sources of stress in people's lives in a rather limited way.

In social models, the context of people's lives is defined by the content of measures of stressful life events and living conditions, an approach which obscures or makes invisible other aspects of the social environment. These neglected contextual aspects come into clearer focus when social models of depression are analyzed from feminist and social constructionist perspectives. In the next section, I explore these concerns and their implications for understanding depression in women in more detail.

A feminist and social constructionist analysis of social models of depression

In social explanations for depression, attention is directed to the circumstances of people's lives and the nature of events which happen to them as important sources of risk factors for depression. These approaches broaden the scope of causal processes hypothesized to be involved in depression beyond internal individual factors (e.g. personality traits and biochemical mechanisms) to include influences external to the individual. However, the narrow way in which the "social" has been conceptualized within these models sets limits on their potential usefulness for understanding depression in women. The circumscribed manner in which the social is conceptualized becomes evident when the following are considered: 1) The scope of what is included as constituting the social context of women's lives; 2) The neglect of structural conditions and political/economic dimensions of women's lives; 3) A tendency to rely on cognitive paradigms for exploring the meaning of events in women's lives; and 4) Use of the stress concept to explain how events originating in the social environment lead to depression.

Conceptions of the social context of women's lives

The social environment is conceptualized in social models primarily in terms of life events, particularly events involving forms of personal misfortune. Included as misfortunes are events which would be expected to have a fairly direct and generally negative impact upon an individual. Examples of adverse (and therefore negative) events include ill-health or disability, the serious illness or death of a spouse or close relative, loss of employment, breakdown of a marriage. When events such as these happen, they often are accompanied by consequences which have adverse effects upon the quality of a person's everyday life.

In the LEDS procedure developed by Brown and Harris, as I noted earlier, emphasis is placed on the gathering of information about the current and past circumstance of a woman's life. This information is considered important for evaluating the degree of contextual threat implied by an event. As conceptualized by Brown and Harris, contextual threat is intended to reflect the meaning of a life event from the standpoint of the woman who experiences it. Based on information collected with the LEDS from many women over a number of years, loss has been identified by Brown and Harris as a key element in contextual threat, where loss is defined broadly as encompassing both actual and anticipated losses involving a person, a material possession, a role, or a cherished idea (Brown and Harris 1989). Thus, Brown and Harris' notion of contextual threat involves a conception of the social environment extending beyond life events to include the circumstances in which they are embedded, although the scope of this attempt to contextualize women's life experiences is still quite restricted. Not addressed is how the circumstances constituting the context of women's lives are themselves structured and organized socially. Brown and Harris' model focuses on more proximal and immediate aspects of women's lives and the meaning of events is interpreted within this local context. Not considered in this approach is how the local circumstances of women's lives themselves are shaped by more distal conditions which govern allocation of social and material resources in relation to gender.

When the social environment is defined in terms of the circumstances of particular women's lives, what remains invisible is how the lives of *all* women are regulated by wider social, political and economic conditions such as lack of recognition for unpaid work in the home, inadequate access to childcare services for women who work outside the home, employment and pay inequities, and so on. When procedures like the LEDS are used in research on social models of depression, a decontextualized view of the circumstances of women's lives is produced. Taken for granted are the gendered dimensions of women's everyday lives and the way these patterns have developed in specific historical and cultural contexts. Ignored, for example, in this way of conceptualizing the social environment are such issues as why unpaid work in the home is performed mostly by women and why this gendered pattern persists. From a feminist perspective, therefore, a serious omission in attempts to develop social explanations for depression in women is the failure to address the conditions underpinning women's unequal and devalued status in society.

Neglect of structural conditions and political/economic dimensions in conceptions of the social environment

In considering how the circumstances of women's lives might be implicated in depression, social models, including the "women's lives" approach, remain focused at the level of individual lives. This individualistic focus, fostered by positivist research traditions, also reflects the established separation between fields of study which take the individual as their subject matter (e.g. psychology, education) and those which address phenomena at the societal level (e.g. sociology, political science). Because of these disciplinary divisions, when explanations for depression in women are framed in terms of social models, political and economic conditions shaping women's lives are excluded from consideration. This invisibility is reinforced by a widespread lack of acknowledgement in western societies of ways in which women are politically and economically disadvantaged, a collective blindspot characterizing researchers and policy-makers alike. For instance, the finding that women caring for young children on a full-time basis are particularly vulnerable to depression is explained by social models in terms of the stressful circumstances of such women's lives, conditions made more stressful when a negative event (e.g. unemployment, a child's illness) is also experienced. The issues of why childcare is primarily a woman's responsibility and why women caring for children receive so little public recognition and support are not addressed by social models of depression.

Explanations derived from the women's lives form of social model point to the isolated conditions of women's work in the home, coupled with financial dependency on a male partner (or the state in the case of many women who parent alone) as factors associated with an increased risk of depression in women who are mothers. Excluded from this type of analysis, however, is any consideration of structural conditions (e.g. pay and employment inequities, lack of adequate childcare services) and how these conditions are implicated in the construction of events such as marital breakdown and unemployment as being particularly negative for women. Despite feminist efforts to gain greater recognition by policy-makers of the important and necessary work done by women in raising the next generation of citizens, public policy in this arena remains stagnant at best and at worst reflects the privatizing tendencies of the "new right" form of economics (Cohen 1997). Thus, the future appears to hold few prospects for addressing structural conditions which make women's work as mothers a potential source of depressive experiences.

Although there is ample evidence documenting a link between poverty and depression in women, public policy in western countries has generally been unresponsive to feminist calls for strategies to redress the persistence of systemic forms of gender discrimination in income distribution and employment. Thus, achievement of gender equity goals recedes further into the future and women's claims for equal pay for work of equal value and access to benefits (e.g. pensions) on the same basis as men are likely to be rejected as undermining the traditional nuclear family. Although many women must work outside the home to earn money to buy food and clothing for themselves and their children, too often policy in the public sphere is based on the assumption that the primary activity of women is, or should be, that of providing care directly for their children. Such caregiving is performed by women as an unpaid "labor of love" and many women readily shape their lives in accord with this assumption, not least because of the insistent reminder provided by their children's needs for affection and attention.

There is also evidence of links between depression in women and being the victim of abusive treatment by a partner and accumulating findings suggest that sexual abuse in childhood may underlie depression in adult women. Although some gains have been made in recent years in bringing the problem of "domestic violence" to greater public attention, public policy has been slow to respond to the evident needs of girls and women who suffer this form of victimization. Thus, women able to gather the psychological resources to leave an abusive relationship too often face barriers posed by lack of material resources to survive on their own without a male partner's financial support. Although shelters and safe houses exist to meet the needs of abused women and their children, usually such respite provides only a temporary solution. For some women, admission to a psychiatric hospital may be the only recourse available to gain relief from an abusive partner (Miedema and Stoppard 1994).

Women's lives undoubtedly represent an important starting point for understanding depression in women, but when analysis remains at the level of individual women and the particularities of their lives, it stops well short of a fully contextualized account. Attempts to develop social explanations for depression in which the focus of inquiry is restricted to the lives of individual women also limit strategies for change to those at the level of individual women and how they cope individually with depression. If social models of depression are to encompass contextual aspects of women's lives more fully, these models need to be expanded to include structural-material conditions regulating the lived experiences of woman, whether married or mothers or paid workers or not.

Reliance on cognitive paradigms for exploring the meaning of experiences

Social models have developed in part as a counterbalance to the relative dominance of intrapsychic orientations in theories proposed to explain depression.

These attempts to incorporate the social environment within explanatory frameworks respond to a longstanding neglect of social influences in causal models of depression. At the same time, an effort is made to address the meaning of events, for instance in Brown and Harris' model through use of the LEDS procedure, although women's experiences provide only an indirect context for interpretation of the meaning of the events in their lives. From a positivist perspective, the strategy adopted by Brown and Harris is considered effective because they have found in a series of studies that depression in women can be predicted by ratings of contextual threat (Brown and Harris 1989). Evidence of a predictive relationship between variables does not constitute understanding of the meaning of women's experiences, however. Unexamined in this approach is the basis on which independent judges make their ratings of contextual threat. In the procedure used by Brown and Harris, the subjectivities of judges are substituted for the subjectivities of the women who participate in their studies, and so interpretations of meaning are based in the experiences of researchers rather than those of women who complete the LEDS interview.

In the diathesis–stress models I discussed in Chapter 3, the meaning of stressful life events also is interpreted from the perspective of researchers, with cognitive approaches currently providing one avenue for conceptualizing how individuals interpret and experience the events happening in their lives. According to cognitive approaches, events in themselves have neutral connotations and the negative meanings attributed to them by depression-prone individuals are explained in terms of their biased interpretational processes. Thus in this interpretative approach, negative meanings are considered as the product of a cognitive style which fosters a pessimistic outlook on the implications of events occurring in a person's life. These cognitive approaches, therefore, equate the meaning of people's experiences with cognitive processes and content. One consequence of this research methodology is that the meanings attributed to events are likely to reflect the assumptions, values and worldviews of professionals whose own backgrounds are middle-class. These meanings then receive the gloss of objectivity through application of procedures endorsed by the positivist version of scientific method (e.g. use of independent raters). This way of proceeding excludes the social and linguistic dimensions of experience from consideration, concerns which from a social constructionist perspective are central to understanding how subjectivity and meaning are constructed in language and social interaction.

In sum, social models fail to address how the meaning of events in women's lives is socially constructed within the broader context of cultural conceptions (or discourses) of femininity within a particular society. Indeed, the notion of women's lives itself is an unexamined social construction. Reliance in social models of depression on cognitive approaches for conceptualizing the meaning of experiences also precludes exploration of how women's lives are shaped by structural conditions, maintained in turn by cultural discourses justifying material arrangements which perpetuate the disadvantaged status of women within society.

Use of stress to explain the depressive effects of negative life events

To explain the process whereby an individual's experiences of adversity (i.e. negative life events) lead to depression, social models draw on the concept of stress. Thus, life events are hypothesized to play a causal role in depression because they engender stress. A stress mechanism also is invoked to explain why more women than men become depressed. According to the women's lives version of social model, the lives of women contain more potential sources of stress than do the lives of men (Nolen-Hoeksema 1990). A drawback in use of the stress concept to explain why negative events lead to depression, however, as Pollock (1988) has argued, is that the form of stress mechanism purported to underlie various mental health and health outcomes, including depression, lacks any clear basis in knowledge of human physiology. Pollock suggests that the notion of stress is a contemporary social construction, a concept whose creation has spawned a "stress discourse" now widely disseminated within the professional literature as well as the popular media. In the LEDS procedure for assessing contextual threat, Brown and Harris (1978, 1989) avoid use of the stress concept and instead pursue the strategy of evaluating the threat implied by life events (albeit based on ratings by independent judges). The intent of this strategy is to capture important aspects of the meaning of women's experiences, but as I indicated earlier the methodology adopted by Brown and Harris limits the ability of their measure of contextual threat to assess meaning from the standpoint of women.

Reflecting the diffusion of the stress discourse within society, women also commonly attribute their mental health problems to stress (Walters 1993), although as Pollock (1988) has pointed out, this discursive strategy potentially creates its own self-fulfilling consequences whereby awareness of stress can lead to feelings of distress. Another consequence of this explanatory move is that when women account for their depressive experiences in terms of stress, they also are able to present their everyday lives as being relatively unproblematic. If stress is identified as the problem, the source of a woman's depressive experiences is located outside the confines of her daily life, as something beyond her control which can affect anyone (and everyone) adversely. Use of the stress concept by researchers and ordinary women alike, therefore, serves to obscure how women's depressive experiences arise in the context of their lives. The meaning of stress is further confused by the frequent use of the term to denote both an external (and socially-located) cause of distress and an internal experience of subjective distress (i.e. as a symptom).

Concluding comments

From a feminist perspective, attempts to develop explanations for depression in terms of social influences appear at first glance to be more compatible than other approaches with analyses which identify patriarchal structures as a key source of women's disadvantaged status within society. As I have argued in this chapter, however, social models suffer from both conceptual and methodological limitations which restrict their capacity to provide a basis for understanding depression in women. The individualistic focus of social models, including the women's lives version, means that the structural-material conditions regulating women's lives remain unacknowledged and therefore unaddressed. Adherence to a positivist epistemological position, moreover, renders these social models incapable of considering how the lived experiences of women are socially constructed. Thus, if social approaches are to contribute to understanding depression in women, they require major modifications to accommodate a conception of women's lives as being both socially produced and socially constructed.

From the perspective of the models discussed in this chapter, depression has been conceptualized predominantly in ways which conform to mainstream definitions of depressive disorder and depressive symptoms. Although descriptions of depressive symptoms for diagnostic purposes include experiences in which the body is centrally involved (e.g. so-called "vegetative signs"), social models of depression do not address the role of female embodiment in depression. Indeed, consideration of the physical materiality of the female body is an omission highlighted with respect to each of the approaches to explaining depression in women discussed so far. In the next chapter, I take up in more detail theoretical issues involved in the problem of combining a focus on female embodiment with a social constructionist perspective.

Notes

1 As well as the semi-structured interview schedule, the LEDS procedure requires familiarity with detailed manuals and codebooks, containing case examples, to use the rating system for coding contextual threat. Thus, use of the LEDS is not a straightforward matter and potential users must first undertake a lengthy training process.

2 In a further refinement of the link between life events and depression, Brown and Harris (1978) identified several "vulnerability" factors as conditions which increase the risk of depression if a provoking event has occurred. These vulnerability factors included having three or more children under age 14 at home, not having employment outside the home, and lacking a confiding relationship (particularly with a husband). For women who were full-time housewives with young children at home, there was an increased risk of depression among working class women but not among those who were middle class. More recently, Brown and Harris have proposed that a woman's self-esteem (particularly a negative self-evaluation) may explain why only some women become depressed following a provoking agent when vulnerability factors are present (Brown et al. 1990).

6

WOMEN'S BODIES, WOMEN'S LIVES AND DEPRESSION

Exploring material–discursive approaches

A limitation shared by each of the approaches to explaining depression in women I have discussed so far is that none addresses the female body directly as a material entity.[1] This is a somewhat curious omission, because the physical body is clearly implicated in the experiences called depression, however such experiences are defined, explained or understood. Whatever else it may be, depression is an embodied experience. For instance, women who identify themselves as depressed, or who are identified in this way by mental health professionals, often report feelings of fatigue or generalized ill-health (Gammell 1996, Schreiber 1996). Moreover, the DSM criteria for diagnosing depressive disorder and the items contained in depressive symptom questionnaires (see Chapter 2) include a variety of experiences, such as weight change, difficulty sleeping, and lack of energy, which explicitly involve the physical body. The body is more or less ignored, however, in the diathesis–stress, psychology of women and social approaches to explaining depression discussed in previous chapters. The question I want to consider here is how these models manage to produce an account of depression in which women's bodies are invisible.

Research in fields concerned with mental health issues has tended to be organized along lines which reflect a division of labor between researchers who focus on experience and behavior (e.g. psychology) and those who take the physical body as their primary subject matter (e.g. medicine). Partly in response to this situation, when the body has been conceptualized, usually it is assumed to best be understood within a biological framework, something which is the prerogative of medical science. This taken-for-granted equation of the material body with the biological body has meant that the body has virtually been ignored in models developed to explain depression by those working within nonmedical fields.

The physical body has not been entirely ignored in fields outside medicine, however. For instance, in the wake of Engel's (1977) articulation of a biopsychosocial framework for conceptualizing health-related phenomena, various multidisciplinary models have been developed in which biological, psychological and social influences are considered in a more integrative framework. Such multifactorial models underpin the cross-disciplinary fields of health psychology, behavioral medicine and medical sociology (Ogden 1997, Yardley 1996, 1997b).

These disciplinary hybrids have emerged in response to perceived limitations of single factor models, whether focused on psychological or social influences or a combination of the two. In addition, biopsychosocial approaches have recently been identified as offering useful frameworks for explaining depression in women (McGrath *et al.* 1990, Gallant and Derry 1995). Inclusion of the physical body in models proposed to explain depression in women represents a departure from the approaches discussed in Chapters 3 to 5, although conceptions of the body in these models have been limited to biological mechanism and processes.

Attempts to develop approaches to explaining depression in women which incorporate the biological domain have followed two main strategies. In one, the body's contribution to depression has been conceptualized in terms of biochemical processes within the brain and genetic influences (Ross and Pam 1995), while the other has focused on the reproductive biology of the female body. When this second approach is used to account for depression in women, researchers have attended primarily to "women's menstrual life" (Gallant and Derry 1995: 199). This latter approach to conceptualizing women's bodies focuses on menarche, menstruation, pregnancy, childbirth and menopause. In this approach, the predominance of women among the depressed is explained in terms of hormonal influences, particularly those linked to estrogen and progesterone and the effects on mood and behavior of changes in the levels of these hormones circulating within the female body. The implications for understanding depression in women of approaches which draw on a conception of the female body derived from these reproductive biological models are discussed in more detail in the first part of this chapter.

Analyses from a feminist perspective of biologically-based approaches to explaining depression in women have revealed these strategies to have a number of shortcomings. A key feminist concern has been that these models function to medicalize women's bodies and women's distress, because the female body is conceptualized solely in biological terms. An issue I take up in the second half of this chapter therefore is how women's bodies can be conceptualized in ways that go beyond a narrow focus on the body as a biological entity. In later sections, I explore an approach in which the body is understood as being both naturally and culturally produced. An understanding of the body as being immersed in culture, rather than a timeless, natural organism (Lock 1993), both transcends dualistic forms of thinking (e.g. the body–mind and nature–culture dichotomies) and avoids the pitfalls of biological reductionism (Ogden 1997).[2]

A central theme of these nondualist and nonreductionist approaches is "the relation between the body as the physical medium of embodied life and the body as the object of sociolinguistic constructions" (Yardley 1997d: 711). In this way of thinking, women's bodies are understood as both material entities and social constructions, a perspective which opens up a range of analytical tools, including ideas developed around the notion of the body as "text" and those addressing the "practical" or "useful" body (Bordo 1993, Yardley 1997b). An important point emerging from these analyses is that women's bodies are the primary means through which women engage in practises of femininity. The term "practises of femininity" is one coined by those working within feminist and social construc-tionist frameworks to refer to activities which constitute women's everyday lives (Bordo 1993). The activities comprising the everyday lives of the majority of women (at least in western countries) are those denoted by the role constellation of wife/mother/housewife. The main focus of these activities is taking care of the physical and emotional needs of children and other family members. This caring work is something women are expected to do, in part because of beliefs held by women as well as those they care about, that caring for others is properly women's work. The larger social context of women's everyday lives also impinges on their experiences of work within the family. Either from necessity or choice, many women are now employed in paid work outside the home, usually in addition to their unpaid caring work within the home.

Although motherhood is no longer viewed as the sole source of a woman's identity, the work involved in mothering still claims a substantial portion of women's lives. And, the well-being of a woman's children is generally attributed by herself and others to the quality of the care she provides. The centrality of nur-turing to notions of women's psychology, as well as being an important value underpinning women's activities in the home, is part of what have been called dis-courses of femininity (Bordo 1993, Ussher 1991, 1997b). This term, which I discussed in Chapter 1 (see footnote 4 in Chapter 1), refers to shared beliefs within a culture about what it means to be a woman. Discourses of femininity reflect implicit cultural guidelines for women on how to behave in womanly ways – how to be a "good woman".

Cultural discourses around what constitutes a good woman are largely taken for granted by both women and men, but are pervasive within society and permeate many domains of everyday life, from assumptions about proper behavior for moth-ers to notions of fashionable modes of dress for women. Discourses of femininity, therefore, play a crucial role in shaping and regulating the activities of women as wives, mothers, housewives, and paid workers, and operate as implicit standards against which women measure the adequacy of their individual efforts to be good women. Discourses of femininity are explored in more detail in the second half of the chapter where I introduce "material–discursive" approaches to understanding depression in women.

A key idea in material–discursive approaches to understanding depression in women is that under certain circumstances engaging in practises of femininity (i.e. doing activities that signify the "good woman"), can exhaust a woman's body, while undermining her morale and sense of well-being. Approached in this way, one way of understanding depression is as the embodied experiences which occur in conjunction with a woman's efforts to achieve the socially constructed ideal of the good woman. Also acknowledged in material–discursive forms of analysis is that a woman's efforts do not take place in a social or material vacuum. Limits are set on women's possibilities for attaining the good woman ideal by social structural conditions and the female body as a finite physical resource.

The biological body and depression in women

Within the practise of medicine, responsibility for diagnosis and treatment of mental disorders, including depression, rests with the medical specialty of psychiatry. As a branch of scientific medicine, psychiatric explanations for mental disorders draw predominantly upon biological models. From this perspective, explanations for depression emphasize biological processes and mechanisms within the brain (Ross and Pam 1995). Contemporary research within psychiatric medicine focuses on biochemistry and genetics, with the presumption that knowledge of this kind will eventually provide answers to the puzzle of depression. Indeed, biochemical changes in the brain have been found to accompany clinical manifestations of depression, although such findings have not yet been well-integrated with evidence of sex-related differences in depression rates (Bebbington 1996). When gender (generally defined as sex of subject) is added to the equation, there is now some agreement among psychiatric researchers that available biological models cannot readily explain higher rates of depression (most usually defined as depressive disorder) among women than men (Bebbington 1996, Russell 1995). Within the field of genetics, for instance, evidence from several large-scale studies has contradicted the hypothesis that a genetic mode of transmission can explain the preponderance of women among the depressed (Bebbington 1996, Weissman and Klerman 1987).

Nevertheless, the search for biological explanations for depression in women continues unabated and in recent years attention has focused on the human endocrine system, especially hormonal differences between women and men (Bebbington 1996). This focus on hormones and reproductive biology has its counterpart in cultural beliefs in which women's behavior, particularly the "emotional nature" of women, is presumed to be governed largely by hormonal influences (Martin 1987, Ussher 1989). The idea that hormonal processes underlie depression in women is one widely shared among both health professionals and the lay public, despite the paucity of findings in support of such a link (Figert 1996, Markens 1996, Nicolson 1992).

Evidence for a connection between aspects of women's menstrual lives and depression has mainly been pursued using the positivist research strategies of the scientific method. Failure to find that hormonal influences and depression are related in women would challenge these biological explanations for depression in women. As indicated in the following brief overview of findings in this area, research so far has failed to yield consistent support for biological approaches. Such research, however, has addressed only one way of conceptualizing women's bodies and how the body is implicated in depressive experiences among women. Later in the chapter, I explore material–discursive alternatives to the equation of women's bodies with hormones and reproductive biology.

Menarche and menstruation

Among researchers, there is some consensus that the time when sex-related differences in depression first clearly emerge is during adolescence (Bebbington 1996,

Gallant and Derry 1995). Findings indicate that from about the age of 15, depression is approximately twice as likely to be experienced by girls than boys (Nolen-Hoeksema and Girgus 1994). This increased vulnerability to depression among girls has been linked to puberty, a biological event marked by hormonal changes (increased production of estrogen) and the onset of menstruation (menarche). Based on their review of research on the links between puberty, gender and depression, Nolen-Hoeksema and Girgus (1994: 434–5) concluded that "there is little evidence to date that hormonal changes are consistently associated with the rising vulnerability to depressive symptoms in girls in adolescence." They suggest instead that hormonal changes might play a causal role in depression in adolescent girls only in conjunction with pre-existing risk factors. Among such risk factors, Nolen-Hoeksema and Girgus included feminine personality traits, body dissatisfaction, rape and sexual abuse. Thus, an increase in rates of depression among adolescent girls cannot apparently be attributed solely to hormonal changes during puberty. Nonetheless, as Nolen-Hoeksema and Girgus point out, there has been almost no research directly investigating the role of hormonal processes in depression among adolescent girls.

Belief in the existence of links between women's menstrual cycles and their moods, especially depressive feelings, is most clearly represented in the diagnostic category of "premenstrual dysphoric disorder" (included in the DSM-IV, American Psychiatric Association 1994) or "premenstrual syndrome" (PMS), the term most often used in the lay and popular literature. Despite a plethora of studies conducted on PMS in recent years, there is little consensus among experts about the nature of this presumed disorder, or even on its existence (Caplan *et al.* 1992, Gallant and Derry 1995, Walker 1995, 1997). The lack of research support for the PMS diagnosis, however, offers little comfort to women who may experience discomfort and distress in relation to menstruation and especially premenstrually.

A factor contributing to the difficulty of doing research on PMS is that women vary quite widely in the degree to which menstruation-related experiences are identified as upsetting or bothersome. Little overlap has been found between women's self-identification as suffering from PMS and observations based on their self-reports of menstruation-related experiences (McFarlane and Williams 1994). Nevertheless, ordinary women, researchers and health professionals alike continue to believe in the existence of PMS. Figert (1996) has analyzed the controversy surrounding the proposal to include PMS (as "premenstrual dysphoric disorder") within the DSM. Based on her analysis, she concluded that while decisions about the existence of PMS as a psychiatric disorder may claim legitimacy from scientific findings, "no matter how scientists and psychiatrists try to portray the development of the DSM, all science is political." (Figert 1996: 172). Despite conflicting views on the existence of PMS, this diagnostic category is not likely to be relinquished easily, because it provides women with a source of medical validation for their distress. Indeed, as Markens (1996) noted, ordinary women have played an active role in the construction of PMS as a medical disease.

Pregnancy and childbirth

Pregnancy and childbirth in particular have also been considered a time of increased risk for depression in women. Once again, a causal link is postulated between hormonal changes accompanying childbirth and depression in women. A biological basis for depressive symptoms immediately following childbirth (referred to as maternity or post-partum blues) is often assumed, because of the significant reduction in levels of estrogen and progesterone which occurs at this time. The main characteristic of post-partum blues is said to be mild depressive symptoms, a short-lived experience often reported by women in the few days after delivery (Whiffen 1992). As Stanton and Danoff-Burg (1995) point out, however, this observation should be considered in the context of other findings on women's moods in relation to pregnancy and the post-partum period. For instance, several studies have found that levels of depressive symptoms are higher among women during the third trimester of pregnancy than during the first 10 days post-partum. Moreover, women typically report higher levels of positive than negative feelings during the post-partum period. Also contradicting a purely hormonal explanation for so-called maternity blues is the finding that a woman's mood during pregnancy is the best predictor of her mood during the post-partum period (Stanton and Danoff-Burg 1995).

Depression in women, defined according to diagnostic criteria for depressive disorder, which occurs during the year following childbirth, also has been the focus of considerable research attention. Recent reviews of this research have addressed the issue of whether this type of depression should be classified as a unique disorder and the conclusion reached is that there is little support for post-partum depression as a separate or distinct form of depressive disorder (Stanton and Danoff-Burg 1995, Whiffen 1992). In addition, there is no clear-cut evidence that depression is more common among women during the post-partum period than among either pregnant or nonpregnant women. As hormone levels are quite different during pregnancy than immediately after childbirth, such findings contradict hormonal explanations for depression in women who have recently had a baby. There is now general agreement in this field that post-partum depression is not a distinct disorder and that depression occurring during the post-partum period is more appropriately referred to as "depression following childbirth" (Nicolson 1986) or more simply as "depression" (Gallant and Derry 1995).

Menopause

Menopause and cessation of menstruation represent loss of fertility and the end of a women's "menstrual life" (menopause, however, may no longer signal the end of a women's capacity to bear a child, with the advent of reproductive technologies). Women in western countries usually experience menopause around the age of 50, although several years may elapse before menstruation ceases entirely. Biologically, menopause involves a reduction in the ovarian production of hormones, especially estrogen. The drop in level of circulating estrogen may be accompanied by various bodily sensations, most notably "hot flushes" or "flashes", characterized by feelings of heat, sweating and facial flushing. Among middle-aged women, depression has been attributed to the reduction in level of circulating estrogen during menopause (Gallant and Derry 1995). Indeed, the now defunct diagnosis of involutional melancholia was used to designate a form of depression believed by physicians to be specific to women during midlife (Busfield 1996: 162).

The issue of whether menopause is a time of increased risk for depression in women has been the subject of a great deal of research in recent years. Based on their review of this research, Gallant and Derry (1995: 232) concluded: "Risk of depression [does] not increase for women experiencing natural (as opposed to surgical) menopause above their likelihood for depression before onset of menopause." An increase in risk of depression has been found, however, among women whose menopausal status is the result of surgery (e.g. hysterectomy) and who therefore experience an abrupt onset of menopause. It is unclear whether this increased risk of depression results directly from a reduction in estrogen levels, because surgery itself is a stressor and women who have a history of depression may be more likely than other women to be referred for surgery by their physicians (Gallant and Derry 1995).

A distinction between natural and surgical menopause implies that when menopause occurs "naturally", it follows a fairly predictable course, marked by recognizable characteristics and experiences. This picture of menopause is somewhat contradicted, however, by cross-cultural findings which reveal a degree of diversity in women's menopausal experiences. For instance, Lock (1993) found that Japanese women rarely report hot flushes, an experience considered emblematic of menopause among North American women and by their physicians. Moreover, neither Japanese women nor their physicians identified depression as a feature of menopause, whereas in North America, depression is commonly believed to be experienced by women during menopause. Evidence that both the experience and meaning of menopause vary across cultures implies that notions of the female body as an immutable biological organism, characterized by fixed and universal physiological processes, are in need of revision.

In summary, as indicated in this brief overview, evidence for a causal connection between depression in women and hormonal aspects of women's menstrual life is almost totally lacking. Why, then, do biological explanations for women's depression continue to be so influential? It is hardly possible to read a newspaper or woman's magazine without finding some reference to the role of hormones in women's health problems or to the potentially detrimental effects on women's mood and behavior of hormonal fluctuations inherent in the menstrual cycle. At the same time, antidepressant drugs are being touted as a treatment for PMS and hormone replacement therapy (HRT) is offered by physicians almost routinely to their women patients when they reach menopausal age. In the next section, issues surrounding this medicalization of women's bodies and women's distress are taken up in more detail.

The medicalization of women's bodies and women's distress

According to Bell (1987: 153), the concept of medicalization "refers to the process and product of defining and treating human experiences as medical problems". Women's bodies, and more particularly women's menstrual life and its landmarks, have long been viewed as properly the concern of medicine. Menstruation, pregnancy, childbirth, and menopause have become part of the domain of biomedicine to be managed by medical means. One consequence of this medical involvement is that otherwise normal aspects of female reproductive biology have come to be conceptualized within a disease framework. It is this tendency to view female bodies as potentially diseased and, by implication, as inherently deviant, which has been the focus of feminist critiques of the medicalization of women's bodies.

Women's experiences of psychological distress in general, and of depression in particular, also have become medicalized. Because medical approaches to explaining depression rest on an assumption of underlying disease or disorder within the biological body, women's experiences of distress also are pathologized. When women's distress is understood from a biomedical perspective it is likely to be viewed as a form of psychopathology within the individual. Feminist psychologists, among others, have raised concerns about the negative consequences for women when their experiences are psychopathologized as part of this medicalization process (e.g. Caplan 1995, Chesler 1972, Ussher 1991). The concerns articulated by feminists are amplified by equivocal empirical support for biological explanations for depression in women. Medical practise involves the application of findings derived from research in the biomedical sciences, yet the bulk of the available evidence fails to support hormonal explanations for depression in women. Why, then, do these biological approaches to explaining women's distress persist? What are the consequences for individual women when they attribute their depressive experiences to biological processes? Why have the medicalization of women's bodies and the pathologization of women's distress been a focus of feminist critiques?

Why do biological explanations for depression in women persist?

In the face of empirical findings which fail to support, and often contradict, biological explanations for depression in women, one reaction has been to search for flaws in the methodologies used in research. For instance, various suggestions have been made for improving the research procedures used to test hormonal explanations. Such proposals have addressed the need for more appropriate control groups, valid measures of depression, and direct rather than proxy assessment of hormonal levels (Caplan *et al.* 1992, Gallant and Derry 1995, Stanton and Danoff-Burg 1995). Recommendations of this kind assume that more rigorous application of research methods is the most appropriate route for proving the "truth" (or otherwise) of hormonal explanations for depression in women. These calls for better research seem to imply that the main obstacle to conclusive findings on the validity of biological theories of depression is faulty research methods.

Nevertheless, efforts to challenge biological models of women's distress on methodological grounds alone are unlikely to succeed. Such efforts, as Parlee (1992) has argued, are misguided, because they are informed by a rather narrow view of scientific practise as operating solely in accord with the rules of logic, uninfluenced by the interests and values of researchers. Numerous investigations of how researchers (including those in biomedical fields) actually go about their work have revealed a somewhat different picture of science as very much a social process (Latour 1987). As an example, the views of critics who also are insiders to this social process are usually more credible to other researchers than criticisms made by outsiders. So, as Parlee (1992: 106) noted with respect to feminist analyses of research on PMS, critics of biological explanations for women's distress are confronted with a certain paradox:

> It is unfortunately true in science (as elsewhere . . .) that in order to be taken seriously a critic has to speak the language (the argument has to be grounded in ways the scientist understands and accepts as serious). But if you speak the language you can no longer articulate a critical perspective.

Others have called for improvements in the "conceptual rigor" of theories formulated to account for women's psychological distress in relation to their menstrual life, advocating more complex theoretical frameworks in which psychosocial influences are integrated with biological factors (Gallant and Derry 1995, Walker 1995). More complex theories, however, are unlikely to be more sophisticated if they incorporate outmoded conceptions of the biology of hormones.

In her recent analysis of the contributions of biological anthropology to knowledge about links between hormones, sex and gender, Worthman (1995: 595) provided the following summary of contemporary understanding of hormonal action.

> Hormones do not directly cause specific biological or behavioral effects. Rather, hormonal action is mediated through an array of other factors. These include: circulating binding proteins, metabolic enzymes, cellular receptors, nuclear binding sites, competing molecules, and presence of cofactors.

Thus, a straightforward causal link between female hormones and women's experiences of depression would appear difficult to reconcile with current knowledge about hormonal action. Unless conceptions of hormones are updated, expansion of biological models to include psychosocial in addition to hormonal influences seems more likely to replicate the conceptual limitations of single-factor biological models.

Another source of the persistence of biological models is support among women for biological accounts of women's distress (Markens 1996). For instance, many women wrote to the DSM committee charged with deciding whether PMS should be included as a diagnosis, detailing their personal struggles with PMS and expressing a keen desire to have their complaints validated by a medical diagnosis. Somewhat predictably, feminist critiques of the proposed PMS diagnosis as medicalizing and pathologizing women's distress were not well-received by the lay women's health movement (Figert 1996).

One reason a woman might seek a medical diagnosis is when her complaints involve troublesome physical experiences and physicians are viewed as the primary source of help with various bodily discomforts. Receiving a diagnosis both legitimizes help-seeking and validates a woman's experiences, while also offering the prospect of some symptomatic relief. Feminist analyses of medical diagnoses for women's distress have focused on the negative consequences of treating women's experiences as symptoms of a psychiatric or mental disorder. Overlooked in such critiques, however, is that accounts of distress given by women often reflect experiences which are both physically debilitating *and* subjectively aversive.

The embodied character of women's distress is illustrated in the following two excerpts taken from interviews with women who were invited to talk about their "depressive experiences".[3] The first is from an interview with "Susan" (not her real name) who identified herself as having problems with depression. "Well, I've sat and cried and cried, most of the time I was laying in the bed, and stuff over nothing. A thought would just come, and I don't know, I'd just break down and cry." The second excerpt is from an interview with "Sarah" who had been medically diagnosed as depressed. "Your self-esteem is very low, um, you withdraw ... You know, like it's not just the emotional part of it, but, but it affects you physically." Similar findings have been reported in other studies in which women's accounts of their depressive experiences were explored (Lewis 1995, Schreiber 1996). The embodied character of depressive experiences may be a source of confusion to women. What do such experiences mean? Are they signs of illness? What kind of illness is it? Are these experiences normal? A woman might respond to her depressive experiences in various ways, depending on how she interprets them and the reactions of those around her. If such experiences have a physical component, a woman might decide that a prudent course of action is to seek the advice of her doctor. Being diagnosed with depression would serve to validate a woman's understanding of her experiences as being caused by a physical disorder within the body, an interpretation likely to be reinforced if her doctor prescribes a medication.

Alternatively, a woman may decide to get on with her life and to cope on her own as best she can without professional help. Responding in this way also means foreclosing on the possibility of having her experiences medically validated. In the absence of a medical interpretation of her distress, a woman may understand her experiences in relation to the circumstances of her everyday life. For instance, as illustrated in the following excerpt from "Jane's" account, a woman may frame her experiences in the context of needing to "keep going" for the sake of her children.

> No matter how depressed or stressed out you are, for me, I know I still
> have to get up every morning and I still have to get them their break-
> fast. . . . I don't know if you'd say that they were my anchor, but I guess
> that's the way you'd put it . . . for me it always comes down to the kids.

Some women, nevertheless, do gain a measure of relief from having their depressive experiences medically validated. From the standpoint of women struggling to
cope with unpleasant and debilitating embodied experiences, feminist critiques of
medical–psychiatric diagnoses associated with women's menstrual life are likely to
be viewed as irrelevant and even counterproductive. And, indeed, women do draw
on hormonal explanations in their attempts to account for unwanted bodily experiences (Lewis 1995, Nicolson 1992, Swann and Ussher 1995). Although such
interpretational strategies may enable some women to make sense of their experiences, biological approaches to explaining women's distress have less positive
implications for women in general.

What are the consequences for women when their distress is blamed on their bodies?

If a woman explains her distressing experiences on hormonal processes associated
with menstruation, childbirth, or menopause, invariably she attributes such experiences to something outside her control. In so doing, however, the possibility that
her own actions are somehow to blame is ruled out. Locating the source of distress
within the body's biology may remove the possibility of self-blame but more negative consequences are not avoided. Although medical treatment may offer a
welcome source of relief to women, such help rests on an assumption that the
female body is potentially disordered and dysfunctional. This view of the female
body fuels cultural beliefs which may be used to justify the exclusion of women
from responsible (and highly-paid) jobs (e.g. airline pilot) and powerful positions
(e.g. political leader) within society. Such beliefs also provide a rationale for the continued search for biochemical cures for women's embodied distress.

Explanations for women's distress in terms of female reproductive biology also
provide fertile grounds for the development of drugs for which women represent a
vast market as well as a source of profits for drug manufacturers (Russell 1995).
Despite the lack of clear-cut empirical support for biological theories of depression,
and the absence of evidence for hormonal explanations for women's distress, psychotropic drugs are the primary form of medical treatment. The widespread
prescription of such drugs to women takes place against a background of ignorance
about their effects on women's bodies. For instance, although women of child-bearing age are the major recipients of antidepressant drugs, little is known about the
adverse effects (euphemistically referred to as "side-effects") these drugs may have
when ingested by women who are pregnant or breastfeeding (Weissman and Olfson
1995). The legitimation of PMS (or "premenstrual dysphoric disorder") as a psychiatric disorder has been accompanied by an increase in the development and

promotion of drugs aimed at PMS sufferers (Figert 1996). Moreover, HRT is now being widely recommended for middle-aged women as a panacea to counteract the subjective distress and physical discomfort expected to occur in conjunction with menopause and its aftermath (Lock 1993).

The dubious record of women's experiences with drugs marketed as providing relief for symptoms associated with pregnancy (e.g. DES, Thalidomide) or to prevent conception ("the pill"), should be cause for serious concern about the continued promotion and medical endorsement of pharmacological cures for women's health problems (cf. Eagan 1985, Figert 1996, Russell 1995). A further consequence of the emphasis on biological explanations for women's distress is that they provide support for medicalized views of women's complaints.

Why does the medicalization of women's bodies and women's distress concern feminists?

Critiques from a feminist perspective of the medicalization of women's bodies and women's distress have focused on the potentially stigmatizing effects for women of being diagnosed with a mental illness. Labels implying a diagnosis such as pre-menstrual dysphoric disorder (or PMS) and post-partum depression refer to conditions defined as mental disorders and like other such terms are associated with connotations of irrationality and craziness. For example, the recent move to include within the DSM several disorders which by definition can only be experienced by women was criticized by feminists because of the increased risk of stigmatization it poses for women, not only for those diagnosed with a particular disorder, but for women generally.

When a woman's distress is interpreted as symptomatic of a mental disorder, attention is likely to focus on her body to the neglect of her social circumstances. Feminists have been concerned that when a medical diagnosis is called into play, links between stressful aspects of women's everyday lives (e.g. poverty, physical or sexual abuse) and their experiences of distress are likely to be downplayed or ignored altogether. An emphasis on the body also undermines feminist efforts to address political and economic sources of inequality in women's lives. When women's distress is attributed to causes within their bodies, attempts to redress gendered inequalities within the public sphere may have less impact. From a feminist perspective, therefore, a major drawback of this medicalization process is that it fosters views in which women's health problems are blamed on their bodies, rather than their lives (Findlay and Miller 1994).

When women's distress is medicalized, usually the response of professionals is to provide treatment for a presumed disorder, a practise which individualizes and personalizes experiences of distress. Medicalization also encourages women to believe that medical professionals are the primary source of expertise on their embodied experiences (including all aspects of women's menstrual lives), so that there is little reason to share experiences with other women. An additional effect of the medicalization of women's distress, therefore, is that it divides women from each other and undercuts feminist efforts to engender a more collective sense of identity among women.

Understanding the distress some women experience in relation to their menstrual life presents seemingly intractable problems for efforts to overcome dualistic and reductionistic ways of thinking. Conceptualizing PMS as a medical problem appears to endorse biological explanations for women's distress. Feminist critiques of medicalization, on the other hand, may seem to deny the reality of experiences which for some women are both physically debilitating and psychologically dispiriting. Regardless of these debates, many women do seek explanations for their distress in terms of biological processes. How can women's accounts of their experiences be respected and validated while avoiding the pitfalls of medicalization? One strategy, proposed by Ussher (1989) is the development of analyses in which both biological *and* psychosocial domains can be included, but without emphasizing one at the expense of the other. A perspective on human health concerns encompassing both biological and psychosocial domains has been referred as "material–discursive" (Ussher 1997a, Yardley 1996, 1997c). Material–discursive approaches begin from a position in which the human body is understood as the "lived body", an organism which is "simultaneously a physical and symbolic artifact" (Lock 1993: 373), rather than the passive biological entity of biomedical conceptions. Thus, material–discursive approaches enable the materiality of the body to be acknowledged, while avoiding dualist and reductionist assumptions about the body's role in human experience and action. In the remainder of this chapter, I explore the potential contributions of material–discursive approaches for understanding depression in women.

Exploring material–discursive approaches to depression in women

Drawing on material–discursive perspectives to develop an understanding of depression in women involves bringing together ideas about women's lives (somewhat analogous to social models) and women's bodies (reformulated versions of biological models) in combination with ideas about women's subjectivity (roughly parallel to psychological and psychosocial models). These ideas are taken up in a transformative way, however, to overcome or transcend the limitations of existing approaches to understanding depression in women.

A material–discursive perspective is grounded in assumptions about the nature of knowledge which are quite different from those informing mainstream approaches (see Chapter 1 where I discussed these assumptions). Concepts such as "depression", "gender", "women's lives", "women's bodies" are re-formulated so that their socially constructed character is made more explicit. For instance, within mainstream research, when "gender" is addressed, usually it is assumed to be something (a biological reality) existing already in the world prior to, and independently from, the beliefs of researchers or participants in research studies. The notion of gender is understood rather differently within a material–discursive perspective. As well as having a gender (normally assumed to be female or male on the basis of physical anatomy) people can also be considered to "do" gender. In this sense, being a women (or a man) involves presenting an appropriately gendered appearance to others (e.g. looking, behaving and dressing like a woman) (cf. Butler 1990).

Doing gender also extends beyond physical appearance to include the activities of everyday life, so it is meaningful to talk about women's lives (or men's lives). Notions of gender encompass ways of being a woman (or a man), where being a woman involves behaving in womanly ways, as reflected in feminine styles of speech, body movements, posture and emotional expression. Thus, from this perspective, gender can be understood as an accomplishment, something achieved on an ongoing basis in the course of daily living, rather than something which is pre-given (fixed at the point of conception and further cemented during early childhood). Conceptualizing gender as a social construction does not mean denying the material reality of human bodies. Instead, when understood from this social constructionist perspective, gender is conceived as something constituted in the context of culturally shared understandings of its meaning.

Women's lives and discourses of femininity

A key assumption of material–discursive approaches is that people's knowledge about themselves, how they understand and make sense of their experiences, is constituted (or socially constructed) in the course of interpersonal interactions. Such knowledge includes what it means to "have a life" as a woman. Within a given sociocultural context, there are certain regularities in the focus and direction of people's lives across the lifespan. Women's adult lives, for instance, have a recognizable shape, typically characterized by involvement in the care of family members, especially children. Notions regarding women's lives have more general meaning because of widely shared understandings of how women should conduct their lives as wives, mothers and housewives. The following two accounts, taken from interviews with women about their depressive experiences, reflect these taken for granted assumptions about women's lives. In the first excerpt, "Linda", who lives in a rural community with her school-age children and common-law husband, describes her daily routine.

> . . . so I get up at 5:30, use the bathroom, make lunches (for children to take to school), make breakfast . . . supper time comes . . . they eat, leave the dishes in the sink and go and they listen to music, on the phone or in bed . . . I get stuck with the dishes, then cleaning up.

"Susan", divorced with adult children living at home and supporting herself with a part-time job, described her family responsibilities as follows: "and I still make their supper, and I would still do their laundry, and I would still do whatever I feel is my duty to do for them".

Women's home-based activities constitute one aspect of what can be termed practises of femininity. Another way in which women enact femininity is through their efforts to produce a feminine style of personal appearance or body shape (using make-up, wearing fashionable clothes, dieting, exercising etc.). Practises of femininity emphasize somewhat different activities at different stages of a woman's life. In younger women, there is heightened concern with achieving an attractive feminine appearance, whereas among older women, more emphasis may be placed on creating a nurturing home environment for family members. The question arising here is how do so many women come to pursue and spend so much of their lives engaging in these practises of femininity? Understanding of a social constructionist answer to this question requires consideration of the concept of discourses of femininity.

From a social constructionist perspective, people's ideas about how to conduct their everyday lives, the options and choices available to them, are formed in the course of their social interactions within the world around them. Such ideas are communicated in language, in conversations with relatives and friends, through exposure to print (newspapers, magazines) and visual (TV, movies) media and during formal education (classroom and textbook materials). Ideas absorbed in the context of social interactions are not necessarily transmitted in an explicit manner but are often taken for granted, forming an implicit cultural backdrop to information circulating within society.

Advertising provides a particularly clear example of this process. An advertisement for a new shampoo, for instance, may extol its virtues (e.g. for controlling dandruff) as superior to those of competing brands. At the same time, the model demonstrating the effects of using the shampoo is a slender young woman, with impeccable make-up, wearing glamorous clothes, and whose hair is styled in the latest fashion. The shampoo ad contains an implicit message focused on women's physical appearance and how to look appropriately feminine, as well as the more explicit message about the shampoo's beneficial effects on personal grooming. The term discourse encompasses both these implicit messages and more explicit directives to which people are exposed in their social interactions.

Shared cultural ideas about the kinds of activities constituting women's lives and the manner in which these activities should be performed also can be understood as social constructions. Discourses of gender and femininity operate around ideals which are central to shared understandings of what it means to be a "good woman". One set of ideals defining the good woman concerns the quality of the home environment created for family members. The myriad forms of caring and nurturing activities implied by the words wife, mother, and housewife are socially constructed as woman's work, and such activities are generally carried out by women.

Women's lives and women's subjectivities

For many women, engaging in activities focused on the caring needs of family members represents an important source of identity, providing a sense of personal satisfaction and fulfilment, as well as feelings of well-being. As constructed within discourses of femininity, a woman's caring work is important for ensuring the health and normal development of her children and also a critical ingredient in sustaining harmonious relations with her partner. Women's caring work on behalf of her family is concretely manifested in a range of daily activities including (but not limited to) cooking meals, washing and ironing clothes, house-cleaning, buying food and other items required by family members, arranging social events to mark family and holiday occasions (birthdays, Christmas, etc.). And "motherwork", the ceaseless responsibility of caring for dependent children, is a central part of the lives of many women.

From a social constructionist perspective, subjectivity is understood as discursively produced and discourses of femininity provide resources from which a sense of self or identity is constructed by women. When a woman defines her identity in terms being a wife, mother and housewife, she is likely to judge the adequacy of her endeavors against the socially constructed ideals of the good woman, which nevertheless are often ambiguous. Are meals prepared from "scratch" more nutritious than frozen dinners? Should towels and sheets always be ironed? What constitutes "quality" time with children? Pronouncements by experts on the potential of inadequate mothering to create child problems serve as reminders (and sources of anxiety) about ensuring that one's own children are properly cared for. A central theme of discourses of femininity is that women's activities in the home should foster a suitably nurturing environment for family members.

Women's subjectivities also are constructed in a cultural context in which the human qualities of caring and concern for others are associated symbolically with femininity (Miller 1986), an association further reinforced by the construction of feminine characteristics as natural womanly traits (Gilligan 1982). Caring work is believed to fall properly within the domain of women's lives, because women are naturally (i.e. biologically) endowed with the propensity to nurture others. The nurturing dimension of women's lives also is underscored by the cultural linkage between food and love (Bordo 1993), a connection in which meal preparation is socially constructed as a tangible expression of women's caring for others (Bella 1992). Thus, women's activities in the home are regulated and governed by ideals of the good woman embedded in discourses of femininity.

According to discourses of femininity, women's work in the home is motivated by feelings of concern and love for family members and so yields its own intrinsic rewards. Such work is constructed discursively as offering satisfactions which cannot (and should not) be measured in the materialistic terms of the public world of money and business. When a woman's identity is shaped in relation to the socially constructed ideals of the good woman, feeling "good", in both subjective and normative senses, is likely to depend on whether she believes the work she performs in the home signifies an appropriate level of care for her family. However, the cultural ideals against which a woman judges herself as a good woman are not fixed and immutable, but rather fluctuate in concert with broader changes within society. For instance, previous views about the relatively benign effects on children of mothers' employment outside the home currently are being contested by the resurgence of a strongly pro-family discourse, in which the importance of a mother's continuous presence within the home is emphasized. Such cultural shifts are likely to generate feelings of uncertainty in women, undermining their sense of identity as a good woman.

Giving an affirmative answer to the question "As a woman, am I good enough?" may be especially difficult for women whose circumstances do not conform to those of the conventional wife and mother. Discourses of femininity provide a background to women's experiences, while at the same time obscuring the material conditions of their lives. For example, when women work outside the home, whether by choice or financial necessity, their childcare efforts are still likely to be judged (and often found wanting) in terms of the socially constructed standards defining the good mother. Such judgments are made without consideration of a woman's material circumstances or the limited availability of good quality and affordable childcare services. For many women, therefore, material circumstances set distinct limits on possibilities for orchestrating their lives in accord with the ideals of the good woman.

Women's lives and women's bodies

Contemporary discourses of femininity now accommodate the figure of the "new woman", one who combines family responsibilities with work outside the home. Thus, in this updated version of the good woman, a woman can have a career (or at least paid employment) while not foregoing the more traditional sources of satisfaction presumed to accompany marriage and motherhood. The addition of paid work to unpaid domestic work, however, does not alter the centrality of caring work within the family to the discursively constructed ideal of the good woman and women who have careers must now juggle the demands of work both inside and outside the home.

To deal with the claims on their time and energy, many women become adept at time management as a way of accomplishing the multitude of daily tasks required of the good woman. Time management, a familiar topic of "advice to women" features in magazines and newspapers, places an emphasis on planning ahead (e.g. making lists), limiting distractions and interruptions (e.g. using an answerphone), and avoiding procrastination (e.g. setting goals for completion of chores). Such advice, exhorting women to use time wisely, putting it to productive rather than wasteful purposes, appears to convey the message that working diligently and efficiently is a sign of being a good woman. The importance of being a effective time manager to a woman's sense of self as a good woman is illustrated by the following excerpt taken from an interview with "Mary" a married woman who worked as a health professional before being diagnosed with depression: ". . . like I used to do fifty things at once . . . I look back and see, not that I want to get back to that person, but even if I could do five things at once I'd be happy."

Women's bodies provide the physical means for accomplishing activities in support of their families. Re-conceptualizing women's bodies as being both culturally and naturally produced make available alternatives to purely biological approaches to understanding the role of the physical body in women's depressive experience. The notion of the "practical" or "useful" body (Bordo 1993, Bourdieu and Wacquant 1992) offers a way to conceptualize the body in which connections between cultural life and bodily dispositions are highlighted. From this perspective, both the activities constituting people's everyday lives and the manner in which such activities are carried out are understood as being socially constructed and discursively regulated. According to discourses of femininity, the good woman is one who invests much of her time and energy in caring for family members. At the same time, the performance on a daily basis of activities in the home shapes a woman's experiences and subjectivity in directions which conform to prevailing conceptions of feminine identity. Through this process, both body and self are transformed, creating an "embodied self" who willingly engages in practises signifying the good woman. One outcome of this process is that when a woman performs her activities as wife/housewife/mother according to the discursively constructed tenets of the good woman, she is likely to feel good too.

The material context of practises of the good woman

A woman's capacity to engage in activities which signify to herself and others that she is a good woman is limited, however, by the finite material resources of the physical body. The material limits imposed by the body may be evidenced by tiredness and fatigue, complaints which are commonly reported by women and typically attributed to burdensome family responsibilities (Popay 1992, Walters 1993). A woman's ability to engage in practises of femininity also is governed by the material circumstances of her everyday life, which in turn are shaped by pre-existing structural conditions. A woman's presence at home, for instance, when her children return from school (a sign that she is a good mother) is likely to depend on the adequacy of the family's financial resources and whether she works outside the home. Perhaps the only jobs available to a woman involve working shifts (e.g. factory work) or the willingness to work irregular hours may be a requirement of her occupation (e.g. nursing).

The material conditions of a woman's everyday life may frequently present situations in which she falls short of her own or others' expectations of the good woman. For example, a woman's work schedule may limit the time she can spend with her children; she may feel too tired after a day spent looking after two preschool children to cook a meal for her husband; she has insufficient time and money to take care of her own appearance; she is irritable with family members because of feelings of fatigue; she is too tired at night for sex with her partner. Under conditions such as these, the feelings of satisfaction a woman might expect to experience from engaging in the practises of the good woman are likely to be diminished, supplanted instead by feelings of demoralization. This scenario is more likely to be the case when a woman's experiences are inconsistent with prevailing cultural conceptions of family life. Perhaps her children are misbehaving or doing badly at school, or her partner is unappreciative and emotionally abusive. For women parenting alone or living in poverty, sustaining a sense of identity as a good mother may be particularly difficult (Lewis 1997). For instance, "Linda", living on a low income, with several children at home, experienced her efforts to be a good mother as a daily struggle:

> . . . and you try and tell them . . . take it easy on the food . . . And then when there's nothing left, of course they sit and cry and of course we get depressed and because it's not there. We don't have the money to get more. And the kids can't understand . . . because you don't know where you're going to come up with anything . . . I just go in the room and cry . . . I'll go sit in the bathtub and read if I get too depressed or just stay in my room.

To overcome her sense of demoralization a woman may increase her commitment to practises of femininity. Perhaps by working harder (and managing her time more efficiently), she can capture the illusive sense of fulfilment which is supposed to be her reward for engaging in activities signifying that she is a good woman. Rather than increased well-being, however, the more likely consequences are continued fatigue and further demoralization. These experiences are brought into sharper focus with a woman's realization that any sense of satisfaction she achieves is hardly commensurate with the effort she expends. Under such conditions, the more probable outcome is exhaustion of a woman's body and depletion of her morale. The following excerpt, from an interview with "Sally", a married woman who worked in a human service field before being diagnosed with depression, reflects one woman's experiences of her failed effort to live up to the ideals of the good woman.

> I still did my daily activities . . . You know, had supper ready, had dinner ready, had their lunches ready. Did the wash. But none of that had ceased, you know. But I did it because . . . well you do it. Then you went to bed. . . . But I think this time I had to allow that because, I ah, I was tired of . . . putting on this mask and . . . keeping going.

A Material–discursive framework for understanding depression in women

When reconceptualized within a material–discursive framework, the embodied experiences labeled in mainstream approaches as symptoms of depression lose their pathological overtones as products of a disorder within the biological body. Within a material–discursive formulation, depression is understood as experiences which arise in conjunction with a woman's embodied efforts to meet socially constructed standards defining the good woman. Thus, from a material–discursive perspective, depression is reframed as the outcome of a process involving reciprocal interactions between a woman's physical embodiment and her discursively constructed experiences. In this ongoing process, female embodiment provides the ground for a lived experience which is both material and discursive. When a woman's endeavors fail to engender feelings of fulfilment and well-being, she is likely to interpret her experiences and actions as signifying her inability to live up to the discursively constructed ideals of the good woman. In this case, a woman may draw the conclusion that she is a bad woman and feelings of powerlessness and hopelessness are likely to mingle with those of self-blame and self-disgust. For many women, the absence of viable alternatives to the identities of wife, mother and housewife, coupled with the lack of social value attached to women's work in the home, contribute to the difficulties posed for women by their lives as women. The lethargy, social withdrawal and lack of interest in usual pursuits which a clinician might diagnose as depression, are better understood, from this material–discursive perspective, as a woman's response to insoluble dilemmas in her life. Constructed within this frame, life indeed may seem not worth living and for some women the material alternative of suicide may represent the only viable solution to the dilemmas they confront.

In this account of a material–discursive approach to understanding depression in women, I have drawn on examples which depict women whose lives follow the conventional adult trajectory of wife, mother and housewife. Similar analyses could be developed with respect to depressive experiences of women at other life stages or whose circumstances differ from those of married women with children. Material–discursive approaches to understanding depression in women are explored in more detail in the next part of the book. The chapters in Part III address respectively depression in women during adolescence, in the context of marriage and the transition to motherhood, and in relation to midlife and old age.

Notes

1 Although female embodiment may have been neglected in approaches to explaining depression in women discussed in previous chapters in Part II, analyses developed by feminist scholars have not been characterized by this omission. In particular, Bordo (1993), Lock (1993), Martin (1987) and Ussher (1989) have made important contributions to development of ways of understanding women's experiences which attend to female embodiment.

2 The term "reductionism" refers to the assumption within a positivist philosophy of science that knowledge about a phenomenon is only achieved when it is reduced to its most elementary constituents (Van Langenhove 1995: 14–15). In the context of attempts to understand the links between women's menstrual life and their experiences of distress, a reductionist outlook implies that experiences, such as those called PMS, will only be understood completely when the physiological processes and mechanisms presumed to underlie them can be mapped empirically.

3 These excerpts and those included later in the chapter, are taken from interviews conducted by Deanna Gammell and Yvette Scattolon, who were doctoral students in psychology at the University of New Brunswick when the interviews were completed. Their contributions and the assistance of the women who agreed to be interviewed about their depressive experiences are gratefully acknowledged.

Part III

EMBODIED LIVES
Understanding depression in women
in context

7

DEPRESSION IN ADOLESCENCE

Negotiating identities in a girl-poisoning culture[1]

Adolescence has been identified as a period with particular importance for understanding depression in women and more particularly for explaining gender-related differences in rates of depression. This is because research findings have indicated that rates of depression seem to increase during adolescence (Culbertson 1997) and this increase is more marked for adolescent girls than adolescent boys (Nolen-Hoeksema and Girgus 1994). Because rates of depression in preadolescent children generally are low and have not been found to be higher (and sometimes are lower) in girls than boys, the gender-related difference in rates of depression reported to be present among adults is now considered to have its beginnings in adolescence (Bebbington 1996, Leadbeater *et al.* 1995, Nolen-Hoeksema and Girgus 1994). For these reasons, depression during adolescence has been identified by some researchers as an important topic for research, because it may hold a key to understanding causal factors in depression, as well as for explaining gender-related differences in depression in adulthood (Cicchetti and Toth 1998).

The issue of why rates of depression are higher among females than males, both in adolescent and older age groups is not my particular concern, however, in this chapter. Instead, I focus on the topic of depression in young women and how such experiences might be understood from a feminist and social constructionist perspective. One reason for side-stepping the gender-related differences in depression issue is because I want to avoid conceptual problems which arise when attempts to understand depression are grounded in mainstream definitions of depressive disorder and depressive symptoms. In most mainstream research on depression in adolescence, these definitional strategies are assumed or taken for granted, and this sets distinct limits on the possibilities for exploring alternative ways to understand depression. Another reason for not considering the gender-related differences in depression issue here is that attempts to address it generally have operated on the assumption that causes of depression are the same regardless of a person's gender. Some causes are just more likely to be present in women's lives than men's or have a greater impact upon females than males. The possibility that qualitatively different causal influences and processes may be involved in depression in females than in males is one which cannot easily be accommodated by mainstream theories. In contrast to such "gender-blind" approaches, the framework I develop in this chapter is one grounded in the everyday lives and experiences of girls, highlighting the particular and gendered character of these experiences.

I begin the chapter by considering what is meant by the term adolescence, pointing to the socially constructed and socially produced character of this period of the life span and the young people who live it. This way of understanding adolescence is contrasted with mainstream notions of this part of life as a developmental stage, marked by puberty as a pivotal event and identity formation as key task in the transition to adult status. Contemporary theories of depression in adolescent girls are then considered, focusing particularly on the model proposed by Nolen-Hoeksema and Girgus (1994). My main reasons for choosing this model for discussion are because it is the most comprehensive of those proposed so far, and also because it exemplifies current mainstream approaches to explaining depression in adolescence. In broad terms, these approaches draw on a combination of biological (e.g. hormonal), psychological (e.g. personality traits) and social (e.g. peer pressures) influences and their interactions to explain depression. Thus, they are in line with the recent shift in mainstream research toward multifactorial, biopsychosocial models of depression as providing the most appropriate framework within which to devise theoretical formulations (see Chapter 6).

In the next part of the chapter, I analyze Nolen-Hoeksema and Girgus' model, identifying ways in which their reliance on the tenets of positivist modes of research shapes the knowledge produced. A limitation which the Nolen-Hoeksema and Girgus model shares in common with other mainstream approaches is the general failure to consider the sociocultural context of adolescent girls' lives, particularly how discourses of femininity are implicated in the lived experiences of young women. A concern with cultural representations of adolescence and their impact on subjectivity and identity in adolescent girls is central to a social constructionist perspective, and these are issues which are not addressed in mainstream approaches. Another area which has been relatively neglected in mainstream approaches is how the experiences of adolescent girls are constituted in gendered ways through girls' interactions with their parents and other adults (such as teachers) and more especially with peers in school and community settings. Such gendered experiences, occurring in the context of culturally shared and promoted discourses of femininity, operate to reinforce and maintain idealized images of adolescent girls as younger versions of the "good woman" discussed in earlier chapters.

Rarely included in mainstream accounts of adolescence is information about the lived experiences of adolescent girls. One consequence of this absence is that depictions of adolescent womanhood have a largely taken for granted character. To counteract and challenge these unquestioned assumptions about young women's lives, in the next part of the chapter, I discuss findings of studies which have explored the lives of adolescent girls from their own standpoint. Research of this kind is beginning to provide a more complete picture of girls' lives and their embodied experiences, particularly with respect to areas such as puberty and menstruation, sexuality and desire, peer relationships and schooling. In the concluding section of the chapter, I consider how an understanding of depression in adolescent girls may be derived from the material–discursive approach outlined in Chapter 6. From a material–discursive perspective, one way of understanding depression in adolescent girls is that the experiences we call depression are part of girls' experiences of subjectivity as they struggle to negotiate identities for themselves in a social and cultural context which has been labelled "girl-poisoning" (Pipher 1994).

The meaning of adolescence: an historically-specific life stage

The term adolescence is routinely used to refer to the stage in the lifespan occurring between childhood and adulthood (roughly the teenage years, and encompassing puberty) and as such its meaning may appear to be self-evident. The familiarity of the notion of adolescence, however, obscures the relative recency, historically speaking, of the identification of a specific life-stage separate from childhood, on the one hand, and from adulthood, on the other. The concept of adolescence as a specific life-stage first emerged toward the end of the nineteenth century (Griffin 1993). As Fasick (1994) has argued, various structural changes, including the movement of young people from the workplace to the school, and increased economic dependence of adolescents on their parents, probably contributed to the invention of adolescence. Rather than signifying an immutable stage or phase of the human life cycle, the term adolescence is better understood as referring to a way of categorizing people which is both socially constructed and socially produced. The term adolescent girls, then, designates a social category which has come to be identified in this way within a historically specific set of social, economic and political conditions.

An important implication of this way of understanding what is meant by adolescence is that when we use this word to describe someone, the images it is likely to conjure up are historically and socioculturally specific. For instance, the image brought to mind by the word adolescence or adolescent may include ideas about youthful energy, freedom to have fun and lack of work responsibilities, involvement in sports, dating, and so on. Such images are part of the meaning of adolescence, what it means to be an adolescent in a specific sociocultural context.

Representations of adolescence

The various images brought forth by the word adolescence are aspects of what have been termed "representations of youth" (Griffin 1993). These ways of representing adolescents are also linked to various discourses around the notion of adolescence. As Griffin has pointed out, however, many of the representations and discourses of adolescence circulating in society reflect the standpoints of adults, particularly those adults involved in doing research and devising social policy in the area of adolescence. Indeed, in some ways, representations of adolescence can be said to be produced by researchers (Griffin 1993). This observation has two main

implications for the points I want to develop here. The first is that accounts of adolescence in textbooks (including this one) and other publications cannot be
understood in a straightforward way as providing a description of the lives and
experiences of actual adolescents. Such accounts do have an impact, however, in
shaping social constructions of adolescence drawn on by adults (e.g., parents,
teachers, career counsellors and health professionals) in their dealings with young
people.

The second point I want to highlight is that images of adolescence also are *gendered*. By this I mean that representations of adolescence vary depending on
whether female or male adolescents are the focus. For example, as Griffin (1993)
has pointed out, certain social problems, such as delinquency and school truancy,
sexual promiscuity and teen pregnancy, are viewed as having both their source and
cause in adolescence. Such problems often are discussed as though they represent
general concerns, when in fact they are gendered. The gendered dimensions of
these social problems may not be acknowledged explicitly, yet gender is clearly
implicated in the construction of some behaviors and activities as problems and
others as unproblematic or normal, depending on whether the adolescents involved
are female or male.

Of course, textbooks written by experts are not the only source of representations and discourses of adolescence. Media of various kinds – movies, television,
"teen" magazines, music videos and other cultural forms – offer myriad images and
portrayals of female adolescents. Such representations both reflect idealized images
of young women and transmit shared ideas about what it means to be a young
woman in a particular sociocultural context. These discourses of femininity, which
have adolescent girls as their object, act as a kind of blueprint for how to be a
young woman, accompanied by a cultural map with directions on how to attain
this goal. Magazines aimed at teenage girls, for instance, place a heavy emphasis on
appearance, clothes and body image. The fact that these topics are singled out for
presentation, not only serves to construct them as properly the concern of girls in
this age group, but also fuels a host of anxieties in individual girls about the size,
shape, and appearance of their bodies.

Representations of adolescence and identity in young women

Representations of adolescence also have implications for identity, or sense of self,
in young women. Gendered images and discourses in relation to adolescence provide a source of raw material from which adolescent girls form their sense of self.
As an aspect of what has been termed subjectivity (see Chapter 1), a young
woman's sense of self includes ideas about the kind of person she is now and the
kind of person (woman) she wants to become in the future.

In mainstream writing on adolescence, "identity formation" is viewed as one of
the central tasks of adolescence, underpinning adolescent adjustment, as well as
setting the stage for adult development (Erikson 1968). Identity formation is

conceptualized as primarily an intrapsychic process, one occurring within the individual personality. In more recent accounts, this intrapsychic process has been reframed in terms of representations of self or "self-schemata" and vulnerability to depression is attributed to dysfunctions within this "cognitive self-system" (Cicchetti and Toth 1998). The process of identity formation generally is assumed to proceed through a series of stages, with each successive stage reflecting a more mature identity than the preceding one (Marcia 1980). Moreover, the ideal end-point of this process is assumed to be that a young person develops a sense of self as an autonomous individual who has self-defined goals and values. Failure to achieve an identity as an autonomous individual who has a coherent (and socially acceptable) sense of direction in life is likely to be viewed as evidence of arrested, deviant or abnormal development (Ianni and Orr 1996, Leadbeater and Way 1996).

This concern with identity formation takes on a somewhat different character when considered from a social constructionist perspective. Rather than a process which occurs solely within the individual, identity formation is seen as very much a social process, one with close links to the social context in which a young person lives and the cultural discourses available within that context (Burr 1995). From this perspective, identity is understood as being constructed in language and social interaction (Burr 1995, Wetherell 1995). For adolescent girls, this means that the ideas a girl is likely to draw on to answer such questions as "Who am I?", "What kind of person am I?" are those available in the social and cultural context in which she lives. So, a girl might glean an answer to the "Who am I?" question from information in the media, from everyday conversations with family members and in the course of her interactions with peers. A girl's sense of self is constituted in the context of the ideas and experiences which she encounters in her everyday life. To the extent that these ideas and experiences incorporate gendered images of what it is to be a young woman, her sense of self also is likely to be shaped in directions that reflect culturally-shared notions of adolescent femininity.

The identity positions available to a young woman also are constrained by the material circumstances of her life (e.g. the social class position and income level of her parents, the area where she lives, the school she attends). They are also shaped by her embodied experiences (e.g. timing of puberty and onset of menstruation, the outward appearance of her physical body) and a girl's physical appearance will have implications for her ability to adopt particular identity positions. For example, an identity based on popularity with peers is hard to sustain in a cultural context in which being thin is a prerequisite for successfully carrying off a "trendy teen" image. The identity an adolescent girl adopts may also have conflicting implications in her everyday life. Doing well in school, for instance, may mean academic success and parental approval, but it may also bring with it rejection by peers and teachers (Bourne et al. 1998, Pipher 1994). Thus, the process of identity formation is far from the clear-cut linear progression often depicted in mainstream writing on adolescence.

As I hope the discussion so far has indicated, the process of forming an identity –

a sense of self which is both viable and valued – is one likely to be fraught with contradictions. For adolescent girls, this process also is one shaped by cultural constructions of femininity (and the various limitations inherent in such constructions). An added complexity in thinking about the meaning of identity is that theorists who work within a social constructionist perspective reject the assumption that the identity a person develops is a "unitary and coherent" one which is the same in all circumstances, in different situations and with different people. In contrast to this unitary conception of identity, social constructionists view identity as consisting of a variety of "subject positions" which not only may contradict each other, but also may be taken up in different ways in different situations (Burr 1995).

Considering the lived experiences of adolescent girls from a feminist perspective also brings into focus the gendered nature of these experiences. Discourses of femininity serve to demarcate and prescribe the identity positions which can be taken up by girls in specific sociocultural contexts. These discourses delineate proper behavior for teenage girls and regulate their activities, as well as shaping social interactions among adolescents. In this social process, both girls and boys can serve as "cultural agents", making sure that each other "toes the line" inherent in gendered identities. In mainstream theories of depression, these aspects of adolescent experience have tended to be lumped together under the catch-all label of "gender intensification". Gender intensification, as depicted in mainstream accounts, is a process occurring during adolescence in which socialization pressures become increasingly gender differentiated. One result of this process is that girls and boys "adopt personality characteristics deemed appropriate for their gender" (Nolen-Hoeksema and Girgus 1994: 428). In the next section of the chapter, I take up discussion of mainstream theories of depression in adolescence in more detail to consider how they have been applied to the problem of explaining depression in adolescent girls.

Mainstream theories and research on depression in adolescent girls

In contrast to the large volume of theory and research focused on depression in adult women, interest in depression in adolescent girls is more recent. This lack of attention by researchers to depression in the adolescent years can be traced to debates centered on the issue of whether children and adolescents experience "the affective quality of depression exhibited by adults" (Leadbeater *et al.* 1995: 5). These debates have been resolved around a consensus that depression (in both its depressive disorder and depressive symptom forms) is properly the concern of the field of "developmental psychopathology" (Cicchetti and Toth 1998).

In the literature on developmental psychopathology, theories proposed to explain depression in adolescents tend to parallel those proposed to account for depression in adults. Like theories of depression in adults, attempts to explain depression in adolescence have drawn on a combination of biological, psychological and social factors, reflecting the contemporary shift to multifactorial biopsychosocial models (cf. Cicchetti and Toth 1998). For example, when applied to the problem of explaining depression in adolescent girls, the hormonal and bodily changes accompanying puberty have been highlighted as a key source of biological influences. Psychological models have focused on personality development in adolescent girls, particularly those aspects thought to increase vulnerability to depression. Social models have also been proposed, with both normative (e.g. the transition from elementary to secondary schooling) and non-normative (e.g. sexual abuse) events identified as sources of stress in girls' lives.

In the paragraph above, I gave a "thumb-nail" sketch of the range of theoretical approaches with relevance to understanding depression in adolescent girls which are represented in the literature on depression in adolescence. This gives a slightly misleading impression, however, because much of this literature addresses depression in adolescents in general, rather than depression in adolescent girls. Typically, in these published accounts, the topic of gender arises only when the issue of "gender differences in depression" is considered (Cicchetti and Toth 1998, Petersen *et al.* 1993).[2] Thus, in the following discussion, I rely mainly on models developed to account for gender differences in depression during adolescence. The most comprehensive of these models is that proposed by psychologists Susan Nolen-Hoeksema and Joan Girgus (1994), which incorporates many of the approaches to understanding depression in women discussed in earlier chapters. This model focuses on gender differences in depression during adolescence and addresses the issue of why rates of depression increase in adolescent girls at this time. In the remainder of this section, I first outline the Nolen-Hoeksema and Girgus model and then analyze its assumptions and limitations from feminist and social constructionist perspectives.

The Nolen-Hoeksema and Girgus model

In their model, Nolen-Hoeksema and Girgus combine several biological, psychological and social factors to form a complex diathesis–stress framework. This formulation is based on the general hypothesis that depression in adolescent girls results from an interaction between pre-existing psychological vulnerabilities (personality traits) and certain biological and social changes (termed "challenges" by Nolen-Hoeksema and Girgus) which girls experience during early adolescence. *The diathesis component* of this model is conceptualized in terms of personality characteristics which have been the focus of psychological susceptibility approaches to explaining depression in women (see Chapter 4). In the case of adolescent girls, a relative lack of instrumental masculine characteristics (e.g. willingness to take on leaderships roles and to take risks) and an absence of behavioral tendencies (e.g. assertiveness) associated with instrumentality are identified as vulnerability factors for depression. According to Nolen-Hoeksema and Girgus' analysis of research findings, these areas of depressive vulnerability reflect a continuation of psychological tendencies already common among girls in childhood. The form of psychological vulnerability termed "sociotropy" or "dependency" in the diathesis–stress models discussed in Chapter 3 is not included in the model because Nolen-

Hoeksema and Girgus found little support for the hypothesis that adolescent girls are particularly likely to be dependent on relationships for their self-esteem. Other researchers (Leadbeater *et al.* 1995), however, have identified dependency, or "inter-personal preoccupation" as a psychological orientation characterizing adolescent girls and which may increase their vulnerability to depression under certain circumstances.

The stress component of Nolen-Hoeksema and Girgus' model is conceptualized in three main ways. First, they suggest that the bodily changes which occur in adolescent girls during puberty (e.g. development of breasts and a more "rounded" shape) may trigger feelings of body dissatisfaction. The occurrence of another normative event, the move from elementary to secondary school, at the same time as many girls may be experiencing feelings of body dissatisfaction is considered by Nolen-Hoeksema and Girgus to represent a potential source of stress. A second source of stress identified in their model is that, during the adolescent years, girls are likely to face an increased risk of becoming a victim of sexual abuse. Finally, Nolen-Hoeksema and Girgus conceptualize stress as having its source in the "gender intensification" process which is thought to be a feature of adolescence. This process is one marked by increased pressures on girls from peers, parents, and other adults to conform to a restrictive and narrowly-defined "gender role". Key elements of this gender role are the development of an identity that is consistent with cultural conceptions of "femininity" and engagement in behaviors considered socially appropriate for females.

Gaps and absences in the Nolen-Hoeksema and Girgus model: a feminist and social constructionist critique

The model presented by Nolen-Hoeksema and Girgus draws on findings on depression in adolescent girls generated by research conducted within a positivist framework. This framework was described in earlier chapters, where I discussed how adherence to the positivist version of scientific method produces particular forms of knowledge about depression. Many of the limitations already identified also are reflected in Nolen-Hoeksema and Girgus' model. At the same time, the assumptions underlying this model have the effect of making invisible the lived experiences of adolescent girls. This way of theorizing, therefore, rests on and also produces what I term "gaps" and "absences" in accounts of the lives of adolescent girls. These various omissions, combined with Nolen-Hoeksema and Girgus' emphasis on mainstream research findings, work together to create a particular way of understanding depression in adolescent girls. The gaps and absences I identify as being most critical in the theoretical model proposed by Nolen-Hoeksema and Girgus concern how depression, gender, the female body, and stress are conceptualized (and in turn operationalized and measured in research).

Depression in adolescent girls is defined by Nolen-Hoeksema and Girgus, in keeping with established mainstream practises, as either depressive disorder or depressive symptoms, in each case assessed using pre-structured criteria defined from the standpoint of researchers. These criteria have been derived, with few modifications, from research on depression in adults. Thus, girls' depressive experiences have hardly been explored at all and so we actually know very little about the experiences of adolescent girls which might be labelled as depression by researchers and mental health professionals.[3]

Apart from this lack of knowledge about depressive experiences from the standpoint of adolescent girls, reliance on mainstream conceptions promotes a decontextualized way of understanding depression. The process of defining certain experiences as symptoms of depression, for example, is one which involves extracting and detaching such experiences from the particular social and cultural context in which they are experienced. By conforming to mainstream practises in their approach to conceptualizing depression, Nolen-Hoeksema and Girgus' adoption of these context-stripping strategies already delimits the kind of knowledge about depressive experiences among adolescent girls which might be produced by researchers.

Gender is conceptualized, within the Nolen-Hoeksema and Girgus model, primarily in terms of individual gender. Other aspects of the gender system, the gendered division of social labor and symbolic gender, described in earlier chapters are not considered in any direct way. Instead, Nolen-Hoeksema and Girgus draw on the notion of gender intensification to account for an increased "feminization" of the behavior and experiences of adolescent girls which seems to occur during early adolescence. What they leave out of this account, however, is any consideration of reasons why gender intensification would occur at this time. Why is adolescence a time when girls increasingly orient their sense of self (or identity) around traditional feminine concerns, such as appearance, and are inclined to relinquish interest in more masculine pursuits? Also unexplored in their model is the contribution of peers, parents and other adults to this process. No explanation is offered for why parents and peers might react toward adolescent girls in ways which reinforce (or intensify) their adherence to culturally shared notions of a feminine gender role.

Like the mainstream models of depression on which their own theoretical approach is based, Nolen-Hoeksema and Girgus' account of depression in adolescence is mute with respect to both structural and symbolic aspects of gender. Thus, there is no discussion of social conditions which operate to channel girls' activities in particular and gendered directions, or of the symbolic associations of these activities with cultural notions of femininity. For instance, some school subjects (e.g. "domestic science" or "home economics", literature and languages) have stronger feminine connotations than do others (e.g. "technical studies", mathematics and science), which are more consonant with cultural notions of masculinity. At the same time, girls' parents, teachers and peers, are likely to share these gendered meanings, because they live in the same social context and are exposed to similar cultural messages. Also, outside the classroom, teenagers participate in a variety of "extra-curricular" pursuits, such as sports, hobbies, and leisure activities. In the choices available to them, the options of adolescent girls are structured along gender lines. For example, some sports are very much part of the male domain (e.g. baseball, soccer, cricket, ice hockey) and for a girl to participate in these activities would require not only a concerted effort on her part, but also strong support (both material and emotional) from adults in her life. When girls do participate in these kinds of sporting activities, it is more likely to be as a spectator or "cheerleader", providing an audience and source of encouragement for the athletic exploits of their male peers. In contrast, figure skating, gymnastics, singing in a choir, or babysitting, activities which are more likely to be engaged in by girls, also are more compatible with cultural notions of femininity.

Beliefs about childcare, for instance, as being a suitable activity for adolescent girls, as well as one for which they are particularly suited, represent aspects of discourses of femininity. Such discourses construct adolescent girls as "women-in-training", apprentices who are trying out, exploring and experimenting with ways of being a woman. Development of an appropriately feminine "gender identity" is presumed to be the end-point of this process, a goal portrayed in many guises through media depictions of women and women's lives (Ussher 1997b). It is hardly surprising that a girl's interactions with her parents and with both female and male peers would be influenced by these cultural constructions pervading many facets of everyday life. What remains invisible in mainstream accounts, however, is the particular form such social interactions take or any understanding of how these interactional experiences are so effective in exerting pressure on adolescent girls to conform to cultural ideals of feminine young womanhood. When mainstream formulations of depression in adolescent girls draw on notions like gender intensification, young women are depicted not only as being passively compliant with "socialization pressures", but also as lacking a sense of agency or autonomous self. To me, this way of theorizing reflects an assumption that adolescent girls are "cultural dopes" whose vulnerability to depression is implicitly attributed to (or blamed on) their tendency to become the kind of person constructed by cultural discourses of femininity.

The way *female embodiment* has been conceptualized in mainstream approaches to understanding depression in adolescent girls is also an area in which gaps and absences are apparent. In the model proposed by Nolen-Hoeksema and Girgus, physical changes associated with puberty are identified as "biological challenges" which may become a source of stress for some adolescent girls. The particular changes focused on by Nolen-Hoeksema and Girgus are those of body shape and appearance, marked by development of secondary sexual characteristics and the consequent loss of "the long, lithe, prepubescent look that is idealized in modern fashions" (p. 435). According to their analysis, body dissatisfaction is commonly present among adolescent girls, because many dislike the changes in their bodies, such as the weight gain ("puppy fat") accompanying puberty. Although Nolen-Hoeksema and Girgus' concept of biological challenges incorporates physical changes triggered by increasing levels of estrogen and progesterone during puberty, they reject purely hormonal explanations for depression in adolescent girls as lacking consistent empirical support.

Beyond identifying body dissatisfaction as a potential source of stress, Nolen-

Hoeksema and Girgus pay little attention to the female body. Curiously omitted from their model are aspects of female embodiment which to me would seem important aspects of the lived experiences of adolescent girls. Surely menarche, the beginning of a girl's life as someone who menstruates, as well as her development of breasts (not merely a "secondary sexual characteristic") might have some relevance, not only for her emerging sense of "bodily self", but more generally for understanding depression in adolescent girls. Perhaps because these aspects of female embodiment are ignored in the Nolen-Hoeksema and Girgus model, sexuality and sexual desire also are not mentioned in their account of the "biological and social challenges" girls are said to encounter during adolescence. The [hetero]sexualization of the adolescent female body is implied, however, by inclusion of "sexual" abuse among the social challenges faced by adolescent girls.

According to Nolen-Hoeksema and Girgus' model, body dissatisfaction increases the chances of a girl becoming depressed only if she also is exposed to some kind of difficulty or *stressful event* at that time in her life. An event routinely occurring in early adolescence is the move from elementary to secondary (or junior high) school. Nolen-Hoeksema and Girgus suggest that this event may be a stressful one for some girls, especially when it coincides with the time of "peak pubertal change". To explain why some girls might experience increased distress at this time, Nolen-Hoeksema and Girgus point to the diathesis component of their model. Thus, school change is likely to be experienced by a girl as stressful if it coincides with pubertal changes and she already is psychologically vulnerable (i.e. lacks instrumental traits). Not discussed by Nolen-Hoeksema and Girgus, however, is the issue of which aspects of the transition from elementary to secondary schooling might be experienced as stressful by adolescent girls. What is likely to be happening during her time at school which a girl finds stressful? A significant gap in mainstream models of depression in adolescence like the one proposed by Nolen-Hoeksema and Girgus is the absence of information about girls' everyday lives from their own standpoint.

Nolen-Hoeksema and Girgus also identify other "social challenges" which may be a source of *stress* in the lives of young women. Included among these challenges is becoming a victim of sexual abuse. Sexual abuse is included as a potential source of stress based on findings indicating that early adolescence is a time when girls face an increased risk of being abused sexually (e.g. Trickett and Putnam 1993), coupled with evidence that risk of depression is increased among victims of sexual abuse (cf. Cutler and Nolen-Hoeksema 1991). According to the diathesis–stress formulation developed by Nolen-Hoeksema and Girgus, an interaction between a pre-existing psychological vulnerability and the stressful event of being sexually abused would predict that adolescent girls who lack instrumental traits are especially prone to depression after being sexually abused. Not addressed, however, is the issue of why adolescent girls face an increased risk of being sexually abused. What is happening in the lives of adolescent girls to increase their risk of becoming victims of such abuse? What role does the sexualization of girls' bodies during adolescence play in their vulnerability to abuse?

123

Also included within the stress component of Nolen-Hoeksema and Girgus' model are social challenges arising as part of the "gender intensification" process. Two aspects of this process are identified as potentially stressful for adolescent girls, those involving parental pressures and peer reactions, respectively. If parents encourage their daughters to pursue educational interests and activities gender-typed as feminine but to avoid those associated with masculinity, girls may be more likely to enter low-paying occupations such as those in the sales/service sector. Occupations of this kind offer young women few prospects for either career advancement or future financial security. One consequence of parental pressures which channel girls' interests in gender-appropriate directions, therefore, is to increase the likelihood that a girl's future will be one characterized by lack of financial independence. Poverty is a risk factor for depression among women (Belle 1990) and opting during adolescence for an occupational choice which is gender-typed may increase risk of depression at a later point in a girl's life. According to Nolen-Hoeksema and Girgus' formulation, the girls most likely to succumb to parental pressures are those who already have the psychological characteristics (e.g, lack of instrumental traits) hypothesized to increase vulnerability to depression.

The gender intensification process is implicated more directly in the reactions of peers toward girls who violate peer-defined standards of acceptable feminine appearance and behavior. Nolen-Hoeksema and Girgus point to evidence that a girl who behaves in gender-inappropriate ways (e.g. outshining her male peers in school work) or for whom conformity with feminine appearance norms is not easily achieved (e.g. because of her bodily physique) is likely to be rejected by peers. Such rejection may take a variety of forms from teasing to "shunning", a form of ostracism which may result in a girl refusing to attend school (Pipher 1994). According to Nolen-Hoeksema and Girgus, peer-rejection not only is a potent source of distress in adolescent girls, it also may play a role in increasing risk of depression. The latter is more likely if a girl also has personality characteristics which increase her vulnerability to depression.

In formulating the stress component of their diathesis–stress model, Nolen-Hoeksema and Girgus focus on a fairly narrow range of normative (e.g. school change) and non-normative (e.g. sexual abuse) events and ongoing conditions (e.g. peer pressure) in the lives of adolescent girls. Moreover, the events and conditions identified as stressful and incorporated within their model are those defined pri-marily from the vantage point of researchers. This positivist definitional strategy parallels that followed by mainstream researchers in conceptualizing stress in the lives of adult women (see Chapter 5), and has similar consequences. When stress is defined in this way, adolescent girls whose bodies conform to feminine appear-ance norms and who are popular with peers are presumed to have "normal" lives. Only those events which fall outside the range of such "normal" experiences are viewed as potentially problematic and as having relevance for explaining why an adolescent girl may become depressed. One result of this way of conceptualizing stress is that the social and cultural context of adolescent girls' lives becomes both taken for granted and invisible. What kind of understanding of depression in young women might be possible if the social and cultural context which prefigures the everyday lived experiences of adolescents girls becomes part of the foreground, rather than remaining an invisible and unexplored backdrop to their lives?

Understanding adolescence from the perspective of girls' lived experiences

Mainstream accounts of adolescence have an almost "disembodied" character. While puberty is certainly highlighted as a key moment defining the adolescent transition, attention is narrowly focused on the effects of hormones and development of "secondary sexual characteristics". Adolescent bodies, moreover, are treated almost as though they are genderless. Rarely is menarche, the onset of menstrual bleeding, and all that this entails, explored in other than superficial terms (usually restricted to discussion of hormonal action). And bodily changes, such as breast development, are mostly ignored altogether. Thus, the cultural significance and social consequences of having a female, rather than a male, body are hardly touched upon in mainstream accounts of adolescent girlhood. In the Nolen-Hoeksema and Girgus model, for example, body dissatisfaction and sexual abuse represent the sole exceptions to this erasure of the female body. Such moves, which signal a partial recognition of adolescence as an embodied experience, have not, however, been accompanied by any loosening of positivist methodological strictures in the direction of considering adolescent girls' accounts of their experiences as a useful source of knowledge.

In this section, I want to explore an alternative, nonpositivist approach to understanding the lives of adolescent girls. This is an approach in which qualitative methods (usually interviews) are used to gather girls' accounts of their experiences. When these accounts are analyzed from feminist and social constructionist perspectives, a rather different way of understanding the lived experiences of adolescent girls begins to take shape.

When analysis and theory are grounded in young women's accounts, the centrality of the female body emerges as a predominant theme. In contrast to mainstream theories of adolescent development, in which the body is conceptualized primarily as a biological entity, these analyses also point to the importance of understanding the body as a cultural entity. In this sense, the body is understood as an organism which is immersed in culture, as a medium through which culture is expressed, rather than being neutral with respect to sociocultural influences (Bordo 1993, Lee and Sasser-Coen 1996, Ussher 1989). Among other things, this means that when girls' bodies undergo the changes called puberty, how girls understand and react to these embodied experiences and the reactions and expectations of others already are shaped by cultural discourses around the female body. These discourses are in many ways contradictory, constructing the female body as signifying both pleasure and danger, as well as a source of "reproductive potential" (Lee 1994).

Whatever cultural meanings are associated with the female body, the subtext seems to remain constant: the female body is judged against standards reflecting a male standpoint and the "woman in the body" is devalued (Martin 1987, Ussher 1989). Collectively, these cultural meaning systems around the female body and women are an aspect of discourses of femininity (Bordo 1993, Ussher 1997b). Early adolescence, then, not only marks the life stage when a girl-child becomes a young woman with a menstrual life. It also represents the time when a girl first encounters, and learns to negotiate, discursively constructed notions of what it means to have a female body and to be a woman in a cultural context in which both are denigrated (Lee 1994, Thorne 1993).

Cultural discourses of femininity not only shape girls' experiences and actions; they also configure the experiences and actions of others, both adults and peers, males and females, and the actions (and inactions) of others play an important part in shaping the experiences of adolescent girls. These experiences also are inter-woven with cultural beliefs about adolescence and expectations about appropriate behavior for adolescents, which can at times create a confusing mix for teenage girls to contend with. I explore these ideas in more detail in what follows, through discussion of recent qualitative findings on girls' experiences in relation to puberty and menarche, appearance and body image, and gender relations in the school context.

Puberty and menarche: becoming a woman

When girls and women who have grown up in western countries are asked to talk about their experiences in relation to menarche and beginning to menstruate, recurring themes are those of embarrassment, shame and secrecy (Lee 1994, Lovering 1995, Ussher 1989). Girls talk about how their menstrual bleeding makes them feel dirty and unclean and they worry about drawing attention to themselves when menstruating (Lee 1994). The cultural message that menstruation is not a proper topic for discussion is reflected in girls' accounts of having difficulty getting information about the practical business of managing their periods (Kissling 1996, Lovering 1995). Although her mother may impart some information when a girl first begins to menstruate, typically such information is quite limited and many uncertainties remain. For instance, based on her analysis of letters published in medical advisory columns in magazines read by girls, Oinas (1998) found that girls' concerns about menstruation focused on normality issues and how to cope with menstrual bleeding in everyday life.

Another source of girls' knowledge about menstruation is "sex education" classes in school, although such experiences are more likely to perpetuate the cultural silence around menstruation, than to increase girls' understanding. As Kissling (1996: 494) concluded, based on her analysis of girls accounts of their menstrual education and the instructional materials used in health education: "Menstruation and other uniquely female functions are apparently presented as a 'special case', implicitly asserting a view of male bodies as the norm." Boys contribute to the aura of secrecy and mystery around menstruation through teasing and taunts, actions which are likely to create a hostile classroom environment for girls (Kissling 1996, Lowering 1995).Thus, girls learn early in their menstrual lives to hide evidence of their menstrual periods from others and to keep their questions and concerns to themselves.

Given the lack of information and generally negative attitudes about menstruation, it is hardly surprising that girls' accounts often reflect a sense of ambivalence about their bodies (Lee 1994). A theme emerging in several studies is that girls and women see the "body which menstruates" as being separate from the self. This "mind–body" split is evident in the passive terms girls and women use to describe menstruation, depicting it as something which happens to them, to be managed and coped with (Lee 1994). A similar dualist discourse is identified by Malson and Ussher (1996a) in their analysis of the accounts of young women diagnosed (or self-diagnosed) as anorexic. These women talked about being annoyed and irritated when they began to menstruate, and of perceiving their bodies as alien and lacking in control. Malson and Ussher suggest one interpretation of amenorrhea (absence of menstruation), a symptom of anorexia, is that it represents a woman's rejection of her body, as something separate from her "self".

For girls who menstruate, the practical business of managing their monthly bleeding serves as a constant reminder (along with cramps and other bodily discomforts they may experience) that they have female bodies. But menarche signifies more than having a female body; culturally it symbolizes a girl's entry into womanhood and the realm of the feminine. Cultural discourses linking femininity with menstruation construct female psychology as inherently unstable, with behavior and mood fluctuating in response to the menstrual cycle (Ussher 1989, Walker 1997). Indeed, many girls believe that "all girls get cranky before they get their periods" (Moore 1995: 94). Constructions of femininity which emphasize women's emotional and unpredictable nature are difficult for young women to contest, and this is especially the case in cultural contexts where premenstrual syndrome (PMS) has been legitimized by the stamp of medical approval (see Chapter 6). Ceasing to menstruate could be interpreted as an extreme form of resistance to these cultural constructions of femininity, and young women who are anorexic are particularly likely to reject this "biologically labile" version of femininity (Malson and Ussher 1996a).

During puberty, girls' bodies also change in ways which are more visible to others. Breasts develop and body shape becomes more rounded, bodily changes which are welcomed and resisted by adolescent girls (Lee 1994, 1997). Girls may both flaunt and attempt to conceal signs of their breast development. As feminist writers have recognized, the female breast is "never innocent" of cultural meaning (Lee 1997, Renshaw 1994), although these meanings are frequently contradictory. The female breast signifies sexuality and desire, while also symbolizing asexual notions of motherhood.

For adolescent girls, breast development is likely to alter both the tone and content of interactions with peers and adults. For instance, girls who develop breasts earlier than their female peers may be viewed as promiscuous (Lee 1994) and breast size (either too big, or too small) becomes a target of sexual jokes and innu-endo by male peers (Bourne *et al.* 1998, Larkin 1997, Lee 1997). Such instances of objectification of the female body, which are commonly experienced by young women, can invoke feelings of shame and embarrassment (Pipher 1994). The fol-lowing excerpt, reported by Lee (1997: 465), is from the account of a woman in her early thirties and illustrates how objectification of the female body, and breasts in particular, can undermine an adolescent girl's sense of self.

> How was I going to be a professional person if I had these big boobs? It would be like people would be just staring at me . . . and they used to instead of talking in my face, they would talk to my boobs, you know . . . it was totally degrading. . . . I don't know if that makes sense, but I felt like my large chest size was a kind of a betrayal of my personhood.

This woman's decision, in her late teens, to have her breasts surgically reduced becomes understandable in the context of her experience of being defined by others primarily in terms of her breast size. As a girl's breasts develop, she also begins to learn about and experience the sexual power associated with the female body. Girls become aware that their bodies can attract the admiration and desire of young men and such experiences may be a source of self-esteem as girls learn to wield their sexual power to attract male attention. As Lee (1997) points out, how-ever, this is an uncertain source of empowerment, because it rests on definitions of a desirable female body from a male standpoint.

When inquiry begins with the accounts of adolescent girls, the picture of girls' experiences in relation to puberty and menarche which emerges is one character-ized by an increasing focus on the body. The body may become a source of anxiety with respect to the normality of a girl's menstrual experiences, as well as how to manage bleeding so it remains hidden from others. At the same time, along with changes in body shape and breast development, an adolescent girl becomes more aware of the social and sexual significance of her body's appearance.

Appearance and body image: the thin ideal

A frequent observation is that the adolescent years are a time when girls become increasingly preoccupied with their appearance (Pipher 1994, Wolf 1991). Concerns about appearance center overwhelmingly on whether the body is too fat, not thin enough. Implicit in a girl's self-evaluation that she is not thin enough are cultural standards defining what is an appropriate and desirable female body shape. In western cultures, as amply documented by feminist researchers, the ideal female body is also a thin body (Bordo 1993, Malson 1998, Szekely 1988). It is now common-place to attribute women's pursuit of the thin body ideal to the influence of media depictions of successful women as also being slender and the eating dis-orders of anorexia and bulimia have been attributed to weight loss regimes carried to extremes (Bordo 1993).

Given the cultural obsession with appearance, it is hardly surprising that body dissatisfaction seems to be endemic among adolescent girls, with dieting and monitoring of food intake and weight being constant concerns within this group. As Tolman and Debold (1994) have argued, however, pursuit of a thin body image implies more than weight loss. The notion of "body image" involves a contradiction in terms, because actual bodies have appetites and desires, whereas images have neither. Thus, body image implies a "no-body body", one which is disconnected from the bodily sensations of hunger and sexual arousal. The goal of achieving a desirable body image also implies a shift to the perspective of others in making judgments about one's own appearance.

When an adolescent girl evaluates herself solely in terms of her body's image, the main criterion becomes the effect her actions have on how she will appear to others. The following excerpt taken from Tolman and Debold (1994: 307) illustrates how a girl's evaluation of her body image also has implications for the way she judges herself as a person. Victoria, a girl in her early teens, attending a school for girls in the US, described facing a "moral" conflict of "whether I wanted the calories of two pastries, or I should only have one . . . whether or not I wanted the calories or to be good". According to Victoria: "Good means not to have too many calories, or you'll be fat like I am." A similar theme in which being thin is equated with being good is reflected in the following excerpt from the account of a young woman in England, which is reported by Malson (1998: 105): "So I just wanted to get rid of all this weight and it made me feel I was better cos there was less fat . . . as if there was less . . . bad".

Adolescent girls' concerns about their appearance also can be understood as part of a cultural process in which the female body is sexualized as an object of male desire (Lee 1997). As adolescent girls become aware of their body's sexual power, concerns with appearance also begin to reflect their interest in attracting male attention. As one of the young women interviewed by Malson (1998: 106) said:

> I felt like guys didn't like me or guys never paid any attention to me as much as they did to my roommates who were, like, gorgeous. And I just felt ignored, like . . . they didn't look at me because I was *fat*. (emphasis in original)

As the following excerpt illustrates, being thin means more than attracting male attention; it also implies future life possibilities: "Things like the media, they seem to connote that if you're slim then you're successful, you're intelligent, beautiful, you get the man of your dreams, dream children, dream house, money" (Malson 1998: 107). Writing about adolescent girls in the US, Pipher (1994: 184) commented: "Unfortunately girls are not irrational to worry about their bodies. Looks do matter. Girls who are chubby or plain miss much of the American dream."

Concerns with appearance and body image among adolescent girls can, therefore, be understood as reflecting an interest in being sexually attractive to men. Being able to attract at least one man is a prerequisite for social success and access to possibilities for achieving "the dream". Tolman and Debold's (1994) analysis suggests, however, that when adolescent girls live within their body's image, rather than their actual body, they are likely to lose connection with their feelings and bodily sensations. Attracting the right kind of male attention not only involves being thin, it also means maintaining a social reputation of sexual purity. As Pamela, a girl in her mid-teens living in a US city, said: "For now, I'd say definitely no [to having sex] because I don't want my husband to be like, 'you are already leftovers'. . . . so I would want to be – I want to wear white when I get married . . ." (Tolman and Debold 1994: 305). Living within the body's image, as Tolman and Debold's analysis suggests, means foreclosing on the possibility of sexual pleasure and living instead according to "the unspoken dictates of a world shaped by future husbands" (p. 306).

One consequence, then, of the cultural construction of the ideal female body as a thin body is that girls lose touch with their actual bodies and their actual appetites and desires. This process is fostered by cultural beliefs which derogate sexual desire in women, constructing it as bad and dangerous, and preferably to be suppressed. While adolescent girls are taught that it is their responsibility to recognize and control sexual arousal in boys, the possibility of their own sexual desire is barely acknowledged: "nice girls" and "good women" are not supposed to be sexual outside the confines of heterosexual, monogamous marriage (Tolman 1994).

Girls and schooling: learning the lessons of gender

During early adolescence, peers begin to play a larger part in the lives of teenage girls. The higher profile of peers as both a reference group and source of identity validation marks the stage in western culture when young people are expected to become more independent and autonomous from parental influences. Early adolescence also is typically when a change from elementary to secondary levels of schooling occurs in most countries. Young people are closer to being "grown-ups" and to gaining access to the social privileges and freedoms reserved for adults. Secondary schooling represents a stepping stone to post-school employment, university and career training. It also represents a social microcosm, in which becoming part of the "in-group" bestows popularity and status on those who make the grade.

Appearance figures large in the social ordering process within the peer group, and the requirements for making the grade are strongly gendered. At the same time, those who fail to measure up or in some way violate peer-defined standards, are likely to become the target of disapproval. Such disapproval can involve teasing, name-calling, and stronger forms of social rejection. School is also where girls first confront and learn to negotiate the social implications of their changing bodies and a girl's bodily appearance has special significance in the peer popularity stakes. For instance, Pipher (1994: 147) described the case of Monica, a fifteen-year old who was highly intelligent, overweight, "homely" in appearance, and also depressed. According to Monica: "Boys get teased if they even talk to me . . . When I walk down the halls I feel like a hideous monster." Most boys ignored Monica entirely, treating her as though she was covered in "invisible ink", while girls teased her. Although Monica was doing well in her school work, she was friendless, lonely and tired of being humiliated by peers.

The reactions of peers, particularly adolescent boys, help to enforce cultural definitions of the female body. Girls wear baggy clothing to hide their developing breasts or face the embarrassment of having their bra-straps snapped by boys (Lee 1997). As their bodies develop more womanly contours, adolescent girls are likely to become the target of verbal comments drawing attention to the size of their breasts. Bourne *et al.* (1998) report an example typifying this kind of comment, which was recounted by a girl attending a Canadian secondary school: "I was walking down the hallway, and I walked past him and he goes, 'hey baby' and when I turned around he goes 'oh never mind, she's got no tits' . . .". Being called "cow", "bitch", "whore" and other derogatory names by boys is an experience frequently reported by adolescent girls (Eyre 1991, Larkin 1997). Another commonly reported practise, which both humiliates girls and sexually objectifies the female body, is the "rating" by boys of girls' bodies and appearance (Bourne *et al.* 1998, Larkin 1997).

Adolescence is also when dating and sex become part of teenage experience and as their bodies develop, girls face increasing pressures to be heterosexual. A dilemma many girls face is how to be sexy and also respected by peers. The rules are confusing and a girl must constantly monitor her behavior to avoid misinterpretation and risk losing her "reputation" (and social status). Girls who violate peer norms for female sexual behavior are likely to be demeaned by being labeled "slut" or "whore", a form of surveillance in which both girls and boys participate (Larkin 1997, Tolman and Debold 1994). As in other areas of social behavior, a gendered "double standard" operates in which a girl who is sexually active is likely to be called a "tramp", whereas a boy is likely to be admired as a "stud". As noted by Tolman and Debold (1994: 306), regardless of how a girl might actually behave, "others (girls as well as boys) have the power to frame how she is seen".

Adolescence is also a time when young women, sexually active or not, face an increased risk of becoming victims of sexual abuse (Koss *et al.* 1994, Pipher 1994). Cultural constructions of female sexuality also shape girls' reactions to abusive experiences. For example, young women may resist framing themselves as a victim, especially when their assailant is known to them, because of the negative connotations this has for their identity. To be a victim means to be weak, passive, and lacking in agency. In their analysis of young women's accounts of being raped, Wood and Rennie (1994) noted how these women's avoidance of the victim identity was implicated in their decision not to report the assault to police or to tell relatives and friends about it. In rejecting the victim identity, however, these young women also faced the implication that they were partly to blame for what happened. Cultural beliefs about women and sex, in which female bodies are constructed as objects of male sexual pleasure while women are responsible for controlling men's sexual desire, add to young women's confusion in sexual situations. Contributing to girls' confusion, as Pipher (1994: 208) indicates, is that "there is no established or easy way [for girls] to stop a sexual encounter". Despite efforts by feminists to promote the "no means no" message with respect to a woman's right to refuse sexual advances, many young people (both girls and boys) hold beliefs condoning the right of a man to force sex on a woman (Pipher 1994).

Girls are subject to other forms of gender harassment which operate to police the boundaries of male gender domains in school settings. Male peers as well as male teachers contribute to this process of "putting girls in their place". For instance, a female student in Bourne et al.'s (1998: 59) study, reported the following incident involving a male high school teacher:

> He really didn't like me because I was doing well in his class on top of all this, I was still getting that 90, and he'd get really upset . . . He said something to me like "you know you're not going to go very far in university. Maybe you'll get a bachelors [degree] if you're lucky".

Although the issue of gender equity in the classroom has received increased attention in recent decades, findings of participant observation studies indicate that girls continue to have less power in classroom settings. Based on extensive observation of classroom practises in a Canadian school, Eyre (1991) noted that classroom interactions were dominated by a relatively small number of boys, who intimidated and controlled girls and less dominant boys. Curriculum content also continues to reflect a male-biased worldview, so that girls' and women's activities and experiences are marginalized and trivialized (Bourne et al. 1998).

As I hope this discussion of girls' experiences in the school context has indicated, the transition from elementary to secondary school also is likely to be accompanied by a marked shift in the social experiences of girls. Gender takes on a more prominent place, and others' reactions are more frequently structured by cultural discourses around female bodies. While young women become more aware of their bodies as they experience pubertal changes, their attention focuses increasingly on their own appearance as a result of peer (especially male) reactions. These peer reactions both enforce gendered assumptions about the female body and femininity and serve to "discipline" young women who show signs of straying from their culturally prescribed gender domain.

As this brief overview reveals, the picture of adolescence which emerges when the focus is on girls' accounts of their experiences is rather different from views of adolescent development conceived from the perspective of researchers. Girls' experiences during adolescence are grounded in their embodied changes and the social implications of these changes are negotiated by girls in a discursive context shaped by cultural constructions of the female body, sexuality and feminine psychology. Girls also navigate the meaning of their embodied experiences in a social context shaped by peer interactions. These interactions, which are structured by patriarchal and "masculinist" assumptions about the place of girls and women in the world, operate to channel girls' behavior in accord with cultural discourses of femininity. The implications of such experiences for girls' subjectivities is the topic of the next section, where I consider how depression in adolescent girls might be understood from a material–discursive perspective.

A material–discursive framework for understanding depression in adolescent girls

Adolescence is when girls learn the "lessons of gender" embedded within cultural discourses of femininity in the course of interactions with peers and adults. Gendered messages also represent a dominant theme in various "popular" media targeted at adolescent consumers ("teen" magazines, music videos, movies etc.). Girls' subjectivities and their sense of self are shaped in the context of this informal cultural curriculum. The "subject positions" available to adolescent girls, ways of defining the person they are now and the kind of person they want to become, reflect a narrow set of possibilities. Nevertheless, whatever the cultural currents shaping the aspirations of young people (e.g., the contemporary "computer revolution" and the "information age"), the body remains the bedrock of identity in young women.

During the adolescent years, girls' identities are tied closely to their physical appearance and how their actions are interpreted by peers. Acceptance by the peer group is a prerequisite for social success both inside and outside the school setting. A young woman's body, and more particularly her body's image, become an important social resource. This resource is an uncertain one, however, because it rests on cultural standards of female attractiveness defined from the standpoint of what boys and men deem desirable. It is also fragile because of the vagaries of embodied changes during adolescence and the unpredictable character of these changes (e.g. breast size). Thus, adolescent girls' identities are formed in relation to a bodily self which simultaneously is discursively constructed and grounded materially in the physical body.

Discursively, the slender body is constituted as the ideal female body shape. Being thin also signifies that a girl is a "good" person and, within the context of adolescent gender relations, will be accepted by peers (both male and female). The boundaries of an acceptable body image are marked by peers through name-calling (e.g. "cow", "bitch") designed to demean and humiliate, and other more explicit forms of social rejection (e.g. "shunning"). The options available to a girl whose body image falls outside the narrow range of peer acceptability are to ignore the reactions of peers or to change her body, neither of which is easily achieved. Even for an adolescent girl who possesses talents which are independent on her body shape (e.g. academic abilities) and whose parents are supportive of alternative constructions of female appearance, facing a continual barrage of peer taunts and rejecting actions is likely to take its toll on a girl's subjectivity. For instance, in the previous section I referred to Pipher's (1994) account of Monica, a depressed teenage girl who was overweight and the butt of peer rejection at school. Although Monica had the support of her parents in resisting cultural definitions of a desirable body image for adolescent girls, she still described herself as a "pimply whale" and a "hideous monster". According to Pipher (ibid.: 149), Monica reported that "I can see people look me over, size me up as unattractive and look away. I am not a person to them." If Monica constructed her sense of self in relation to these real (and imagined) peer evaluations, it is hardly surprising that she felt "bad" about herself, and saw herself as a social misfit.

Adolescent girls who already "look the part" are more likely to subscribe to cultural definitions of a feminine appearance and desirable body image and so reap the rewards of peer approval and acceptance. In this case, the goals of achieving and maintaining an attractive (and thin) appearance are likely to take center stage. Appearance may be a critical index of a girl's popularity in peer social status hierarchies, but the limits of an acceptably feminine body image are narrowly defined and easily transgressed as a girl's body changes with puberty. The goal of achieving a desirable body shape is a difficult one to attain, not least because of the actual material body, which tends to be recalcitrant to weight loss efforts. Thus, a girl's sense of embodied self is tied to a material body which is likely to resist her efforts to control and change its shape and size.

One consequence of contemporary concerns about the "problem" of body dissatisfaction among adolescent girls is that they create a picture of young women as falling victim to a potentially self-damaging (and, therefore, irrational) "body fixation". Girls are depicted as "cultural dopes", blindly conforming to whatever body size is considered the fashionable vogue, regardless of their actual bodily make-up. However, as I discussed earlier, the accounts of teenage girls reveal their awareness of the implications of having a suitably feminine appearance for their present and future social success. Girls draw a connection between their body's image in the present and the kind of life (and lifestyle) they hope for as adult women. Their accounts are constructed in relation to what some feminist theorists have identified as a "romantic" discourse (Malson 1998, Wetherell 1995). This romantic discourse reflects the traditional narrative of meeting the "right" man (handsome and wealthy) and falling in love, which is followed by the white wedding. In due course this blissful wedded state is complemented by children, punctuated by holidays in exotic places, and the action takes place in a home (and driveway) appointed with the usual material possessions of a consumer-society. In short, this romantic discourse constructs the "dream" in terms of a middle-class lifestyle. Thus, for many young women, "having a life" beyond adolescence continues to be constructed as a variant of the fairy-tale fantasy of a handsome prince rescuing "Cinderella" from a life of drudgery and poverty.

A girl's prospects for achieving the "dream" are indeed closely linked to her appearance. Media images of women who are "successful" in conventional terms (having a lifestyle which depends on money) overwhelmingly depict such women as thin and attractive to men. During adolescence, overweight girls and those with a "plain" appearance are likely to be the last to be invited to parties or on dates (if at all) and may be actively rejected by peers. Thus, a girl's appearance not only has specific social consequences in her own life; it also has implications for her future possibilities for gaining access to material resources. As well, other less socially acceptable, and personally damaging, routes are available to girls for gaining peer acceptance. Drugs and alcohol may be used by girls as both a means to "fit in" and to cope with feelings of distress (Pipher 1994). In a culture in which the youthful female body is constructed as an object of male sexual desire, young women may also seek affirmation of their self-worth through sexual activity, with the consequent risks of pregnancy, sexually-transmitted diseases, and sexual abuse.

From a feminist perspective, the variety of ways in which a girl may be "put-down" and humiliated by peers if she shows signs of resisting socially constructed standards of feminine appearance and behavior can be interpreted as the noxious side-effects of growing up in a culture in which male domination and female subordination are taken for granted. Nevertheless, many adolescent girls learn the lessons of gender well, and willingly adopt the practises of femininity (e.g., use of "make-up"). Rather than rejecting cultural constructions of feminine appearance, young women are more likely to reject feminist critiques.

Young women's willingness to engage in the practises of femininity is illustrated by Harrison's (1997) account of young Australian women's involvement in the "deb ball", a social event with roots in the English upper-class practise of "debutante (or "coming-out") balls". Apparently, in some parts of Australia, the deb ball is a key social moment in the lives of young women. In spite of official, feminist-informed, criticism of deb balls, large numbers of young women continue to participate in this practise, which may involve a considerable financial outlay. Rejection by girls of the relevance of feminist critiques is based in a media-shaped interpretation of feminism as representing a puritanistic opposition to fun and pleasure. These young women continue to enact a "fluffy fantasy" version of femininity, because of the enjoyment they derive from dressing-up to look like "real princesses" (Harrison 1997: 507). In a similar vein, Bourne *et al.* (1998) reported in their Canadian study that "feminist" was considered a negative term, one equated with the equally pejorative label "lesbian", and the latter was routinely applied to anyone who openly identified as a "feminist". For these Canadian girls, the meaning of feminist seems to include foregoing sexual relations with men.

If adolescent girls interpret femininity and feminism as being in opposition, a potential resource for constructing alternative identities to peer-defined subject positions is also foreclosed. So long as young women continue to construct their sense of self in relation to cultural discourses of femininity, they risk becoming the target of demeaning, belittling and rejecting peer reactions. Lacking counterpoints to this devaluing treatment, adolescent girls are likely to devalue themselves, a form of self-diminishment which may be part of what is now called depression. Thus, one way of understanding "depression" in adolescent girls is as an experience of subjectivity produced in the context of girls' struggles to achieve a viable and self-affirming identity in a cultural context which has been characterized as "girl-poisoning" (Pipher 1994).

Although young women may look back with pleasure upon their moments in the spotlight of adolescent social success (Harrison 1997), leaving school signals a shift to a different set of expectations and responsibilities. Central among these new challenges are the business of earning a living and finding one's place in the world. Early adulthood also marks the point in the lives of most young women when marriage and motherhood become paramount concerns. In the next chapter, I turn to an exploration of women's experiences as wives and mothers and the contributions which knowledge about these aspects of women's lives can make to understanding depression in women.

Notes

1 The phrase "girl-poisoning culture" is taken from Pipher (1994).
2 In their recent review of research on depression in children and adolescents, Cicchetti and Toth (1998) include a single paragraph (less than half a page) on the topic of "Gender differences" in an article with more than sixteen pages of text. Petersen *et al.* (1993) devote less than a page to a section headed "Variations by gender, ethnic group and cohort" in their review of research on depression in adolescence.
3 In our searches of bibliographic databases in psychology, social science and health fields, my doctoral student Deanna Gammell and I were unable to find any studies in which qualitative methods were used to explore the depressive experiences of adolescent girls. Some limited information concerning depression from the perspective of adolescent girls is provided in the case studies described by Pipher (1994: see Chapter 8) and in Nylund and Ceske's (1997) account of narrative therapy with a depressed adolescent girl.

8

WOMEN'S LIVES AND DEPRESSION

Marriage and motherhood

During adolescence, the activities of many young women are governed by a desire to gain popularity with peers. In the social context of the peer group, male attention, in particular, is an important prerequisite for "dating", in western countries, usually considered a preliminary to marriage. Once a woman becomes a partner in a heterosexual couple, married or not, parenthood is often the next step in creating a "family". Because of the centrality of marriage and motherhood to the lives of adult women, attempts to explain depression in women also have focused on these twin social institutions, and this is the topic of the present chapter.

Women's lives and depression: alternative frameworks

In Chapter 5, I discussed social explanations for depression in women, where the burdensome nature of women's work in the home as wives and mothers has been identified as a source of stress. Childbirth also has been identified as a specific precipitant of depression in women. Within the framework of biological theories, depression following childbirth (referred to as post-partum or post-natal) has been explained as a consequence of the rapid shifts in hormone levels accompanying pregnancy and childbirth (see Chapter 6). Depression in women also has been explained as one outcome of stress associated with raising children alone, whether motherhood is preceded by marriage or not. As single-parents, women are more likely to live in poverty, a source of stress which itself increases risk of depression (Belle 1990, Graham 1993). A link between marriage and motherhood and depression in women is also drawn in the social model developed by Brown and Harris (1978, 1989). These researchers identified "the cultural importance of the role identity of wife and mother" as a key influence determining whether a woman will join the "conveyor belt to adversity", and in turn her chances of becoming depressed (Brown and Harris 1989: 381).

Thus, a substantial body of research and theory now seems to converge on the conclusion that marriage and motherhood are not always good for women's well-being and indeed may account in large measure for susceptibility to depression among women. This position would seem to imply that strategies for preventing depression in women might focus on discouraging so many women from becoming wives and mothers. Perhaps if more young women could be encouraged to pursue careers and to forego motherhood, or at least to combine employment with being a wife and mother, this would have the dual advantages of fostering economic independence in women and reducing stress in their lives related to economic hardship. An important goal of gender equity programs in education and employment has been to increase the proportion of women in male-dominated occupations, which also are better paid than those traditionally entered by women. In a similar vein, one aim of sex education is reduction of pregnancy rates among teenage girls, based on the assumption that becoming a mother "too early" interferes with a young woman's ability to avoid the "conveyor belt to adversity" (Griffin 1993, Leadbeater and Way 1996).

Although claims commonly are made that depression in women arises in the context of their roles as wives and mothers, it is also the case that remarkably little is known about women's experiences as wives and mothers from the perspective of women themselves. As I indicated in Chapter 1, this knowledge gap can be attributed in part to reliance on methods informed by a positivist epistemology in research on depression in women. In this chapter, I want to focus on women's experiences in relation to marriage and motherhood for the purpose of exploring how such knowledge can contribute to understanding depression in women. From feminist and social constructionist perspectives, attempts to understand depression in women need to begin with women's experiences. Knowledge about women's experiences in the context of marriage and motherhood would certainly seem important for understanding depression, not least because many women's experiences are constituted in relation to the identities, as well as the activities, of wife and/or mother.

In mainstream approaches, when women's lives, or more particularly their activities as wives and mothers, are considered as possible causal factors in depression, the explanations developed generally have taken the form: "x" (some aspect of women's lives) causes "y" (depression). A drawback of this type of approach is that it tends to promote a conception of depression as something separate from women's lives. This way of thinking implies that depression is something which can be studied in isolation from the lived experiences of women who are depressed. Such methods also foster a conception of depression as something (a condition?) that exists within individual women. At the same time, when depression is explained in terms of "women's lives", there is a tendency to view women as comprising a homogeneous group. When women are assumed to be more or less the same, this obscures diversity in the lived experiences of women related to their age, social class, race-ethnicity, and sexual orientation.

Furthermore, when aspects of women's lives as wives and mothers are conceptualized as causal factors in depression, the reality that most women do become wives and/or mothers at some point in their lives is taken for granted, rather than something which itself requires explanation. In contemporary theories of depression in women, it tends to be assumed that women become wives and mothers because of "socialization pressures" or as the result of having a "feminine gender identity". In such formulations, women are characterized as individuals who passively comply with social expectations that their adult lives be shaped in conformity with the identities of wife and mother, presumably in keeping with their gender identity. Such approaches, then, depict women as largely devoid of agency, blindly pursuing a life course which both expresses their gender identity and is expected of them by others. Explanations for depression focused on women's lives appear, therefore, to rest on the unexamined assumption that marriage and motherhood are primary routes to expression of a female gender identity.

Toward a material–discursive framework for understanding depression in women

In the remainder of this chapter, I explore how depression in women in relation to marriage and motherhood can be understood from a material–discursive perspective. In this approach, depression is understood as an embodied experience produced at the intersection of women's bodies and women's lives. From this perspective, rather than assuming that women get married and have babies *because* they are women, the identities of "wife" and "mother" are understood as being both socially constructed and socially produced. This way of thinking involves a reversal of the usual assumptions. For example, instead of understanding marriage as a normal consequence of femininity in women, from a social constructionist perspective the identity of wife is understood as something which is shaped in the context of a heterosexual relationship with a "husband". Thus, rather than being preordained, the meaning of wife is constructed in cultural discourses about marriage (its purpose and ideal form) *and* the actual practical business of being a wife (i.e. "wifely" activities). Similarly, rather than motherhood being the result of a woman's "maternal instinct" or "natural drive", the conventional identity of "mother" can be understood as a sense of self which is created by having children. As McMahon (1995: 3) concluded based on her analysis of women's experiences as mothers: "the experience of motherhood *produces* a gendered sense of self in women." (emphasis in original)

A place to begin in understanding how and why women become wives and mothers is women's accounts of their experiences in relation to marriage and motherhood, and this is the focus of the first part of the chapter. In discussing women's experiences of marriage and motherhood, I draw on three conceptual tools to make theoretical sense of women's accounts. First, I consider the meanings of marriage and motherhood, followed by the practises involved in being a wife and those of mothering. Meanings and practises are interlinked with a third concept, discourse, in this case what I referred to earlier as discourses of femininity (see Chapters 1 and 6). In formulating this conceptual framework, I have drawn on the analysis of motherhood developed by Phoenix *et al.* (1991). I apply this framework first to understand how and why women become wives and mothers and then to explore how depressive experiences arise in the context of women's lived experiences as wives and/or mothers. Based on this analysis, I suggest that depression in women can be understood as a set of experiences arising at the intersection of women's lives and their bodies. These experiences are socially constructed in relation to cultural meanings of marriage and motherhood and socially produced by the practises of being a wife and a mother. These meanings and practises are both shaped and regulated by discourses of femininity, as well as by structural conditions characterizing the societal context within which women live their lives as wives and mothers.

Young women's experiences in relation to marriage and motherhood

Not all women who marry become mothers and not all women who are mothers are married. Nevertheless, conventionally, marriage and motherhood are closely linked and, indeed, often legitimize each other. The desire to have children and to establish a "family" are reasons given by both women and men for getting married. After marriage, parenthood generally is assumed to be the next step, although this sequence may be reversed, for instance, when a woman and her male partner decide to get married following discovery of her pregnancy. To the extent that the marriage-motherhood sequence is truncated (e.g. through infertility), disrupted (e.g. because of divorce) or rejected (e.g., a lesbian woman's use of artificial insemination to have a child), a woman's ability to take on the identities of wife and mother is circumscribed. Motherhood outside the confines of heterosexual marriage is likely to be judged as deviant and a married woman unable to have a child may view herself as failing as a wife.

The assumption that the marriage-motherhood combination will play a large part in structuring women's lives is clearly present in adolescent girls' accounts of their post-school plans. McLaren and Vanderbijl (1998) provide substantial evidence of this in their analysis of findings from a Canadian study involving interviews with a large sample of adolescent girls (and boys) during their final year of schooling. Although interviewers avoided use of the terms "wife" and "husband", none of the girls spontaneously discussed alternatives to heterosexual marriage and most of these young women envisaged a future life "stretched between waged work and motherhood" (ibid.: 131). The kind of paid work young women typically imagined themselves doing was predicated on the assumption that they would also be a wife and mother, as the following excerpt illustrates:

> Um, I don't really think it'll [a potential family] affect my working life because I think [as] a dental hygienist it's pretty flexible and I've heard that you can . . . work three days a week, you can take maternity leave if you have to . . .
>
> (ibid.: 132)

Although these young women expected their adult lives to involve a combination of waged work and family life, their plans were characterized by a fluidity and lack of closure absent in adolescent boys' accounts, which focused on their career plans. As McLaren and Vanderbijl (135–6) point out: "Many of the girls . . . felt themselves likely to be dependent on either the approval or understanding of their partners to negotiate the shape of their family and career lives."

The option of paid employment without marriage and motherhood was one not considered by any of these young Canadian women. Nevertheless, their accounts reflected an awareness of the difficulties likely to be encountered in combining waged work and family life, goals which are structurally incompatible. As one girl said:

> . . . if I have any children I might . . . [give] more attention to my family, or I can always go back to work later, right? After a while. Or, I don't know, I'll compromise and talk to my husband.
>
> (ibid.: 136)

The accounts of these adolescent girls were characterized by a sense of inevitability, resignation, and futility about making plans, as they struggled with the realization that any plans they made would probably be modified by actual family practises. McLaren and Vanderbijl argue that gender educational reforms focused on encouraging more girls to pursue nontraditional occupations as a route to enhancing girls' futures will be misdirected, unless such efforts also attend to the implications of cultural discourses around family life and normative heterosexuality. Otherwise, girls seem likely to continue to envisage future lives contingent on their family circumstances and, in particular, on the preferences and cooperation of a future male partner.

These young women seemed to be aware of fundamental contradictions between actual family practises and the notions of individual self-determination and autonomy underpinning western concepts of gender equality. Despite this awareness, most girls still anticipated becoming wives and mothers. McLaren and Vanderbijl (ibid.) also observed that the young women they interviewed were relatively accepting of gender-based inequalities (such as pay differentials between men and women). Such inequalities were justified by girls as inevitable consequences of males being "breadwinners" in the traditional nuclear family. As one young woman said:

> I think because the responsibility is on the man to get a good education because he is the one that he feels has to support the family, pay the bills and things like that, so he obviously has to have a better paid job, he has got to have the education to get the better paying job you know.
>
> (ibid.: 132)

Thus, these young Canadian women seemed cognizant of inequitable structural arrangements which underpin conventional marriage and motherhood. At the same time, most expected traditional family life to be a central aspect of their adult lives. Why does this happen? What is the attraction for young women of becoming a wife and mother? Are young women simply following cultural scripts about "women's roles" as a route to gaining social approval? Is the prospect of having a career an unappealing one for many young women? Perhaps answers to these questions can be found in the meanings that marriage and motherhood have for women, the topic I turn to next.

The meanings of marriage and motherhood

In Chapter 7, I discussed the romantic love discourse and its importance in shaping young women's concerns with appearance and attractiveness to men. Rather than interpreting adolescent girls' preoccupations with their bodily appearance as irrational, I suggested that such concerns make sense when understood in relation to cultural ideas around what constitutes a "good life". For many young women, a prerequisite for "having a [good] life" is being able to attract the attentions of a man. A romantic relationship with a man is discursively constructed as a precursor to the fairy-tale dream of "living happily every after" (Malson and Ussher 1996b).

Having a relationship with a man offers women something in addition to romance. It also represents a cultural resource for female identity. The possibility of marriage and becoming a man's wife brings with it both social status and the material advantages which can accrue from being a married woman. Without marriage, these avenues for identity development are foreclosed. Thus, part of the appeal of romantic love is that it makes available to women the prospect of a transformed identity, one offering more positive social and material possibilities than an alternative future outside marriage. For many women, therefore, marriage represents a set of cultural resources for constructing a new identity. It also offers women the chance of rescue or escape from a female identity position which is culturally devalued: that of "single woman". Being unattached to a man implies that a woman lacks qualities deemed desirable by men. In addition, as a partner in a heterosexual relationship, a woman potentially can access identity resources associated with conventional notions of the family and her opportunities for participation in community life will be enhanced by being part of a "couple" and having an identity as someone's wife.

Being in a sexual relationship with a man opens up other identity possibilities, particularly that of mother. Studies of women's experiences in relation to motherhood have revealed the importance for female identity of being a mother. For instance, based on her interviews with women living in central Canada, McMahon (1995) characterized women's experiences of becoming a mother as a form of resocialization akin to a "moral transformation". Becoming a mother not only involves giving birth to a child, it also has important implications for a woman's subjectivity. McMahon suggested that the process of becoming a mother enables women to develop a gendered sense of self, one defined by the valued qualities of caring and responsibility, character attributes culturally signifying femininity. The women interviewed by McMahon believed that becoming a mother had made them better, more human, persons. Motherhood was seen as a source of personal growth and maturity, as illustrated in the following quote:

> I've grown up a lot [by having children]. I have gotten rid of a lot of problems I didn't know about. . . . So it's been very helpful for my personal growth. That was sort of the unexpected benefit with each child. . . . It can be quite surprising how you can change *yourself* as a person – the growth you experience as a person.
>
> (ibid.: 148 emphasis in original)

The positive identity resources which motherhood offers are further underscored by considering the meaning of childlessness. If a young woman has not yet had a child, motherhood remains a possible option, unless infertility or sterilization intervenes. Permanent childlessness, however, eliminates mother as a potential identity. As Woollett (1991: 63) has pointed out: "a major task for childless women and women with fertility problems is one of maintaining a positive self-image of themselves as adults and as women." Deciding to have a child, therefore, may have as much to do with a woman's desire to avoid the identity of "nonmother" as it has with her wish to become a mother. In women's accounts, being childless, not being a mother, is portrayed in very negative terms, as almost unthinkable. For instance, while conducting interviews with mothers living in California, Hays (1996: 108–9) found herself unprepared

> . . . for the intensity of feeling mothers expressed at the mere thought of not having children. Nearly one-quarter of the [38] women I talked to actually cried when I asked them this question. And the answers of nearly all mothers – "lonely", "empty", "missing something" – were stunningly consistent.

The accounts of the Canadian women interviewed by McMahon (ibid.) also reflected negative images of themselves as nonmothers. When asked how she would feel about being childless, one woman said: "I'd be heartbroken – empty. I don't think I'd feel *whole*. . . . I don't think I would have any self-confidence or respect. . . ." (p. 173 emphasis in original).

Thus, women's accounts reflect their negative perceptions of the identity of nonmother compared to that of mother. In some ways, as McMahon suggests, the meaning of nonmother is the cultural equivalent of being a "nonwoman". Reflecting on her childhood experiences of growing up in Ireland, McMahon (1998: 190) recalls her unmarried aunts:

> [T]hey were considered nuisances by my mother and those others who interpreted the world for me. And they were, I was told, selfish. But they were not called selfish because they did unkind things or failed in some expected performance of aunt-like behaviour. Nor were my aunts seen as selfish because they refused to marry and have children. Rather, my aunts

were considered selfish *because they had not had the children who would have made them unselfish*. That is, in not having children, my aunts had not been transformed into that other category of woman – mother. (emphasis in original)

The negative connotations surrounding the figure of the unmarried, childless woman would seem sufficient reason why many young women would want to avoid the identity of nonmother. As McMahon (1995) found in her interviews with Canadian mothers, women were readily able to give reasons for *not* remaining childless, but becoming a mother was often justified solely in terms of "always wanting" to have children. That they would become a mother was taken for granted by these women, something requiring little justification.

Becoming a mother offers other identity benefits to women. The identity of mother is a more enduring one than other potential identities (such as wife) and it provides a sense of continuity, as well as giving meaning to life. A participant in McMahon's study said the following when asked how she would feel if she was childless:

It's like knowing death, to never have a child – to experience your own death as you are living. It's not so much that *I'm* going on with [my daughter], it's just that *everyone is going on*. That life goes on. And that's important for some strange reason.

(ibid. 141–2 emphasis in original)

Not surprisingly, women contrast the identity of the childless career woman in very unfavorable terms with that of being a mother. The American women interviewed by Hays (1996) judged childless women harshly as being shallowly preoccupied with money and material possessions. The Canadian women in McMahon's study perceived childless women with careers as lacking an important source of meaning in their lives.

As I hope the foregoing discussion has indicated, long before a young woman has a child, the cultural identity of mother is likely to play an important part in shaping her sense of self. Given the contemporary dominance of profamily senti- ments in most western societies, together with parental expectations that, like them, their own children will have children, it hardly seems surprising that so many young women anticipate becoming wives and mothers. By comparison, the alternative of constructing a future as an autonomous career woman, the identity implied in school-based discourses around equality, appears to offer women little which is positively valued. An important reason, therefore, why most young women expect to marry, as Phoenix *et al.* (1991: 6) pointed out, is that few realistic and sat- isfying alternatives are available for women. At the same time, both before and after they have a child, women do acknowledge that mothering may involve some negative aspects. For instance, McMahon (1995) noted that among the middle-class mothers she interviewed, many had not been committed to the idea of becoming a mother earlier in their lives. As one woman said: "I thought kids would be an infringement on [my] lifestyle. I saw . . . mothers with children, you know, shuffling kids to parties and I felt sorry for them . . . It did not look like my cup of tea" (p. 57). After having a child, women may evaluate the work of caring for their children in quite negative terms. Many of the British mothers interviewed by Boulton (1983), for instance, expressed dislike for childcare activities. McMahon (1995) also found that the women she interviewed often had been unprepared for the reality of childcare. For example, in describing her reactions to motherhood, one middle-class woman said: "I think the biggest thing was I had no idea of how much work was involved. I had *absolutely no idea*. It's an incredible amount of work. . . . I found the work load absolutely incredible" (p. 132 emphasis in original). As this last comment indicates, once women have children, their actual experiences of mothering may conflict sharply with the more positive images of motherhood reflected in women's accounts before they have a child. The promise of marriage and motherhood as a source of positive identity resources for women seems to overwhelm and trivialize any consideration of the actual realities of being a wife and mother. From a material–discursive perspective, these practical aspects of women's lives have particular relevance for understanding women's experiences of depression and these activities are the focus of the next section.

Housework and childcare: the practises of wives and mothers

In the nuclear family, conventionally women do much of the domestic work involved in maintaining the home and caring for family members (cooking, cleaning, childcare, etc). This arrangement is most pronounced after a woman becomes a parent (Croghan 1991, Fox 1998, McMahon 1995). Thus, women who are wives *and* mothers typically have responsibility for activities within the private sphere of home and family, and as McLaren and Vanderbijl's (1998) findings illustrate, adolescent girls are well-aware of this prospect.

In most western societies, a gendered division of social labor exists in which women do much of the unpaid caring work in the home, even if they also work outside the home, and men's efforts are usually concentrated on paid work outside the home (Doyal 1995, Graham 1993, Lorber 1994). Women's heavy involvement in unpaid work in the private sphere of the family has been identified by feminists as a major source of the disadvantaged economic status of women, as well as underlying gender inequalities in employment. As long as a major portion of a woman's everyday life is spent doing housework and looking after children, she has little time or energy available for other activities outside the home, such as further education or paid employment. Lack of access to financial resources poses a serious impediment to women's ability to support themselves while caring for children, especially following marriage breakdown, and poverty among older women often has its roots in the limited income earned by women earlier in their lives (i.e. inadequate pension provisions).

In light of these analyses, the persistence of such patterns is somewhat puzzling. Why do so many women continue to engage in the activities of being a wife and mother? Why do so many women apparently willingly engage in practises which restrict their adult lives? Partial answers to these questions undoubtedly lie in the positive meanings of marriage and motherhood for women and in the absence of equally valued alternatives to the adult identities of wife and mother. Attempts to explain women's involvement in the activities of wife and mother have also drawn on the notion of socialization. Perhaps women devote so much time to housework and to the care of their children because this is what women are supposed to do. But such approaches construct women as devoid of agency, as passively complying with social prescriptions about women's "roles". A different way of understanding why women engage in the practises of mother and housewife emerges when research is grounded in women's accounts of their experiences as wives and mothers.

The importance of acknowledging women's agency in understanding the gendered division of work in the home is highlighted in Fox's (1998) analysis of the accounts of a sample of Canadian women who were first-time mothers. Fox suggests that gender inequality in the family is partly reproduced through women's practises as mothers, particularly in the context of the shifts in social support relationships which occur in conjunction with the transition to motherhood. A woman's ability to take on full responsibility for childcare, especially when her children are very young, depends to a large degree on having the cooperation and support of her partner. As one of the women interviewed in Fox's study said:

> Yes, I'm more dependent on him . . . I couldn't do it without him. I just couldn't. He has to be there. I don't know, he has to tell me a lot that I'm doing a good job, that the kids [twins] are good. Yes, I am very dependent on him.
>
> (Fox 1998: 165)

A mother's ability to provide child-centered care also depends on the availability of others, such as her own mother, to provide additional help. The support and assistance of others enabled many of the first-time mothers interviewed in Fox's study to adopt an "intensive" form of mothering.

An exclusive and intensive form of mothering, in which children's needs take precedence over other activities in a woman's life, is particularly characteristic of the lives of middle-class mothers (Hays 1996, McMahon 1995). Working-class mothers may aspire to a similar form of mothering practise, but worry about spending enough time with their children if they also work outside the home (McMahon 1995). Because a mother's ability to spend time caring for her children depends on freedom from other responsibilities (such as paid work), when a woman becomes a parent she is likely to become more dependent, both emotionally and financially, on her partner. Engaging in intensive mothering also involves spending more time in the home and as Fox (1998: 168) notes, the more time a woman spends at home, the more likely she is to become aware of housework which needs doing. A mother's attention to home cleanliness, for instance, is likely to increase because of concerns about her child's welfare (e.g. having clean floors becomes important when an infant begins to crawl).

More than exposure and familiarity, however, are needed to explain why women take on primary responsibility for housework when they become parents and Fox suggests two additional considerations which come into play. The first involves a mother's desire to foster her partner's relationship with the child. In order to facilitate a "bond" between father and child, a woman is likely to encourage her partner to engage in pleasant activities requiring close physical proximity with the child (e.g. play, bed-time care routines). At the same time, the partner's involvement with the child frees the mother to engage in other household chores, such as cooking and cleaning, unencumbered by childcare responsibilities. Secondly, because intensive mothering depends on having a partner's financial support, a woman is likely to give priority to ensuring that her husband's ability to work is not jeopardized by fatigue or ill-health. For instance, a woman interviewed in Fox's (1998: 166) study explained why she was the one to get up with her infant while her husband slept: "I'd much rather have him stable and healthy so that he can help me when I really need it." The availability of a woman's own mother to help with childcare also creates a situation where less help is required from the partner, and as Fox found, a partner's attempts to help may even be resisted.

In the transition to parenthood, therefore, changes in the patterning of family relationships, partly initiated by women's actions, reproduce housework and childcare as the domains of mothers. These changes also operate to construct such practises as women's work, activities for which men have limited responsibility. Women justify this process in which they define themselves as the person ultimately responsible for childcare on the grounds that their male partner not only has less time but also is less attuned to the needs and temperaments of their children (Croghan 1991, Fox 1998, McMahon 1995). As Croghan's (1991) study with British mothers revealed, during the early months of motherhood, women attempt to resolve contradictions between their child's need for care and their own increased workload by doing more and sleeping less. Such coping strategies are adopted by mothers as a way of avoiding conflict with their partner, especially when he is reluctant to negotiate a more equitable sharing of work in the home. For the sake of her children, a mother is likely to put family harmony ahead of conflict with her partner. As one of the British women interviewed by Croghan (1991: 234) said:

> I did talk to him about it all [helping with childcare]. And he's a really lovely bloke, very understanding. Even when I said that I was really angry with him, he was so kind, he is such a kind and lovely bloke.

Adoption of such conflict avoidance strategies probably explains why mothers are more likely to evaluate their partners' contributions to the family in terms of "relational equity" (based on the notion of "equivalent roles"), rather than that of gender equality (Croghan 1991, Fox 1998).

Of course many women willingly engage in childcare activities and mothering is experienced as rewarding, because it provides an important source of meaning and purpose in their lives. The British women interviewed by Boulton (1983), for example, described their involvement in childcare as something which was intrinsically worthwhile and valued, because it was for the benefit of their children. In McMahon's (1995) analysis, a central theme was the strength of the women's sense of emotional connectedness with their children. As one woman said: "I really was not prepared for the emotional impact on myself of having a child – it was *profound*. I mean just *profound*. . . . The whole experience was very overwhelming." (ibid.: 134 emphasis in original). The theme of "overwhelming love" also was identified by Weaver and Ussher (1997) as an important element in the accounts of mothers of preschoolers living in London.

Hays (1996) also observed in her analysis of accounts of mothers living in California that many wanted their male partners to be more involved in childcare. At the same time these women also worried about the quality of the care their partner would provide if he was more involved. Hays interpreted this aspect of women's accounts as reflecting a "guilt gap", the outcome of a situation in which women are considered to have ultimate responsibility for their children's care, while childcare is viewed as optional by their partner (if they have one). The account of one mother interviewed by Hays (ibid.: 104) captures this theme:

> See, my kids are my world. I would not do anything without thinking of them first. I think a lot of men do, think more about themselves than what they're doing or leaving behind. . . . Not that it's the right thing to do. But, you know, once in a while, I'll feel like I want to just walk out and leave for a couple of hours. I got to find a baby-sitter. If [men] want to walk out, it's like, "I'll be back". They don't have to think about who's gonna take care of the kids.

What is it about becoming a mother that creates in women such an overpowering sense of responsibility for their children's care and welfare? Fox (1998), Hays (1996), and McMahon (1995) all identify the intensive character of contemporary mothering practises as both producing women as mothers and a key source of women's disadvantaged social status. As I will argue later in the chapter, the practises of intensive mothering also are strongly implicated in understanding women's depressive experiences. Why do women so readily (and apparently willingly) become "intensive mothers" when they have a child? To answer this question, it is necessary to consider not only how mothers are socially produced through contemporary mothering practises, but also how notions of the good mother are socially constructed in discourses of femininity.

Discourses of femininity and the social construction of the good mother

As I outlined earlier, becoming a mother has important implications for a woman's sense of self. The identity of mother is central to adult women's conceptions of the kind of person they are. Culturally, the qualities associated with the "mother figure" – those of being a caring, empathetic, loving person – are positively valued. These qualities also are socially constructed in western cultures as critical aspects of femininity. Without such qualities, a woman is less than a proper woman, a bad mother, almost a nonwoman. Becoming a mother provides women with a ready-made avenue for demonstrating in a convincing fashion, to themselves and others, their inherent womanliness, and by implication, their femininity. Closely linked with discourses of femininity is the "ideology of motherhood" (Hays 1996, McMahon 1995, Phoenix *et al.* 1991), a term denoting the set of ideas around the core cultural belief that motherhood is both the ultimate source of a woman's fulfilment and a requirement for women.

While it certainly is true that women have always borne children, analyses of women's lives in past centuries reveal the relative historical recency of the set of practises which now are so closely associated with the identities of wife and mother (Phoenix *et al.* 1991, Hays 1996). The intensive form of mothering typifying the lives of many middle-class women, and to which working-class women often aspire, is a phenomenon of the twentieth century (Findlay and Miller 1994, Hays 1996, Tizard 1991). The "occupation" of housewife for women began to take its current shape in the early 1900s in conjunction with increased public concerns about the health and welfare of children as future workers in the factories of the industrial revolution. Following the pattern which characterized the lives of more privileged women (who also had servants to perform household chores) mothers were identified as being in the best position to monitor and promote the health and welfare of family members. In the wake of the later "mental hygiene" movement, mothers gained the added responsibility of fostering the development of their children. This expanded conception of motherhood also received impetus from theories in which the development of a close mother–child attachment during infancy was emphasized as an important precondition for psychological health in adulthood (Tizard 1991). Thus, a good mother came to be seen as someone who was part housekeeper, part nurse, and part teacher and the place of married women was firmly established as being in the home. By the 1950s, the figure of the stay-at-home housewife and mother, whose daily life was dedicated to housework and meeting the needs of family members, was well established in the public imagination (Friedan 1963).

Although women no longer face legal impediments to combining motherhood with employment outside the home, women are still expected to be good mothers once they have a child. Being a good mother also encompasses the process of becoming a mother, pregnancy and childbirth, in addition to practises of mothering. For instance, the accounts of the women interviewed by McMahon (1995) reflected a belief that not only is there a "right time" to become pregnant, but some life circumstances are more appropriate than others for having a child. Women's views about readiness for pregnancy also varied with social class, with the right time to become pregnant being somewhat later for middle-class than working-class women. Middle-class women defined readiness in terms of having achieved some degree of financial and career stability, in the context of a settled relationship with a man. As one middle-class woman said:

> We were mature enough. We had satisfied a lot of other needs. We were ready to make a commitment to children. We were very sure in our relationship . . . Emotionally both of us were ready. . . . We both wanted to have a baby. . . . It seemed like the right thing to do.
>
> (McMahon ibid.: 66)

In contrast, the main precondition for readiness among working-class women was having a sexual relationship with a man. Neither marriage nor financial security was considered necessary. The following account reflects this understanding of readiness among working-class women:

> Well, I guess we'd been together for a couple of years. We seemed more like, you know, the married type, and I just thought, like, it was a good time to have a baby. Get married first, but then have the baby.
>
> (McMahon ibid.: 103)

Both pregnancy and childbirth have become highly medicalized in recent decades (Findlay and Miller 1994; Oakley 1986). As a reflection of this trend, the information provided to pregnant women by health professionals and disseminated in print form (e.g. as pamphlets, advice manuals, etc) generally present medicalized accounts in which a central theme is that of normality (Woollett and Marshall 1997). Certain experiences during pregnancy such as nausea and sickness are depicted as normal, whereas others might signal a need for medical intervention. An understanding of pregnancy sickness as medically normal is so well-established that a pregnant woman may be concerned if it is not part of her experience. In recent years, as well, increasing emphasis has been placed on the pregnant woman's own actions as being important for ensuring a normal pregnancy and a healthy child. Having a good diet and following healthy lifestyle practises are seen as paramount in this regard. So, if problems are encountered during childbirth or with the baby, the woman's behavior while she is pregnant may be partly to blame.

Childbirth itself represents a critical moment for women in becoming a mother. The idea of "natural childbirth" (i.e. without medical intervention) has gained wide currency as a standard against which women evaluate their own delivery experiences. At the same time, women are concerned that they will have a safe delivery and their baby will be healthy, so a role for medical intervention is also acknowledged. Nevertheless, in anticipation of a birth which is eagerly awaited, a woman

150

and those around her, may expect her to feel an immediate sense of love for the baby. Anything short of positive "bonding" with the newborn is likely to be experienced as shameful and as a source of guilt. In her analysis of post-partum depression, Taylor (1996) gives the following excerpt taken from a woman's account of her experiences in relation to childbirth:

> I had in mind this cooing, laughing baby, someone I could love and have that special kind of close relationship with that you can't have unless you're a mother . . . so I was a bit let down when in the hospital I was handed this sleeping infant who didn't seem to care whether I was there or not. It just wasn't what I expected. Here was this baby I was supposed to love, and I just didn't feel a thing. I literally went numb. I can't tell you how guilty I felt.
>
> (Taylor ibid.: 39)

Once the baby arrives, childcare becomes the central focus of a woman's life and cultural ideals about what constitutes a good mother regulate how women engage in their practises of mothering. In McMahon's (1995) analysis of mothers' accounts, several key themes emerged and these varied by the social class background of the women. Working-class mothers were more likely than middle-class mothers to emphasize their own actions in relation to their children. Thus, providing for their children's material and physical needs and spending time with their children were key criteria against which the working-class women judged the adequacy of their mothering. McMahon suggested that working-class women's preoccupation with these outward signs of good mothering reflects the relative visibility of their family lives to others. Concerns about how their mothering might be perceived by others stemmed from lack of privacy afforded by often cramped living arrangements and also was linked to public discourses constructing young, poor, or unwed mothers as social problems. These women were well-aware of the risks which "official" surveillance could pose for them, especially if a woman was receiving social assistance ("welfare"). The identification by working-class women of "patience" and "lack of irritation" as qualities of good mothers was interpreted by McMahon as a way for these mothers to distance themselves from images of neglectful or abusive mothers. Similar themes emerged in the accounts of the working-class mothers interviewed in Hays' (1996) study in California. Mothers were seen as "bad" if they were "too lazy or too preoccupied" with their own lives "to properly supervise their kids" (p. 87).

The accounts of the middle-class mothers interviewed by McMahon (1995) reflected somewhat different concerns, focused on the *quality* of the mother-child relationship. Being a good mother involved showing the "right feelings" toward, and interacting in a loving way with, their children, as well as providing the "right environment" for the development of their children's potential. Good mothers, therefore, not only *show* appropriate feelings (love and care) toward their children and do so in a sensitive and empathetic manner, they also *enjoy* their children. The following account of one middle-class mother illustrates this notion of good mothering:

> [A good mother] is really just able to unconditionally love and accept their child for who they are and where they are and what they are all about, and not try to mold them into something to meet their expectations. I think it's someone who can be there but in the right context.
>
> (McMahon 1995: 157)

This more child-focused form of mothering, in which the quality of the time spent with children and the special connectedness characterizing a close mother–child relationship, was also emphasized in the accounts of the middle-class mothers interviewed by Hays (1996).

Key themes emerging from the accounts of both middle-class and working-class mothers are that good mothers act "with their children in mind" (McMahon 1995: 184) and with "loving attention" (Hays 1996: 111). Being a good mother is something accomplished on a daily basis through the particular ways in which a woman engages in the practical activities of looking after and caring for her children. How a mother goes about her mothering, therefore, signifies the kind of mother she is. Her children's appearance and behavior in turn provide evidence of the quality of her mothering. For working-class women, children who are poorly dressed, dirty, or behave in an unruly way reflect negatively not only on the character of their mother, but also on the adequacy of her mothering practises. Appearance and cleanliness play a less critical part in the concerns of middle-class women, because their material conditions usually enable such things to be taken for granted, although their children's welfare remains a central focus. Middle-class women are more likely to interpret their child's development of special talents and individual achievements as signs of good mothering. The broad similarities between middle-class and working-class women's ideas about what constitutes good mothering can be interpreted in another way. As Phoenix *et al.* (1991) have pointed out, in prevailing conceptions of the good mother, the practises of middle-class women are given more emphasis than those of working-class women. Although working-class mothers may struggle to emulate such patterns, their material circumstances set distinct limits on their ability to do so. Thus, the mothering practises of working-class women more often may be judged, both by themselves and others, as falling short of the culturally defined ideal of the good mother, which reflects middle-class practises.

A more fundamental theme also has been identified in cultural conceptions of motherhood and this has to do with how children and childhood are perceived. Zelizer (1985) has traced the shift which has occurred during the twentieth century from seeing children as potentially unruly and troublesome to seeing them as "sacred gifts", repositories of innocence and virtue. In concert with this shift in the cultural valuing of children, mothers increasingly have come to be seen as "facilitators of this boundless potential and as protectors of priceless innocence"

(McMahon 1995: 190). As McMahon points out, this shift also has influenced the conception of the good mother in a direction which moves the focus from mother to child. The moral value attached to motherhood is now somewhat eclipsed by the social worth children represent, a trend which may signal a diminution in the cultural value of motherhood. Nevertheless, mothers are still firmly tied to their children's caring needs and are still the first to be blamed when their children behave in ways which are less than innocent or fail to develop their "boundless potential".

To summarize the chapter so far, I have discussed women's experiences of marriage and motherhood and their associated meanings, practises and discourses. Central to the meanings of marriage and motherhood are the positively valued identities of wife and mother. Such identities not only offer women social status; they also make available avenues for relational connectedness, especially with children. These identities, I suggest, are constructed discursively and also produced through engaging in the activities, or practises, constituting women's everyday lives as wives and mothers. Caring for others is a key aspect of these practises and women view the work they do in the home, and more particularly the care of their children, as a way of expressing maternal feelings. In recent decades, these practises have taken shape increasingly as an intensive style of mothering, in which a mother's life is child-centered. Such mothering practises are supported by cultural discourses which construct caring as a core aspect of femininity and mothers as having ultimate responsibility for their children's welfare. In the final section of this chapter, I consider how experiences labeled as depression can arise in the context of women's everyday lives as wives and mothers.

Depression and women's lived experiences as wives and mothers

As I pointed out earlier in the chapter, mainstream approaches to explaining depression in women conceptualize depressive experiences as something apart from women's lives as wives and mothers. When the problem is defined as a set of symptoms called depression, women's lives tend to fade into the background and become taken for granted. Social approaches which focus more directly on women's lives as wives and mothers (see Chapter 5) are based in a similar assumption. When stressful aspects of the everyday lives of women who are wives and mothers are identified as causal factors in depression (e.g. McGrath et al. 1990), this assumes that a reduction in these sources of stress also would lead to a decrease in rates of depression among women. Thus, social approaches seem to rest on a presumption that marriage and motherhood have inherently benign implications for women's well-being. The problem is the stressful nature of some women's lives as wives and mother, rather than marriage and motherhood. Attempts to explain the depression experienced by some women following childbirth reflect a similar assumption. The problem is depression, not motherhood, and a woman's treatment for depression will restore her satisfaction with motherhood (Taylor 1996). The assumption made here is that motherhood is inherently a positive experience for women and failure to experience expected maternal feelings is a sign of depression.

A more pervasive conceptual problem characterizes explanations for depression among women who are wives and mothers. Such theories are based in ideas about women's lives which are derived from the perspective of researchers and mental health professionals, rather than reflecting women's experiences from their own standpoint. What kind of understanding of depression might emerge when women's experiences, rather than the views of experts, are the starting point? In the next part of this section, I discuss studies in which the focus has been on women's accounts of their depressive experiences. Then, I draw on this information to consider how women's accounts reflect the influence of "discourses of depression". These discourses shape how women interpret their experiences and their responses to them. Often overlooked, however, when research has focused on women's accounts of their experiences are the material realities of women's lives. These material realities include women's bodies and the structural conditions shaping their lives. I conclude the chapter by discussing how depression in women who are wives and mothers can be understood from the material–discursive perspective developed in Chapter 6.

When studies have focused on depressive experiences among women who also are mothers, key themes to emerge from analyses of women's accounts include ambivalence, disappointment and loss. Women express ambivalent feelings about motherhood, are disappointed with their experiences of being a mother, and feel that in becoming a mother they have lost their sense of identity (Jack 1991, Lewis and Nicolson 1998, Taylor 1996). Such themes are present in the accounts of women who have been diagnosed with depression by mental health professionals as well as among those who identify themselves as having difficulty with "distress" or "emotional problems". For instance, a woman interviewed as part of a British study with distressed mothers who were receiving support from a voluntary agency described her predominant reaction to motherhood as one of "shock".

> And the whole sort of ideas are there, certainly for the first child – not having had much contact – and it's quite a shock, you know, a horrible shock to find you've been bombarded with all this wonderful "Mothercare" image – and it was so much more difficult and exhausting because I hadn't had any kind of contact with children and parenting.
>
> (Lewis and Nicolson 1998: 184)

This woman's experiences of becoming a mother would seem consistent with the information that she was distressed and her feelings of distress probably color her negative evaluation of motherhood. Such an interpretation is difficult to sustain, however, when the accounts of women who have not been identified as distressed are considered. The experiences recounted by the nondistressed mothers interviewed in Weaver and Ussher's (1997) study in England reflected very similar themes. For example, one woman said:

I mean, you can read about it and you can talk to friends, but . . . there's nothing that can prepare you for parenthood particularly. I mean I think it really is a complete and utter shock to the whole system. Definitely.

(Weaver and Ussher ibid.: 58)

The following account is taken from Taylor's (1996) study, based on interviews with American women who identified themselves as having "emotional problems" in the year following childbirth.

I was so anxious that . . . I couldn't give her a bath because I was afraid I would drown her. I didn't want to change her diaper because something made me afraid I would stick her with the pin. Everything I did with that baby I was afraid to do.

(Taylor ibid.: 42)

This account can be compared with the following excerpt taken from McMahon's (1995: 209) study with Canadian mothers: "[For me the worst thing is] worrying – anxiety, I guess, about the responsibility. . . . I focus on them and worry about doing the right thing". Or contrast the next two excerpts, the first from an interview with a young single mother in Taylor's study and the second from an interview with a single mother in McMahon's study.

I felt like some of my youthfulness left. If I wanted to go somewhere and do anything, I've got to think about having a babysitter or getting my Mom or my brother to take care of her. I've got to think about coming back in an hour or two to feed her. I can't go on dates, to the mall, the movies, or do any of the things my other friends are doing. I feel restricted and tied down.

(Taylor ibid.: 46)

Sometimes I get frustrated and tired of it . . . I just want to go out and have fun, leave [my son] John at home with a sitter. But I'm a *Mom*. I have a child that I've got to support. [I used to be] fun and crazy. . . .

(McMahon ibid.: 169, emphasis in original)

As I hope this comparison of excerpts from the accounts of different women in different studies and in different countries illustrates, negative feelings are commonly experienced by women who are mothers. Does this mean that such experiences are simply a normal part of becoming a mother? Are mothers who experience negative reactions to motherhood in some way inadequate? Do the accounts above indicate that these women have made a poor adjustment to an adult female identity or are deficient in feminine, maternal traits? Are the negative experiences of these women signs of individual pathology?

An alternative interpretation of these accounts, one which makes more sense to me, is to view them as reflecting the lived experiences of women in the context of particular, and historically specific, ways of organizing the work of mothering. Not only is mothering socially constructed as women's responsibility but both this work and women's experiences of motherhood are regulated by pervasive cultural discourses constructing what it means to be a woman and a mother. Before addressing the implications of this way of understanding women's experiences, I consider the explanatory strategies women use to account for their negative experiences as wives and mothers.

Women seem to draw on two main approaches for explaining their negative experiences. One approach involves attributing negative feelings to stressful aspects of their lives as wives and mothers and the other focuses on their bodies as a source of feelings of distress. Elsewhere (see Stoppard 1997), I have referred to these explanatory approaches as the "women's lives" and "women's bodies" strategies. The following excerpt is from an interview with a mother who had previously been depressed and illustrates the first strategy.

> It was background panic. I've felt that I haven't had time to get depressed.
> I'm alright as long as I'm busy and I see a lot of people. If I was in the
> house with just him and not seeing anyone, then I don't think it would be
> hard to get depressed.
>
> (Lewis and Nicolson 1998: 188)

This woman links her depressive feelings with the social isolation involved in caring for an infant. A middle-class woman interviewed in McMahon's (1995) study expressed a similar idea about the connection between having negative feelings (in this case "irritation") and spending too much of her time at home with her children:

> Nowadays, it's all right . . . I [used to] get irritated by about 8:00 at
> night . . . The little one has been getting up a lot at night and that's when
> I get irritated. . . . Otherwise I don't get [irritated] anymore because
> [now that I'm working full-time] that's the only time I spend with them.
>
> (McMahon ibid.: 220)

Women also draw on bodily explanations for their feelings of distress, attributing such feelings to hormonal fluctuations and other biochemical changes in their bodies. In a study with Canadian women who had been treated for depression by a mental health professional, Gammell and Stoppard (1999) found that women often attributed feelings of distress to their bodily processes. For instance, one woman explained her depression in the following way: "It's a chemical imbalance and to me it just happened, it may have had something to do with my menopause." (p. 121). Walters (1993) also found in her Canadian study that women drew on a "women's bodies" form of explanation in accounting for feelings of stress and depression, as reflected in the following excerpt:

At that time [of menstrual period] I am always very depressed and down and almost going to cry. That's the point, you want to do things you shouldn't do. Every month it comes up, what's happening in my life, all the bad things at that point, and if I am really lonely and by myself, that's the point I could do something.

(Walters ibid.: 400)

One way of interpreting these explanatory approaches is that they represent the strategies which culturally are available to women for making sense of their experiences. Women make sense of their negative experiences by accounting for them in various ways. Explanations focused on women's everyday lives or on women's bodily processes are different accounting strategies. These accounting strategies also can be characterized as discourses, sets of beliefs about the causes of negative experiences and how they can be explained. In some ways, these discourses parallel the more formal explanatory models developed by researchers and mental health professionals to account for depression. When women attempt to make sense of their negative experiences by drawing on these discourses of depression, the accounting strategies they employ reflect popularized versions of experts' theories of depression (Stoppard 1997). For instance, the women's lives explanatory approach has similarities with the social stress models considered in Chapter 5 and the women's bodies approach overlaps with the biological theories discussed in Chapter 6.

The type of accounting strategy a woman adopts also has implications for her sense of self as a woman and a mother. If she attributes negative experiences to her everyday life, this may imply that she is unable to cope very well with the responsibilities of being a mother – perhaps she is not a good mother. Rather than following this accounting strategy, which would have unfavorable implications for her character (and identity as a mother), a woman is more likely to "normalize" her negative experiences (Walters 1993). Typically, this normalization is accomplished through a process in which women attribute their negative experiences to the burdensome nature of their everyday responsibilities, while simultaneously taking their lived experiences for granted as an expected part of being a wife and mother. The following account, taken from Gammell and Stoppard's (1999: 120) study with women who had been treated for depression reflects this normalizing strategy: "I still did my daily activities of daily living. You know, had supper ready, had dinner ready, had their lunches ready. Did the wash. But none of that had ceased, you know." When this woman became depressed, she decided to reduce her involvement in paid employment, rather than making changes in her activities in the home as a wife and mother. Adopting this coping strategy also enabled her to retain an identity as a good wife and mother.

If a woman draws on discourses around women's bodies as a way of accounting for her feelings of distress, this also avoids threats to her identity as a good woman. When women attribute negative feelings to their bodily processes, they ascribe them to something outside their control and thus remove the possibility of self-blame. The source of the problem lies within her body, not her practises as a wife and mother and, therefore, her problem is one most appropriately dealt with by consulting a medical professional. Although a woman's distress is likely to be interpreted by a health professional as a symptom of a mental disorder, possibly depression, for some women this may be preferable to jeopardizing their identity as a good wife and mother.

Discourses around women's bodies as a source of negative feelings are particularly likely to inform women's understanding of distress experienced after childbirth. Taylor (1996) analyzed the explanatory strategies employed by American women involved in the post-partum depression self-help movement. This movement in the US has the aim of gaining increased medical recognition for post-partum depression as a disorder which may affect some women following childbirth. According to Taylor's analysis, one reason for the growth in support for this movement is that it allows the negative feelings (or absence of positive feelings) a woman may experience when she has a baby to be legitimized as symptoms of an illness. Rather than signifying that a woman is a bad mother, negative feelings following childbirth are interpreted as a sign that she is suffering from the disorder of post-partum depression. By adopting this explanatory strategy, a woman's identity as a good mother can remain intact.

A woman's efforts to maintain her identity as a good mother also can be threatened by lack of material resources. When the practises of being a good mother are defined in terms of an intensive form of mothering and childcare is socially constructed as a woman's responsibility, a situation is created where women are caught between the demands of motherhood and the material realities of their lives. Women face a variety of dilemmas rooted in contradictions between the material conditions of their lives and the socially constructed image of the good mother. As McMahon pointed out:

> The mystification of the work of caring for others as not being real work that requires adequate preparation, material resources, social support and organizational responsiveness leaves women vulnerable to ambivalence and anxiety, feeling they are not doing enough for their children or that they are not doing it right. And it leaves women who do not have the personal or material resources to approximate the ideals of good parenting feeling like failures.
>
> (McMahon 1995: 214)

An important material resource which sets limits on a woman's ability to engage in the practises of the good mother is her own physical body. The themes of sleep deprivation, fatigue and tiredness repeatedly emerge in women's accounts of their experiences as mothers (Croghan 1991, McMahon 1995, Popay 1992, Walters 1993). Intensive mothering is an exhausting undertaking, even if a woman has the help and support of others (Hays 1996, Fox 1998). But a mother may lack help, because her partner is unwilling to assist with childcare or she has no partner.

Under such conditions, a woman may still strive to engage in the practises of the good mother and interpret her chronic fatigue as part of the "price of motherhood". So long as a woman is rewarded with the emotional benefits of a close relationship with her children, who are developing in socially desirable ways, she is likely to consider the price of constant tiredness and lack of time for herself one she is willing to pay. After all, raising children is something which is inherently worthwhile and valuable.

Material conditions have an impact on a woman's experiences of mothering in other ways. The form of intensive mothering which currently defines the good mother reflects a middle-class conception of appropriate maternal behavior (McMahon 1995, Phoenix *et al.* 1991). Women who lack material resources cannot easily engage in the middle-class variant of motherhood, intensive or otherwise, as they struggle to provide the basic necessities of life for their children. Mothers whose lives are shaped by structural inequalities of class, race and ethnicity are particularly vulnerable to being judged as inadequate mothers, although the source of any maternal failings is more likely to lie in lack of adequate material resources. Under such conditions, continuing to claim the identity of a good mother, while avoiding others' judgments that they are bad mothers, may lead women to redouble their mothering efforts. More energy may be expended on caring work in the home or more time spent in doing paid work to enable the financial needs of the family to be met. Whatever strategy is followed, some aspect of the good mother ideal is likely to be threatened, increasing the likelihood that a woman will evaluate herself negatively, while also depleting her own energy resources and health.

A woman's mothering efforts undoubtedly are made worthwhile by the close and emotionally connected relationships she has with her children. And a woman's children may represent more than sufficient compensation for the material deprivations of her everyday life. But other aspects of her lived experiences may undermine her sense of herself as being a good mother. Despite her efforts, family life may not be harmonious, her partner may be neglectful and abusive or abandon her, and her children may fail in school or behave in antisocial ways. Under such conditions, a woman can hardly avoid acknowledging that her efforts to be a good wife and mother are unappreciated and unrecognized. Such feelings are likely to be exacerbated in a cultural context in which women are blamed for their children's shortcomings as well as for discordant family relations (Caplan 1989, Tizard 1991). In failing as wives and mothers, women are likely to judge themselves as being bad women.

From a material–discursive perspective, a woman's subjective and embodied experiences which may be labeled as depression by mental health professionals can be understood as arising in the context of the lived experiences of being a mother. The lived experiences of women who mother children are created in relation to the practises of intensive mothering, regulated by discourses in which the good mother is equated with an intensive mother. As constructed by discourses of femininity, a good mother is one whose everyday life is organized "with her children in mind" and who puts her children's needs ahead of her own (Hays 1996, McMahon 1995). At the same time, cultural beliefs in which motherhood is represented as the ultimate source of personal fulfilment for women, coupled with the construction of childcare as ultimately women's responsibility, set limits on both the material and identity resources available to many women. This is especially likely to be the case under social conditions in which motherhood is assumed to be a matter of personal choice and the responsibility of caring for children is relegated to the private domain of the family (McMahon 1995, Phoenix *et al.* 1991).

In reflecting on the circumstances in which many women strive to be good mothers, McMahon (1998: 197) observes that "[m]others often pay a high price for what may be transitory or illusory moral or emotional rewards. They may come to feel unappreciated, isolated or abandoned rather than connected." I concur with McMahon's analysis and would modify it only to suggest that another way of conceptualizing the "high price" women pay for being mothers is in terms of depressive experiences. The problems women face in being mothers lie not with motherhood, nor necessarily with the meaning motherhood holds for women, but with the *intensive* form of mothering which has come to dominate cultural constructions of the good mother.

The caring imperative, which structures the everyday activities of many women's lives during the years dedicated to child-bearing and child-rearing, also extends to include the lives of older women. As women's bodies age, the focus of discourses of femininity also shifts. The practises of older woman are constructed in relation to cultural meanings of the menopausal and post-menopausal female body. In the next chapter, I turn to a consideration of how depressive experiences can arise in the context of older women's lives.

9

WOMEN AND AGING

Depression in midlife and old age

The topic of depression is an element in the rather negative image conjured up by the term "older woman". As characterized by Gergen (1990: 477), the narrative form of women's lives implicit in theories of psychological development is one in which the trajectory "is basically downhill, or regressive from 40 on". Against such a dispiriting backdrop, feelings of depression among older women would not seem especially surprising. These negative connotations of women's aging are compounded by myths surrounding menopausal changes and pervasive ageism in a patriarchal cultural context in which the social value of women is defined largely in terms of reproductive potential and the sexist equation of attractiveness with a youthful appearance (Gannon 1999).

As I read material on depression in older women, two things stood out for me. First, the lived experiences of older women are virtually invisible in the literature on depression. Second, experts' views on depression in older women often seem to reflect diametrically opposed positions. For instance, HRT (or hormone replacement therapy) currently is being promoted for use by midlife women to counter the presumed negative health consequences of menopause, among which depression and mood swings are included (Hunt 1994, Lock 1993, Rostosky and Travis 1996). At the same time, researchers have pointed repeatedly to the lack of evidence for a direct association between menopause and depression (e.g., Kaufert *et al.* 1992, McKinlay *et al.* 1987). A similar paradox is apparent in the literature on depression in women's later years. Some researchers conclude that rates of depression are relatively low in older women compared to rates in younger age groups (Cappeliez 1993, Culbertson 1997), whereas others suggest that depression often goes unrecognized and untreated in older adults (Katona 1994, Kennedy 1996). Rather than indicating disagreements among researchers about how research findings should be interpreted, these conflicting positions probably reflect the more general problem of a lack of information about the experiences of women as they age, a gap in knowledge noted by others (cf. Day 1991, Gibson 1996, Rostosky and Travis 1996).

Two central preoccupations dominate the research literature on women and aging. The first is the presumed centrality of the menopausal transition to women's midlife experiences (Rostosky and Travis 1996). The second is the problem posed by the growing number of old women in a world in which the overall population is aging and women live longer than men (Gee and Kimball 1987, Gibson 1996). The problematic character of women's aging is an unspoken assumption in much of this work, as is the supposition that the source of this problem lies within women themselves. As I read this literature, I was struck by the taken for granted character of this picture of aging in women and started to wonder whose interests it serves. Who benefits from such negatively-toned depictions of what amounts to almost half the life span of many women alive today? What is missing or left unsaid in published accounts on the health and mental health concomitants of aging in women? I found a partial answer to these questions in analyses of aging informed by more critical and feminist perspectives (e.g. Ginn and Arber 1995, Calasanti and Zajicek 1993, Coyle 1997, Gibson 1996). What these analyses indicate is that widely shared notions about aging in women and the lived experiences of older women are shaped by cultural discourses around what it means to be a woman and old in a historical context characterized by particular social, economic and political conditions. In important ways, then, the categories of midlife and old woman are better understood as being socially constructed and socially produced than as clearly distinguishable groupings of individuals already present in the world before research is conducted or social policy is formulated.

I begin this chapter with a discussion of how the categories of midlife and old women are constructed and produced socially. This involves tracing the way these categories are linked to conceptions of aging and old age and how each is conceptualized in relation to the category woman. Next, I consider approaches to research on depression in older women, linking the analysis to critiques developed in earlier chapters. This analysis reveals the virtual absence of older women's voices in existing work on depression, with the consequence that much of the available knowledge is at best limited and partial, and at worst distorted and misleading (as well as damaging to women in general). In the remainder of the chapter, I discuss what we know about the lives of midlife and older women from research based in exploration of women's experiences. Such knowledge is beginning to yield a picture of women's experiences during midlife and beyond which challenges taken-for-granted assumptions in mainstream accounts of aging and depression in women.

Midlife and old women: socially constructed and produced categories

Those working in fields which take aging and age-related changes as their central focus (e.g. developmental psychology, social gerontology, old age psychiatry) tend to emphasize different aspects of concepts such as age and old. While chronological age (calendar years) provides a common sense index of aging, whether a woman is categorized as midlife or old rests on more than a simple count of years since birth. Two other ways of defining age also need to be considered. Thus, age can be defined with respect to physiological (e.g. medical) and social (e.g. age-related norms) criteria (Ginn and Arber 1995). When age is defined physiologically, attention is focused on the body as a medical entity, a biological system manifesting fairly predictable regularities in structure and functioning over the life span. Socially, age is conceptualized in terms of characteristics attributed to an individual by virtue of the age they appear to be or acknowledge being. Although conceptually distinct, these three ways of conceptualizing age (chronological, medical, social) merge in everyday use. In recent decades, the medical-biological approach has become the dominant way of defining aging, largely overshadowing its social aspects (Lock 1998, Matthews 1979). The overlapping character of these different conceptions of aging is evident in the difficulty researchers have in distinguishing the categories of midlife and old, and the categories of young and midlife (Ginn and Arber 1995, Day 1991, Matthews 1979). In practise, this means that distinctions made between these age-related categories are always somewhat arbitrary.

In western countries, chronological age generally is taken as an indicator of when a person is legally defined as "too old to work" (for pay) and must cease paid employment, taking on the status and identity of a "retired" person and becoming an "old-age pensioner" or "senior citizen". Thus, the age when most people are no longer in paid employment usually is taken as the lower boundary of the category old. As Matthews (1979) has pointed out, however, use of chronological age to define the dividing line between "able to work" and "too old to work" is rooted historically in the beginnings of industrial modes of production and in more recent demographic shifts marked by increased life expectancy and reduced birth rates. I draw on key points from Matthews' analysis in what follows.

Up until the late nineteenth century, people were considered old when they were physically incapable of working, because of ill-health or infirmity, and therefore could no longer participate fully in their social world. Toward the end of the nineteenth century and the early part of the twentieth, large numbers of people were drawn from rural areas to jobs in the factories of the industrial revolution. With the influx of people to urban areas, controls became necessary to both stem the flow of those seeking work and reduce pressures on resources (housing etc.). Such controls were exerted in two ways: by defining a lower age below which people were too young to work and by setting an upper age above which people were too old to work. Historically, these age boundaries have tended to fluctuate in concert with economic conditions. A current example is the shifting downwards of the upper boundary, with early retirement programs instituted in response to economic downturns (sparking a trend in the opposite direction because of concerns about the burden on pension funds). From these earlier socially-based efforts to control the size of the working population, children and old people became classed as dependents, with the rest of society (i.e. parents in the first case and working adults in the second) being responsible for providing assistance. Economic support becomes a key form of assistance when both the young and the old are prohibited from working for pay. It was from such considerations that the concept of a "pension" for retired workers was born.

While too old to work is no longer defined by an individual's physical incapacity, such a link is still assumed, buttressed by entrenched beliefs in the inevitableness of declining abilities with age (Ginn and Arber 1995). Although the correlation between chronological and physiological age is far from perfect, the former has come to be treated as an indicator of physical and, therefore, economic dependency on the rest of society (Ginn and Arber 1995, Day 1991). When chronological age is taken as an indicator of a person's physical condition, biological aspects of aging are highlighted, while the social context of older people's lives is taken for granted. In this process, effects produced by extrinsic influences, unrelated to physiological age, nevertheless may be interpreted as signs of aging at the individual level.

As a result of attempts to control the size of the labor market by designating some portion of the population as too old to work, chronological age is now a key criterion for defining who is old. But the extent to which those in the category old are dependent is a state partly created by legislation. The conditions characterizing the lives of many older people (women, in particular), such as poverty and social isolation, also have come to be construed as part of the meaning of old. Over time, a set of conditions which are socially produced have operated to construct the meaning of oldness as implying not only physical dependence, but also financial impoverishment and isolation from mainstream society. Advanced age, therefore, has come to be understood as *causing* the very conditions stemming from the way in which old age has been socially defined (Matthews 1979).

The meaning of old age also intersects with the meaning of gender, so that the connotations of older woman are somewhat different from those of older man. Because of the gendered social convention that women marry men who are older, and the fact that on average women live longer than men, married women are much more likely than married men to be widowed in later life. Among women, widowhood itself may be a time of increased financial dependency, the result of a husband's pension benefits being curtailed. As widows, women also face dislocation of their social networks, because they are no longer part of a couple and may be dropped by erstwhile friends who are married (van den Hoonaard 1996). Along with a reduction in income, widows may find themselves taking on unfamiliar responsibilities (e.g. family finances and car maintenance).

Reproductive capacity (fertility) is also a central component of cultural definitions of what it means to be a woman. The time in the female life cycle when pregnancy ceases to be a possibility is labeled menopause, or more euphemistically midlife. As Lock (1998) notes, middle-age as a distinctive period of the life span is a fairly recent discovery, one which has emerged from a growing interest among social scientists in developmental stages beyond childhood. The term menopause itself only entered the professional vocabulary in recent decades, and has become popularized as a term to describe midlife women during the last 10 to 15 years (Lock 1993, 1998). Although women are involved in all facets of social life, a woman's primary purpose is still likely to be viewed as that of reproducing the next generation of human beings. This reproductive function may be seen as extending into later life through a woman's involvement in caring for younger family members (e.g. as a grandmother), as well as for older relatives who are sick or infirm.

With increased awareness of population aging, a theme identified by feminists has been the tendency to characterize women who are beyond childbearing age as a superfluous sub-population, devoid of meaningful purpose in life (Gergen 1990, Gibson 1996, Lock 1998). This view of older women is fostered by a distorted (yet widely shared) understanding of earlier historical periods as a time when few women survived beyond midlife. Although the average life span was considerably shorter than it is nowadays, nevertheless, as Lock (1998) points out, women who survived childbirth and disease lived well beyond midlife and into old age. In some interpretations of the historical record, menopause has been depicted as a con-temporary phenomenon, a product of increased human longevity (and reduced risk of mortality during childbirth). In these accounts, the menopausal and post-menopausal body is constructed as unnatural and abnormal, a form of evolutionary anomaly (Gergen 1990, Hunt 1994, Lock 1998). At the same time, the ending of a woman's menstrual life now dominates understanding of what it means to be an older woman (Lock 1998). Such ideas about the aging female body, in combination with the social construction of old age as a time of increased dependency, portray older women as beset by a range of increasingly debilitating problems as they age. This depiction is also one fostered by medicalization of the aging female body, with menopausal and post-menopausal bodies, in particular, becoming the target of medical efforts to prevent and ameliorate a variety of adverse physical conditions associated with aging in women (Hunt 1994). Use of HRT is the best known example of this expanding medicalization, although the benefits (or otherwise) of such biochemical forms of prophylactic continue to be debated (Hunt 1994, Lock 1998, Lupton 1996).

Initially promoted as an anti-aging remedy (to prevent wrinkles and other phys-ical signs of aging) (Hunt 1994), HRT is now being touted as a key medical strategy for preventing ill-health in later life, with heart disease and osteoporosis leading the list of threats to older women's physical well-being (Hunt 1994, Lock 1993). Although the longitudinal studies required to support such claims have yet to be completed, HRT is being prescribed by physicians to large numbers of women. Long-term use of HRT is often justified on the grounds that it will reduce the "burden" on health and social services expected to occur as the proportion of older (and potentially dependent) women in the population increases (Hunt 1994, Lock 1993). Aging among women is now taking place in a cultural climate in which midlife and older women are constructed not only as lacking social purpose or ability to contribute usefully to society, but also as representing a growing depen-dency burden on the rest of the population (Gibson 1996, Lock 1998). Recent analyses suggest, however, that concerns about the "costs" of meeting the needs of the older segment of the population are exaggerated (Denton *et al.* 1998). Issues posed by an aging population may have more to do with decisions around resource allocation than with resource insufficiency. When aging in women is conceived pri-marily in biological terms, however, and social aspects are ignored, discourses of "dependency burden" and "resource insufficiency" seem likely to dominate public policy discussions. Gibson (1996) has sketched in somewhat stark terms the implications for women when analyses begin from a position in which old women are constructed as a social problem.

> The problems likely to be encountered by particular old women in particular social and historical contexts have become so central to scholarly discourse on this topic that there is a danger of viewing old women only in terms of those problems, and hence, there is a danger of taking the short step to constructing old women as a problem for society. The problems that society poses for old women may thus disappear, as the problems that old women pose for society take hold.
>
> (Gibson ibid.: 434)

Research on depression in midlife and older women

Efforts to estimate the prevalence of depression among older adults have proved difficult, not least because there has been so little research on depression in older age groups (Cappeliez 1993, Kennedy 1996, McGrath *et al.* 1990). Studies with community residents apparently are hampered by a reluctance among older adults to report symptoms which might label them as mentally ill (Kennedy 1996). Debates around rates of depression in older adults have focused on the issue of how depression should be defined for clinical and research purposes (Formanek 1987). Thus, when depression is defined in terms of diagnostic criteria for depressive disorder, rates seem to be relatively low, whereas depressive symptoms and more diffuse forms of psychological distress may be more prevalent (Cappeliez 1993, Kennedy 1996). Another obstacle to assessing the extent to which depression is experienced by older people is the blurred distinction between depressive symptoms and signs of what may be considered normal aging, with a commonly held idea being that depressed feelings are likely to be part of the aging experience, a predictable response to the vicissitudes of becoming older (Kennedy 1996). This viewpoint appears to rest on the assumption that being old and being unhealthy are equivalent, a belief which also can lead to misinterpretation of an individual's reactions to the social consequences of aging as signs of depression (Day 1991, Matthews 1979).

In conducting research on depression in older adults, researchers generally have relied on measures used with younger adults, a strategy which assumes a degree of homogeneity in depressive experiences independent of age. In contradiction to this view, Mohide and Streiner (1993) have suggested that some of the symptoms included on depression measures may assess experiences which are more specific to younger age groups, as well as ones confounded with aspects of a person's everyday living situation. For instance, rather than being symptoms of depression or related to the aging process, changes in sleep and appetite patterns may reflect changes in daily routines associated with caring for a sick or infirm family member. Although attempts to distinguish between features of depression in older and younger age groups are at a relatively early stage, it has been suggested that a subset of depressive symptoms, termed "depletion syndrome", may be more characteristic of older people (Culbertson 1997). Indicators of this age-specific form of depression are said to include loss of interest in everyday activities, social withdrawal, and thoughts of death and dying (Cappeliez 1993).

Despite the lack of research on depression in older age groups, a familiar pattern is evident in the available work – either gender is ignored altogether or discussion tends to focus on older men. For instance, the topic of depression in older adults recently seems to have attracted research attention in part because of an increase in rates of suicide among elderly men in the US (Schneider 1996). To consider old age without regard to gender, however, means ignoring the fact that women represent the majority of elderly persons as well as a significant percentage of those with incomes falling below the "poverty level" (Brotman 1998, Gee and Kimball 1987). Despite important differences in the social circumstances of the lives of older women and men, relatively little attention has been given to non-biological explanations for depression in older age groups. Within mainstream accounts of depression in the later years of life, the dominant paradigm remains that of biological psychiatry. Depression is explained as a concomitant of age-related deterioration in neurotransmitters and proposed interventions emphasize use of drugs and ECT (electroconvulsive therapy) (Katona 1994, Kennedy 1996).

When the topic of depression in older women has been addressed by researchers, another kind of homogeneity is apparent. Older women have tended to be considered as a group whose experiences are essentially similar and determined largely by advancing age. Diversity among women is either ignored or attributed to aging itself. The relative neglect of influences which are extrinsic to bodily processes no doubt is fostered by the biomedicalization of aging in women. One effect of this biomedicalization is that the aging post-menopausal body has become imbued with a form of "normal pathology" to which all manner of female characteristics and ills have been attributed (Hunt 1994, Lock 1998). In her analysis of psychological accounts of women and aging, Gergen (1990: 478) identified the main theme implicit in much of the work in this field as being that "a woman is her body". When the female body is conceptualized according to male-defined standards of physical attractiveness and reproductive potential, it is hardly surprising that many women approach their own aging with some trepidation. Such foreboding is underwritten by the cultural equation of old with "awful" (Healey 1986: 59) and the figure of the "old woman" as signifying someone who is less than a person, almost a nonperson. Writing about the situation of older women in the US, Healey has described the stereotype of the older woman in overwhelmingly negative terms:

> Think of all the adjectives that are most disrespectful in our society. They are all part of the ageist stereotyping of old women: pathetic, powerless, querulous, complaining, sick, weak, conservative, rigid, helpless, unproductive, wrinkled, asexual, ugly, unattractive, and on, ad nauseam.
>
> (Healey ibid.)

The attribute "wise" is the sole positive characteristic associated with old women, but such "wisdom" is easily discounted as an "old wives tale" or "gossip" when the source is an old woman (Healey 1986, Matthews 1979).

Regardless of diversity among women, as they age, all women face the homogenizing influences of ageist and sexist discourses. When being old is stigmatized, being both old *and* a woman is likely to leave its mark on a woman's subjectivity (Gibson 1996, Healey 1986). Signs of aging are readily visible, so however a woman may view herself (as "young at heart") she is likely to confront on a daily basis evidence of her diminished social status in the eyes and reactions of others. Older men may partially escape the marginalization and sense of "social obsolescence" accompanying aging through their continued involvement in the public sphere (e.g. by holding a powerful public office) (Ginn and Arber 1995, Matthews 1979). Few strategies are available to older women, however, for protecting their identities from the stigmatizing consequences of ageist discourses. The impact of ageist and sexist discourses in the lives of older women and the contribution of such discourses to depressive experiences in this age group have not been considered in mainstream research on depression.

Rather than contesting ageist and sexist discourses, older women are more likely to be depicted in terms which more befit their social status as "reproductive has-beens" who are "over the hill". In this case, proper womanly attributes for older women include maintaining an appropriately "feminine" appearance, one in which signs of aging are hidden, but at the same time "acting their age", which involves passively fading into the background of younger people's lives. Thus, the ideal older woman seems to be one who makes few demands on others, is independent, and expects little from the world around her (Day 1991, Healey 1986).

As I hope this brief exploration of mainstream research on depression in older women indicates, the information currently available does not reflect women's lived experiences as midlife or old women. In the next section I consider aging and depression from the perspective of older women's experiences. What does it mean to be a woman during midlife and old age? How do older women account for their depressive experiences? How do the material conditions of older women's lives shape their experiences and how are such experiences interpreted in the context of prevailing cultural discourses on women and aging?

Women's experiences at midlife

In this section, I draw on recent qualitative studies which have focused on women's experiences in relation to menopause and midlife. I begin by discussing depressive experiences in the context of menopause, because bodily changes, particularly hormonal, have been constructed in both biomedical and lay accounts as an explanation for depression in women. Following this, I discuss women's menopausal experiences, identifying discourses drawn on by women in constructing their accounts. Based on this discussion, I suggest that understanding women's menopausal experiences is best accomplished from a perspective which can encompass both the material and discursive conditions shaping women's embodied sense of self at midlife.

Depressive experiences and menopause

Debates around whether menopause is a cause of depression in midlife women parallel those discussed in Chapter 6 concerning the existence of a psychiatric syndrome, popularly known as PMS, attributed to fluctuations in hormonal levels related to women's menstrual cycles. In the case of PMS, depressive experiences are explained by the *presence* of hormones. It is indeed ironic, as Hunter and O'Dea (1997: 217) point out, that when women reach midlife, their depressions are then explained in terms of *absence* of hormones. Nonetheless, as I suggested earlier when discussing medicalization (see Chapter 6), exposing the "Catch-22" nature of discourses constructing women's bodies as problematic provides little comfort to those women who experience considerable distress in relation to menopause. Deconstructing women's attributions of depressed feelings to menopause as examples of medicalized accounts not only invalidates women's experiences, but also may undermine women's efforts to get help for their distress (Daly 1995, Kaufert 1994). Older women who receive standard medical-psychiatric treatment for depression do attribute their depressive experiences to menopause (Gammell and Stoppard 1999), but if the goal is alleviation of women's distress, to suggest that these women's understanding of their experiences is misguided hardly seems therapeutic.

In her study of midlife and menopausal experiences among Australian women, Daly (1995) identified a subgroup of women who complained of problems they attributed to depression. Most commonly, these women described their depressive experiences as an extension of "premenstrual stress". Daly gives the following account as typical of these women's experiences:

> For two weeks I would be all right and the next two weeks leading into the period, I was getting suicidal. . . . I was really thinking of sitting in the garage and putting a hose in the car. . . . I suppose the past few months has been when I wanted to suicide, because the depression would get longer, not just a few hours to a few days, they're longer, into a month.
>
> (Daly ibid.: 120)

As Daly and others (e.g. Gannon 1993) have pointed out, when health professionals attribute depressive experiences to menopause, women's distress tends to be dismissed as "just menopausal". In this case, treatment may focus on menopause itself rather than depression and a woman is likely to be left without the help she needs. While medicalized discourses linking depression with menopause may offer women a route for accessing treatment services, these same discourses also can operate as barriers to treatment. For instance, one of the women who was interviewed in Daly's study identified depression as her main problem, but instead

169

her treatment focused on menopause.

> She [doctor] put me on HRT but I didn't think it was doing me any good
> and I've been on it for a few years. I went back to tell her about my
> symptoms, you know, that they were getting worse . . . She just sort of
> fobbed me off and just sort of got huffy with me. So I didn't go back . . .
> I've been getting worse and worse . . . I just don't know what to do any
> more. I don't know where to turn.
>
> (Daly ibid.: 121)

Another woman experienced depression in relation to severe "hot flushes" which
seriously disrupted her life, but these concerns were dismissed by her doctor.

> [Y]ou have to get past the doctor who thinks you are neurotic when you
> ask for help or tell them anything. You are labelled as neurotic and you
> don't need anything. "Get out and get some more social life. Take your
> mind off yourself, dear!"
>
> (Daly ibid.: 122)

Although HRT may be useful in overcoming some of the physical problems which
women experience in relation to menopause, as Daly points out such treatment
may exacerbate other problems, not least because one of the "side-effects" of
HRT is depression.

When treatment does focus on a woman's depressive experiences, additional
benefits may be derived if the source of such experiences is attributed to
menopause rather than some other source. Believing that their depressive experiences have a physical cause (i.e. menopause) may be preferable to some women,
because it avoids the implication that their problems are "neurotic" and so due to
a mental illness or that they are somehow to blame (Kaufert *et al.* 1992). As well,
explaining depressive experiences as menopausal, and therefore as having a physical cause, may be convenient for both a woman and her doctor. Focusing on
bodily causes of depression directs attention away from the social conditions of a
woman's life, which can then be constructed as unproblematic. For instance, in our
recent study with Canadian women (Gammell and Stoppard 1999), one older
woman, who was a full-time homemaker, attributed her depression to physical
causes, including menopause. When asked for her thoughts on what caused her
depression, she said:

> [I]f I had something that brought it [depression] on or something to keep it
> here . . . but like I said there's nothing. I have a really good life with my
> family. And I have my car to drive and no problems. If I want to go shopping
> and buy something I can go shopping . . . so it's, there's nothing, not a thing.
>
> (Gammell and Stoppard: 122)

When the women interviewed in our study made changes in their lives to reduce "stress", typically they curtailed involvement in activities outside the home, which had the effect of re-instating them more firmly in lives oriented around family responsibilities.

In her recent analysis of discourses on aging and the female body, Lock observes that

> [t]heories about a close relationship between menopause and madness, melancholia and depression, all fashionable over the course of the century, have been consigned to the waste basket. In creating a [menopausal] deficiency disease it proved helpful to strip it of the messiness of psychiatric disorder or negative emotions.
>
> (Lock 1998: 43–44)

The views Lock identifies presumably reflect the failure of attempts to establish an empirical link between menopausal status and depressive experiences in women. Nevertheless, one cannot help wondering whether the recent severing of theoretical links between menopause and depression is motivated in part by an interest in capturing within the net of this newly created "deficiency disease" (and its treatment with HRT) all women of menopausal age, rather than only those who experience depression. One consequence of an increased emphasis on biological accounts of women's aging, as Lock (ibid.: 44) points out, is "that emotional issues that may arise for some women are in danger of being ignored". Moreover, when biological discourses around menopause dominate both lay and professional accounts of women's experiences, not only are the physical aspects of problems experienced by women likely to be overlooked, but the discursive conditions of women's lives also remain unexamined.

Women's experiences of menopause

In western societies, women commonly report a fairly characteristic set of bodily changes in conjunction with the "menopausal transition", the chief marker of which is cessation of menstrual bleeding. A long list of symptoms has been associated with menopause, including heavy or irregular menstrual periods, hot flushes (or flashes), night sweats, weight gain, memory problems, dizziness, and assorted aches and pains, among others. The occurrence, frequency and intensity of such symptoms vary widely among women, as does the degree of discomfort experienced by individual women (McKinlay et al. 1992).

Whether a woman experiences her "menopausal symptoms" as bothersome or upsetting seems to depend on both their severity and the extent to which they disrupt her everyday life. For instance, hot flushes (or flashes, the term used in North America) as the name suggests, typically are experienced as increased feelings of warmth, sweating and flushing (usually, but not always, facial). A woman's reaction to such experiences is likely to depend on the social context within which they occur. The bodily changes accompanying hot flushes, especially if observed by others, may be interpreted as signs of anger, embarrassment, or illness.

> There is no hiding when you have a hot flash. If you are in a very serious conversation with a mixed group and you turn beet red, people tend to stop and say, "Are you alright?" I found that very distracting.
>
> (Dickson 1991: 119)

> The first time I got it I felt everyone was looking at me; I used to go bright red and feel embarrassed. It only lasted a few minutes but does happen sometimes when I'm talking to people now. I feel uncomfortable. All the blood rushes to my face.
>
> (Hunter and O'Dea 1997: 206)

As these two excerpts illustrate, hot flushes are not experienced in a social vacuum. A woman's reactions depend on shared social meanings of these experiences, as well as others' responses. No longer confined to the relative privacy of the home, women's menopausal experiences have entered the public domain of the workplace, with its expectations of emotional control and rationality. Experiences, such as hot flushes, seem to create additional discomfort for women, because they cannot readily control or hide these bodily reactions.

The main conclusion to emerge from studies of women's menopausal experiences is that the character of these experiences varies widely, both across and within individual women, and with time and place (Avis *et al.* 1993). Nevertheless, women evaluate their own experiences in relation to a stereotypical "menopausal woman", an image largely informed by a biomedicalized discourse of menopause as an "oestrogen deficiency disease". In disclosing her own experiences of menopause, for example, Cole, an American woman, begins with a description of her "hot flashes".

> I have no idea, of course, how my hot flashes compare physiologically to those of other women, but I can tell you that I do not mind them. I can even say, although I hesitate for fear of sounding ridiculous, that hot flashes are fun.
>
> (Cole 1994: 313)

She goes on to say:

> I have yet to experience vaginal dryness or a reduced interest in sex. Nor am I aware of depression or unusual mood swings. . . . So that is my experience with the "big six" symptoms of perimenopause: irregular periods, hot flashes, sleeplessness, vaginal dryness, changes in sexual desire.
>
> (Cole ibid.: 314)

Cole's account gives the sense that she is expecting to experience various "symptoms" of menopause, and although these have so far failed to make an appearance, they may still do so in the future.

Feelings of uncertainty about what menopause entails also are apparent in the accounts of British women reported by Hunter and O'Dea (1997). Most commonly, the women described their experience of menopause as a "nonevent", a "natural developmental stage" having little impact on their sense of self. Although many of these women viewed menopause as relatively inconsequential (something which "happens to the body, not the self" [p. 209]), their accounts also reflected the influence of a medicalized discourse. This theme was identified in Hunter and O'Dea's analysis as "staving off the unknown" (p. 214), an aspect of which was the women's avoidance of the word "menopause" in their accounts (referring instead to "it" or "this"). A similar tendency among older women to refer to their bodies as "it" also was noticed by Lee and Sasser-Coen (1996: 165) in their interviews with American women. In talking about their bodies as something separate from their subjective experiences and identity, these women's accounts reflect the body–mind form of dualism which underpins biomedical depictions of menopause, as well as more popularized renditions (Lee and Sasser-Coen 1996, Rothfield 1997).

Hunter and O'Dea (1997) suggest that women tend to talk about their experiences of menopause using somewhat vague, nonspecific terms in order to avoid positioning themselves as "menopausal", an identity status which nevertheless is alluded to in their accounts as something negative. As a way of distancing themselves from the devalued identity of menopausal woman, women tended to emphasize the unproblematic character of menopause. For these women, menopause was viewed as a natural process which could (and should?) be managed by having an appropriate attitude and approach to life.

> You have to occupy your mind. So I think for some women who have nothing to do it must be really terrible for them. They must sit down and think about it and become depressed.

> Not to let it get to you basically. I mean it's something that you can't particularly stop. It's something that you're going to have to deal with and accept presumably and accept it gracefully.

> (Hunter and O'Dea: 215)

Like Cole (1994), these British women seem to construct menopause as largely unproblematic, at least in their own case, although it might present problems for some other women.

In popularized accounts of menopause, the importance of following a healthy diet and exercising regularly are lifestyle strategies often suggested to women as ways of weathering the menopausal transition and for staving off its negative consequences. What are the negative consequences that women are concerned to stave off? Women's accounts point to physical appearance issues as integral to women's perceptions of menopause. For instance, as one of the American women interviewed by Jones said:

> I do notice the definite middle-age spread and sagging. It drives me crazy to see that my legs are going. I mean the broken little veins and the sagginess and the cellulite and all those ugly little things . . . I find myself covering up more . . . and not wanting to be visible.
>
> (Jones 1994: 53)

Also based on a study with women in the US, Lee and Sasser-Coen present the following excerpt from an older woman's account:

> It was like something taken away from you, that maybe men wouldn't think of you as a whole person. Your facial features are changing . . . getting wrinkles, and not being young again . . . I try to take care of my complexion, and my hair and my weight. I don't want to be big and fat.
>
> (Lee and Sasser-Coen 1996: 162)

The ending of a woman's menstrual life also is a key signifier in constructing post-menopausal women as lacking a social function. Rather than feelings of loss or sadness in relation to this aspect of menopause, however, women's own accounts typically are characterized by themes of relief that menstrual periods are over and risk of pregnancy is no longer a concern (Daly 1995, Hunter and O'Dea 1997, Lee and Sasser-Coen, 1996).

In these analyses of women's menopausal experiences, one theme which seems to stand out is the emphasis on hiding from others any evidence of bodily processes signifying a woman's reproductive status and by implication her age. "Passing" socially as younger than her chronological or physiological age may allow a woman to retain a degree of "youth privilege" (Copper 1986: 51) and with it some of the benefits associated with being perceived as young. Although a woman may successfully present herself as "young", she still faces the task of making sense of her embodied experiences as she ages. Culturally, two main discursive alternatives seem to be available to women. On the one hand, a woman can interpret her experiences in terms of a biomedical discourse of decline and pathology, and on the other, she can draw on a discourse in which menopause is constructed as a normal, natural and largely unproblematic phase of life (Daly 1997, Hunter and O'Dea 1997). For women whose menopausal transition does not fit comfortably with either of these alternatives, their bodily changes are likely to seem confusing, unpredictable and mysterious.

As Hunter and O'Dea (1997) suggest, one source of the difficulties women encounter in making sense of their embodied experiences during menopause is the absence of emancipatory discourses available to women. In a similar vein, Martin (1997) argues that pathological interpretations of menopausal bodies are reinforced more generally by the cultural metaphors underpinning medical conceptions of women's bodies. The images currently dominant within medical conceptions of the menopausal body are those of a failed (re)production system or a faulty information processing network. Martin proposes that such images be replaced by ones derived from "chaos" or "complexity theory", thereby encouraging a view of the female body as a flexible, adaptive, and responsive system. A metaphoric shift of this kind, she suggests, could foster more positive self-images for women undergoing menopause. The prevailing discourses on menopause do not offer very promising conditions for women's construction of positive midlife identities. Nevertheless, recent studies of women's midlife experiences suggest that women are resourceful in fashioning more hopeful, celebratory and empowering midlife narratives (Healey 1986, Jones 1994, McQuaide 1998a), enabling them to resist negative and limiting cultural images. At the same time, the possibilities for such inventions are hampered by the restrictive nature of the material conditions (social and economic) governing the circumstances of many women's lives as they age (Copper 1986, McQuaide 1998b).

Being an old woman: possibilities for aging (dis)gracefully[1]

If becoming "a woman who no longer bleeds" (Lee and Sasser-Coen 1996: 166) signifies the beginning of old age with its intimations of mortality, how do women who already are old, and nearing the end of life, understand their experiences? To what extent is depression part of these experiences? In this section, I first consider women's depressive experiences in old age and then discuss the lived experiences of old women.

Women's depressive experiences in old age

Although old age is predominantly a female experience, little attention has been given to gender in studies of depression in older age groups. When gender has been considered, usually it is conceptualized as individual gender and research focuses on the issue of sex differences in rates of depression. Interest in gender-related influences has been limited to exploration of links between depression and the stressful life events and conditions older women experience, an association presumed to originate in the greater longevity of women. Because old women are more likely to live alone, often in circumstances of relative poverty, researchers have tended to assume an increase in vulnerability to depression with advancing age. This view of the lives of old women is exemplified in the following excerpt from a frequently cited overview of research findings on depression in women.

Because women are over represented in the aging population, this problem [depression] is of special concern . . . Depression in older women may be related to factors different from those seen for younger women, for example, increasing poverty, isolation as adult children move away and friends and family die, changes in biochemistry as aging occurs, role changes with retirement, and moving to new locations. Two major causes for depression in older women are the loss of physical health (more than 80% of people over 65 have at least one chronic illness) and the loss of a spouse.

(McGrath *et al.* 1990: 84–5)

In such accounts, emphasis typically is placed on what is absent from the lives of older women and in an almost taken for granted way it is then assumed that depression also is likely to be a feature of older women's lives. In her analysis of research on aging in women, Gibson (1996) argues that potential sources of advantage in women's lives are commonly misconstrued as weakness or disadvantage. For instance, women's greater longevity compared to that of men is often identified as a factor underlying the social and economic disadvantages faced by many women as they age. In such accounts, women's longer life span is perceived as a problem, a proposed solution to which is improvement of men's health in later life. So, even in old age, women's lives are compared against a standard defined by male lives – and found wanting – in this case, because women live too long!

The assumption that problems encountered by old women arise from absence of a male partner is virtually unquestioned in much of the literature on women's aging, an assumption rarely evaluated against the actual experiences of women during widowhood or old age more generally. When the experiences of widows have been explored, the picture which emerges frequently contradicts the negatively-toned depictions in the mainstream literature. For instance, based on her Canadian study with widows, van den Hoonaard (1996) points to gains as well as areas of strength in the lives of the women she interviewed.

As they assimilate into their new single state, most of these women master the chores and tasks they previously left to their husbands, increasing their levels and feelings of competence. They also learn new rules for interacting as single women. It is their creativity and resilience that most impressed me.

(van den Hoonaard 1996: 295)

Negative images of older women's lives also are challenged by the findings of Day's (1991) study on "successful aging" among American women. For a small minority of the women in her study, Day (p. 296) found that "aging has meant sliding into oppressive conditions from which there seems no escape and very little chance of relief". Markers of the "oppressive conditions" identified by Day (p. 252) included "depression, dependency, deterioration of functional capacity, and loss of autonomy". She goes on to point out that "these markers are not particularly associated with age, but it may be harder for people in later life to withstand their devastating effects in combination."

The oppressive conditions identified by Day are not confined to the lives of women who are widows or who never married. Day describes one of the married woman in her study, selected as a case study to illustrate "unsuccessful aging", in the following way:

> She is deeply unhappy, incapacitated by numerous physical complaints, alienated socially, and abjures [rejects] the person she lives with, her husband, as a main bulwark [source] of day-to-day companionship and practical help.
>
> (Day 1991: 246)

Although widows may no longer have their husbands as a source of support, availability of children may offer some compensation. Having a family often is justified in terms of support for parents in old age, but evidence from several sources suggests that children may contribute to, rather than detract from, "oppressive conditions" in old women's lives. Children's concerns for a elderly parent may be expressed as overprotection and by attempts to limit an older woman's autonomy. Based on her British study with adults in advanced old age, Wilson identified the family as an important constraint on an elderly person's freedom.

> Children were recorded as disapproving of new relationships or constantly requesting parents not to take the risks involved in travelling to visit friends or going on holiday. Women were requested not to do their own housework or not to become vegetarian. Children were reported as being generally controlling and anti-change.
>
> (Wilson 1995: 111)

Contrary to the notion of children as providers of a home for parents in their later years, among the older American women in Day's (1991) study, living with a child was the option "of last resort". Children may contribute to the oppressive conditions of an old person's life by behaving in hurtful or even abusive ways. The woman mentioned earlier who was identified by Day as an example of "unsuccessful aging" described the following incident after her husband (of a second marriage) had been hospitalized for a serious illness.

> He's [husband] got four children, but they won't do anything for him . . . And what they were doing was planning on contesting his will – and what they wanted and what they didn't want – and what belonged to them and what didn't. That's when I started to get upset. His son came and he wanted to go through the trailer [home] and see what he could get.
>
> (Day 1991: 4)

Changes do occur in women's lives as they age which may be perceived and experienced as losses. Whether such losses are an inevitable accompaniment of aging, and whether they result in depression, is likely to depend as much on the larger social context as it does on the perspective from which changes are interpreted. Day makes the point that the oppressive conditions she identifies are better under-stood as social problems rather than as being "an indelible characteristic of old age." She concludes that misinformation and "[f]ears about old age have con-tributed to making the situation of older women invisible, and to discounting the genuine dilemmas they face" (p. 296). There is little doubt, as Gibson (1996: 442) acknowledges, that "old women really do have a number of problems." Consistent with Day's conclusion, Gibson also argues that what passes as knowledge about the lives of old women often reflects inaccurate and misleading stereotypes, con-structed from a vantage point which takes little account of the actual experiences of old women.

Women's experiences in old age

A rather different perspective on old age emerges when the starting point is old women's experiences. From this standpoint, aspects of old women's lives which are either invisible or treated as disadvantages are revealed as assets and sources of strength. For instance, rather than widowhood being a time with few positive con-sequences for women, women report appreciating the freedom to organize daily life in line with their own tastes rather than in accord with spousal preferences (Day 1991, Furman 1997, Wilson 1995). Although women's involvement in caring work has been characterized as a burdensome and stressful responsibility, mentioned less often (or invisible) is that such caregiving also is predicated on the existence of well-developed social networks. Overlooked in mainstream accounts of women's lives are the resources inherent in women's capacity to develop and sustain connections with others, assets which women continue to draw on in old age (Day 1991, Furman 1997, Matthews 1979).

Thus, contrary to depictions of old age as a time of social isolation, women's accounts reflect their continued involvement in relational activities, especially ongoing friendships with other women (Furman 1997). During old age, many women continue to be involved in extensive social networks and even to develop new contacts. Equating living alone with social isolation is to misinterpret old women's experiences and to overlook the relational context within which the lives of many old women are embedded (Day 1991, Gibson 1996). Furman's (1997) ethnographic study of one "informal community" which developed around a "beauty shop" in the US midwest provides a particularly rich example of how a group of elderly women maintained their social connections with other women during their weekly visits to the hairdresser.

The lives of older women also reflect continuity in their involvement in activi-ties of daily living and their ability to look after themselves. As Day (1991: 55) points out, "although housework is still not defined as 'productive activity,' the capacity of older women to 'do for themselves' greatly reduces the costs to [American] taxpayers of providing subsidized home maintenance services." Old women's ability to live independently also is evidenced by relatively low rates of institutionalization compared to their rates of widowhood (Gibson 1996). Thus, absence of a male partner does not weaken (and may even enhance) women's capacity to take care of themselves in old age. Women's experiences outside the formal economy of the public sphere also are important in sustaining independent living, with bartering and exchange strategies used to meet their needs for assistance. One of the old women identified by Day (1991: 10) as aging successfully, described her use of such strategies: "When I go and pick strawberries, maybe, I pick four quarts – one quart for the lady that picks me up for church. I think of her."

One strategy which widows seem universally to reject as an option in later years is that of remarriage. Although lack of available marriage partners for older women is often cited as a disadvantage, limiting women's chances of remarriage, widows typically evince little interest in becoming somebody's wife again (Day 1991, Furman 1997, van den Hoonaard 1996). In her British study, for instance, Wilson (1995: 110) found that older women preferred to remain unmarried, having friendships with men in which they exchanged services (e.g. cooking and gardening), and taking trips together, while retaining control of their own lives.

In sum, there is abundant evidence that many old women cope well in old age, living lives characterized by resourcefulness and resilience and a level of well-being which outside observers might judge to be mismatched with their material conditions (Gibson 1996). Nevertheless, it would be a mistake to overemphasize positive interpretations of old women's lives without also considering conditions undermining women's ability to enjoy their later years. These conditions, both material and discursive, can be conceptualized as aspects of ageism (Copper 1986, Healey 1986) or what Day (1991: 157) calls "'the bads' of aging".

> Aging is a real process, which takes place differently in each individual. Ageism, on the other hand, is a constriction that rearranges power relationships, just like any other kind of discrimination or prejudice. When one ages, one may gain or lose. With ageism, one is shaped into something that is *always* less than what one really is.
>
> (Copper 1986: 54, emphasis in original)

> It is not aging that is awful, nor whatever physical problems may accompany aging. What is awful is how society treats old women and their problems. To the degree that we accept and allow such treatment we buy the ageist assumptions that permit this treatment.
>
> (Healey 1986: 62)

Being old, as Matthews (1979: 61) has pointed out, "spoils" identity, because "[o]ld people are possessors of a stigma that is in a middle ground between discrediting and discreditable". To become an old woman is to age in a cultural context in which being younger is constructed as better than, and preferable to, being older.

179

As women age, increasingly they confront concrete manifestations of their devalued status in the reactions of others and in their reflections in the mirror. The effort
to maintain a positive sense of self is continually eroded by reactions which "at best
involve patronizing acknowledgement" and at worst, treat an old woman as though
she no longer exists:

> I attended a WAND (Women's Action for Nuclear Disarmament) meet-
> ing at which a young MD spoke about his research. . . . His talk was
> stimulating, and after the meeting I went up to him to comment on his
> research. I had the most peculiar feeling of being looked through, as
> though, what could I, this gray-haired woman in very casual dress, know
> about research design. I felt patronized, a feeling I wasn't used to.
>
> (Healey 1986: 58)

Older women can attempt to offset their social powerlessness in various ways, for
instance by dissociating themselves from stereotypical images of old women by
attempting to pass as younger than their age. Women with the financial means can
employ a variety of beauty practises to avoid appearing "too old". One 72 year-old
woman, a participant in Furman's study of a beauty shop community, explained
why she continued to color her hair:

> You've got to do it or you'll look like "yik." I don't want to take the
> chance, I'm afraid. You know, I have enough problems, and I look bad as
> it is. . . . Without makeup I look like death warmed over.
>
> (Furman 1997: 111)

Women also attempt to undercut the negative impact on their identity of discrediting stereotypes by distancing themselves as atypical exceptions to an otherwise
general pattern (e.g. more active, more independent, and less conservative than
other older women). Maintaining an identity position as exceptional may lead
however to increased social isolation, if a woman avoids situations in which she
might encounter disconfirming evidence. A different strategy for retaining personal
power capitalizes on the old stereotype by playing on others' assumptions about
age-related incapacity. Examples of this strategy are pretending deafness as a way
of ignoring others' requests and exaggerating physical limitations to get one's own
way. Miller (1997) has described such strategies as those of the "underdog", a
form of "power from the underside" available to those "who speak from a position
of structural inequality". Some older women have exploited underdog strategies
with more explicitly feminist and political goals, for instance by self-identifying as
old (rather than older) and using music and humor. For instance, the Canadian
"Raging Grannies" groups provide musical entertainment, singing about social jus-
tice issues, and in the process re-valorize the demeaned figure of the old woman.

If the problems faced by women as they age are to be addressed in ways
enabling "successful aging" to be a prospect for all women, clearly something

quite different is needed than the current preoccupation with biomedical techniques and technologies around the female body. Understanding depression in midlife and older women means recognizing how inequitable conditions in the social environment which deprive women of needed material supports combine with oppressive discursive conditions constructing old as useless, pitiful and ugly to produce a context in which feelings of self-hatred, hopelessness, and despair are likely to be engendered.

Note

1 Inspiration for the wording of this subheading came from reading the anthology *Women and Aging* (Alexander *et al.* 1986).

PART IV

IMPLICATIONS FOR THEORY AND PRACTISE
Feminist social
constructionist approaches

10

WOMEN OVERCOMING DEPRESSION

Coping, treatment and politics

The focus of this chapter is women overcoming depression. The wording I eventually chose for the title of the chapter is intended to reflect the range of strategies which might be drawn upon by women to address the "problem of depression" in their lives. A discussion of strategies available to women for dealing with their depressive experiences might imply that I attempt to answer the question "What is the best treatment for depression?" Framing the discussion in this way, however, takes for granted the assumption that depression is something experienced by an individual and a problem that needs to be rectified. Such an assumption would shift attention to individual women who "have depression", and ways to remedy this problem. It follows that the goal of this process would be to alleviate or cure "depression" – to return women to the presumed normality of a nondepressed state, or at least to help them "feel better". Since it is assumed that individuals cannot do this by themselves, "treatment" must be something done by those with special training – experts who have knowledge and skills unavailable to ordinary people. If depression is defined as a health problem, then treatment is presumed to fall within the domain of medicine and the expertise most likely to be sought is that dispensed by medical doctors.

In this chapter, I outline a range of responses to the problem of depression in women's lives, responses which may include interventions at the individual level. A focus on interventions with individual women is too restrictive, however, because from the outset it precludes other possibilities from consideration. For instance, one option is for a woman to do nothing. By "nothing" I mean that a woman may decide not to seek help from an expert. The reluctance of people to seek treatment for depression is a concern which often has been highlighted in the professional literature, because of evidence that many individuals who might be diagnosed as depressed by a professional do not seek outside help (Regier et al. 1993). In recent years, professional and health service organizations in various countries have responded to this concern by mounting public education campaigns with the goal of encouraging more people to seek treatment for depression. One might wonder, however, about the intentions which lie behind such efforts, when it is realized that a major source of funding (at least within North America) is the pharmaceutical companies manufacturing antidepressant drugs.[1]

185

If a woman chooses not to seek professional help, this does not mean she is doing nothing at all, as avoidance of outside help may reflect a reasonable decision, given her circumstances. Accordingly, in the first part of the chapter, I explore how women cope with depression without professional help. Even if a woman decides to seek professional help, this does not necessarily imply that she becomes a passive patient who acquiesces to her therapist's injunctions. Women can play an active role in determining both the form and content of their treatment. Thus, the notion of "coping" itself also needs to be examined from the perspective of women. These and other issues are explored in the first part of the chapter. Following this, I discuss the experiences of women who do seek professional help. Treatment, including therapy, by a professionally-trained expert is the focus of the second part of the chapter. Medication is one form of treatment with which women are likely to be familiar. It involves taking pills, usually some type of "antidepressant" drug, such as Prozac or Elavil (the trade names of two antidepressants). Before embarking on this type of treatment, a woman has first to be seen by a medically-trained professional, normally a family physician or a psychiatrist, who determines her diagnosis. If the doctor decides medication would be the appropriate treatment, a prescription is written for the selected drug.

There are ongoing debates among experts about use of prescription drugs in the treatment of problems such as depression (Breggin 1991, Hamilton and Jensvold 1995, Wade and Wade 1995). Concerns raised include the potential for over-prescription of drugs and the medicalization which occurs when women's experiences are attributed to biological causes. Also, when drugs are prescribed, non-biological influences are less likely to be explored or to be viewed as an inevitable part of women's lives. Nevertheless, many women do choose to use antidepressants and some find them helpful. Although drugs are now fairly routinely prescribed to women, little attention may be given to the effects of antidepressants on the female body. Issues involved when antidepressant drugs are used to treat depression in women are discussed later in the chapter.

Prescription of medication does not occur in a psychological or social vacuum and drugs may have various "side-effects" in addition to those attributable to their biochemical action. One side-effect has to do with the length of time required for drugs to have any influence on a woman's mood. A woman, those around her, and/or her doctor may consider her depressive experiences to be severe enough that an intervention with more rapid effects is desired. Under these conditions, a physician might recommend ECT (electroconvulsive therapy), a form of treatment involving the passing of an electric current through the brain in order to trigger a convulsive seizure.[2] Although use of ECT has been criticized by those who work in mental health fields (Johnstone 1993, Ussher 1991), for some women this treatment may represent a "lifeline", offering them the possibility of relief from feelings of distress which have become unbearable (Perkins 1994).

Another side-effect of drug treatment is that a woman may decide she wants more, or a different form of, help than is provided by taking a pill. This need may be articulated by a woman in terms of "wanting to talk to someone" about her problems. In this case, she may arrange to see a therapist or counsellor who offers some kind of therapy. Although various types of therapy have been developed for use with people suffering from depression, currently cognitive therapy is most often recommended (Hughes 1997, McGrath *et al.* 1990). Regardless of their starting assumptions, the goal of most forms of therapy is to change some aspect of a woman's psychological functioning or behavior. For instance, therapy may focus on a woman's thought patterns and beliefs (cognitions), her underlying personality, or her interpersonal skills. A further difference between types of therapy concerns how a therapist understands a woman's problems. Some therapists practicing from a feminist perspective base their therapy approach (whether cognitive or some other type) on a feminist analysis of women's problems. In feminist approaches to therapy, typically a therapist attempts to establish a relationship with a woman client which is equal and collaborative. Thus, rather than the therapist assuming a leadership role, a woman client is invited to be a co-therapist as the person who is most knowledgeable about her own experiences. This relational strategy is adopted by feminist therapists with the goal of fostering the "empowerment" of women clients (Worell and Remer 1992). Within therapy, empowerment involves helping a woman to take greater control within her own life, through identifying choices and enhancing "self-esteem". Like other approaches to therapy, therefore, feminist therapy focuses primarily on individual women.

A rather different feminist position is one in which the target of change efforts is identified as the social system, in order to address inequitable conditions shaping women's lives (and also the presumed source of their depressive experiences). The claim in this case is that the origins of women's depressive experiences lie within the societal domain, rather than women's bodies or minds, and therefore overcoming depression in women requires collective political action. Conventional individual therapy, in this feminist view, operates as a form of perpetual "repair" work performed by therapists on individual women (Kitzinger and Perkins 1993). Therapy may help a few women feel better, but it does little to address the oppressive conditions which shape the lives of women in general.

These differing feminist positions reflect rather different interpretations of the slogan "the personal is political".[3] This phrase encapsulates the belief derived from feminist analyses that women's experiences (including their depressive experiences) are grounded in the conditions of their lives, and these conditions in turn are regulated by patriarchal beliefs and social structures. In the final part of the chapter, I suggest that strategies for overcoming depression need to draw on approaches in which consideration is given to both the material and the discursive conditions of women's lives. As Heenan (1996: 55) has pointed out, the kind of approach needed is one fostering an understanding of "the ways in which not only is 'the personal political' but also how the 'political *becomes* personal' " (emphasis in original). The conclusion I reach is that a reconciliation of these apparently disparate feminist positions on how to overcome depression in women will be achieved by developing a perspective which can encompass both the personal *and* the political.

Women coping with depression on their own

Many women never seek professional help for their depressive experiences, preferring to cope on their own. From the perspective of mental health professionals, some women's eschewal of professionally-mediated help (or "treatment") is perceived as a problem requiring solution. The assumption appears to be that without professional assistance, a woman will remain depressed or at best function less than optimally in her everyday life. Professionals also seem to believe that if women do not seek help, it is because they lack information about what is available or are misinformed about what is involved. Such views remain one-sided, however, without considering why women decide not to seek professional help and, instead, cope with depressive experiences on their own.

Few attempts have been made to explore why some women choose to cope with depressive experiences on their own. A major difficulty in pursuing this kind of inquiry is the practical problem of making contact with women who have not sought professional help. An additional deterrent to this kind of study is that whatever the findings, they are likely to be dismissed by experts, because the women involved were not diagnosed with depression by a mental health professional, in essence that the women were "not really depressed". This catch-22 dilemma is virtually insoluble within the framework of mainstream positivist research, so that such studies are unlikely to be carried out. Inquiries of this kind become quite possible, however, when research is freed from positivist methodological strictures.

How women cope on their own with depressive experiences was the focus of a recent study, with which I was involved (see Scattolon and Stoppard 1999). The women who participated in this study live in rural communities in eastern Canada. All of the women identified themselves as coping with stress, but none had sought professional help for depression.[4] Many of the women had young children at home and in most cases their main source of financial support was social assistance ("welfare"). Although basic health and mental health services are publicly-funded in Canada (and so more-or-less "free"), these women could not easily afford the costs (transportation, babysitting) involved in making use of these services. But in any case, they did not interpret their feelings of distress as signifying that professional help was needed. Typically, the women understood their depressive experiences as being a part of their lives, something to be endured and coped with. In keeping with this understanding, they explained these depressive experiences as arising out of the particular circumstances of their everyday lives, conditions which could not be changed by seeking professional help. The following excerpts are representative of these women's accounts.

> I still think that my problem would have been that I had no money, I don't even care for help. I know what my problem is. But if I went to the doctor, he probably would have said, well, you're depressed or something. And I probably would have said, yeah, and said, what's the use,

whatever, you know. I know I am depressed and I don't know how you can help there. Are you going to give me some money?

(Scattolon and Stoppard 1999: 211)

I didn't think I was depressed, I just thought it was the way of life. . . . the only reason really, I would have said I was depressed was because of my parents . . . because of the way it [abuse] went, it would go at home.

(ibid.: 213)

Other obstacles to help-seeking identified by these women were specific to life in a rural community. Contact with professional caregivers tended to be avoided because of concerns about lack of confidentiality and the stigmatization associated with the depression label. As one woman said:

I don't feel comfortable to go to the doctors here because I know their wives and ah, so we don't want to expose ourselves . . . especially some of the doctors go to our church, nobody wants to talk about it.

(ibid.: 216)

Professional help also may not be pursued by women if their initial contact with a service provider proves to be less than helpful. In a study by Schreiber (1996), which involved women who identified themselves as having recovered from depression, some had never sought professional help and others reported that their contacts with health care providers had not been particularly helpful.[5] Nevertheless, all of the women interviewed by Schreiber considered themselves to have overcome depression, even though their contact with professional caregivers had been minimal.

How do women cope with, and overcome, their depressive experiences without the help of experts? The mass media, reinforced by professional accounts, promulgate the view of depression as an illness or disorder characterized by an inevitable downward spiral of dysphoric mood and feelings of hopelessness, eventually culminating in suicidal thoughts or actions. This gloomy depiction is contradicted somewhat by women's accounts of their experiences of coping with, and recovering from, depression without professional help. For instance, a Canadian woman living in a rural community described how she overcame her depressive experiences in the following way.

I went on Income Assistance and got my act together and got a job and got you know, a life, and got on with life . . . so I was forced on Income Assistance, which was another, in my eyes at that time, was another step down to the bottom of the barrel.

(ibid.: 215)

This woman was able to overcome her depressive experiences on her own, contrary to notions of depression as something which can be alleviated only with professional treatment. Many of the women interviewed by Schreiber (1996) also recounted having had suicidal experiences at an earlier point in their recovery from depression. Coming close to suicide had served to motivate them to engage in a process which Schreiber called "(re)defining my self" (p. 488). In a similar vein, the accounts of women in the study by Scattolon and Stoppard (1999) reflected the theme of "getting on with life" as a way of overcoming their depressive experiences, a process illustrated in the following excerpt.

> But I just said, somebody's got to look after the house, somebody has got to look after the lawn, and it was me who had to do it . . . I got through that by realizing that somebody had to do stuff around here, you knew it, stuff wasn't getting done.
>
> (ibid.: 214)

What coping strategies did these women use to overcome their depressive experiences? One explanation proposed for higher rates of depression in women than men is in terms of gender-related differences in coping (McGrath *et al.* 1990). Nolen-Hoeksema (1990), whose research on coping is often cited, has suggested that women are more likely than men to respond to depressive experiences by "ruminating" on them. This "passive" coping style is contrasted (usually unfavorably) with the more active coping responses of men. Use of active coping strategies is considered "antidepressant" by theorists such as Nolen-Hoeksema, because they distract a person's attention from their depressive experiences, whereas rumination is likely to exacerbate them. Thus, higher rates of depression in women compared to men have been attributed to the tendency of women to use less effective coping strategies. Within this explanatory approach, women are characterized as "deficient copers". However, such judgments about the effectiveness of the coping strategies used by women may simply reflect the perspective of experts, rather than the actual experiences of women. For example, Banyard and Graham-Bermann (1993: 306) have pointed out that "[n]o mention is made of the fact that women seem to employ other strategies such as negotiation and forbearance more often than men".

Mainstream conceptions of effective coping strategies, like Nolen-Hoeksema's (1990) formulation, also rest on the assumption that a person has access to various resources, such as money, status, and power, sources of privilege which many women lack. If women tend to cope with depressive experiences by drawing on more contemplative (or "ruminative") strategies, one reason for this may be that more "active" alternatives are unavailable to them. For instance, a woman who is living on welfare is unlikely to have enough money to engage in activities which might take her mind off everyday difficulties, especially if she has young children to care for. Spending time outside the home, even for a few hours, whether to visit friends or to pursue leisure interests, is likely to require advance planning, as well as financial resources.

Like I say, my friend down the road, we need to just get out. Her and I just need to after the kids are in bed . . . because you get too busy and you get caught up in things . . . you're already stressed out from you know, having the daily routine . . . you know you still need that time for yourself. I used to . . . go out one night a week . . . I don't do that anymore, but . . . once a month or once every two months, I call her and say, let's go out for a coffee . . . you still need that out away from it all for like an hour.

(Scattolon and Stoppard 1999: 215)

Use of the rather demeaning label "ruminative" to describe a form of coping which involves reflecting on one's situation and searching for meaning in one's experiences would seem to devalue the more "discursive" coping strategies which women may employ (and which may be the only ones available to them). Schreiber (1996: 484), for instance, highlights the contribution of "cognitive and emotional knowing" to the process of "(re)defining my self" in women's recovery from depression. The women interviewed by Schreiber also emphasized the importance of having someone willing "to listen, to hear their experiences and to validate that their experiences were real" (p. 484). Being able to talk to other women about their experiences was also identified by Scattolon and Stoppard (1999) as a coping strategy used by women living in rural communities, as the following brief excerpts illustrate:

Thank god I had a friend two doors away . . . before she went to work, and then when she came home, she'd run over and have a cup of tea or something . . . I give her all the credit for pulling me through that because I didn't go to a doctor.

(Scattolon and Stoppard 1999: 215)

They meet once a week and the idea is mothers come . . . just to socialize with each other . . . but a number of them have said to me this has been a life saver . . . just to talk to another adult.

(ibid.: 216)

Although the circumstances of many women's lives may preclude use of more active, problem-oriented coping strategies, this does not mean that women have coping deficits. The coping strategies typically adopted by women have been characterized as "passive", "problem-avoidant" and "emotion-focused" by mainstream researchers. Labels such as these, as Banyard and Graham-Bermann (1993: 313) note, "may mask a variety of actions that are discovered only by looking out through the eyes of various groups of women". When research begins from women's standpoint, a rather different picture emerges, revealing the range of strategies drawn on by women in overcoming depressive experiences on their own without professional involvement.

Professional help for depression: treatment alternatives

Seeking help for depression depends on both the availability of services and the social context in which a woman lives. Women living in rural communities may avoid use of professional services to protect both personal privacy and their family's standing in the community. In urban settings, where services are likely to be more readily available, privacy and confidentiality concerns may recede in importance. Nevertheless, women may seek professional help only with the prompting of those around them. Based on interviews with Canadian women who had received treatment after being diagnosed with depression, we (Gammell and Stoppard 1999) found that most of the women interviewed had sought professional help only after being encouraged to do so by a friend, co-worker, or family member. For example, one young woman said:

> My mom . . . was just shocked, and I was just like you know, I have to quit school, I can't do this you know . . . then they ah suggested that I go see my medical doctor, so I went to see my medical doctor and he recommended me to a psychiatrist.
>
> (ibid.: 117)

Even if a woman did seek help from her family doctor, she rarely gave depression as the reason.

> I just thought it was more like a burn out, like I thought maybe it was just my job . . . I thought maybe it had partly to do with that, you know, thinking oh, I can't handle this anymore . . . I kind of blamed it on that initially, thinking OK, it's maybe I'm not handling my job in perspective.
>
> (ibid.: 116)

Our study involved women living in the eastern part of Canada, an area where few mental health professionals practice on a fee-for-service basis, so the first contact these women had with the health services system usually was through their family doctor, often followed by referral to a psychiatrist. Subsequently, some of the women had seen non-medical professionals for therapy or counselling. Initially, however, all had been encouraged to take antidepressant medication by either their family physician or a psychiatrist, and almost all had agreed to use these drugs.

Medically-oriented treatments: antidepressant drugs and ECT

Despite critiques of drug treatment for problems such as depression, use of antidepressant drugs is widespread among women (Ashton 1991, Hamilton and Jensvold 1995) and likely to increase as the marketing efforts of pharmaceutical companies extend into "less developed" areas of the world (Doyal 1995). In western countries, for example, the antidepressant drug Prozac is being promoted in women's fashion magazines, using advertisements with seasonal themes. Although drug treatment has been criticized as a pernicious form of "biopsychiatric attack" on women (Wade and Wade 1995), such depictions are not based on women's accounts of their use of antidepressant medications. When attention shifts to women who have used these drugs, a somewhat different story emerges. Rather than having negative feelings about drugs, some women find them helpful in alleviating their depressive experiences, as indicated in the following excerpts taken from Gammell and Stoppard's study and a study by Brandt (1998) based on interviews with American women.

> And I know I do need medication . . . we've tried three, well four different drugs now and this is the one that seems to be working, you know, the best.

> (Gammell and Stoppard 1999: 122)

> I was afraid that she [her physician] was going to say that I didn't need an antidepressant drug . . . I think I would fight tooth and nail if anybody refused to prescribe it for me.

> (ibid.: 119)

> He wanted me to try Zoloft [an antidepressant] . . . I didn't even want to think about it. In my mind, people who were on them were wacked out. But now I know better. . . . Within two weeks, I felt like I had never felt in my entire life. I was more confident . . . I just felt better about things.

> (Brandt 1998: 5–6)

> I . . . actually did not use any type of antidepressant until I was 34 . . . The reason I decided to go on something was because I found out that I had gotten herpes from my ex-husband . . . and to find out medically that I would be stricken for the rest of my life was just overwhelming. My depression was just not changing and my counselor felt that that [an antidepressant] would help me, and it does.

> (ibid.: 6)

The picture is a bit more complicated than implied by these brief excerpts, however. Women are aware that they will probably be offered a prescription for an antidepressant if they visit a doctor and this is one reason that some avoid seeking help for their depressive experiences. Others may comply with a physician's suggestion that they try an antidepressant, but then decide on their own to stop taking the drug.

> And then I got thinking about like the medication, I was just like, so what does this mean if I have to take this medication in order to be, in order to be normal? Like it just felt so weird . . . I haven't told my doctor but I'm, I have stopped taking my medication.

> (Gammell and Stoppard 1999: 119)

Other women may be worried about the long-term effects of drugs.

> And I'm not really, at this point I'm still deciding . . . I think partly it's fear
> of the drugs themselves. Like I'm not really sure what, in terms of side
> effects and in terms of sort of like and addiction . . . I guess the idea of
> needing, whatever drug to feel okay is a really, I don't know, it's kind of a
> nasty idea.
>
> (ibid.: 119)

Although the rationale physicians give to patients for taking antidepressants is usually couched in terms of "biochemical imbalances in the brain" (ibid., Karp 1993),
a woman's decision to use them may have nonpharmacological benefits. Receiving
a prescription for a drug from a physician provides a source of validation, con-
firming a woman's perception that something "really is wrong with me". Also,
being able to attribute her problems to a biochemical disturbance serves to locate
their source within her body, rather than her personality or behavior.

While the medicalization process which accompanies use of drugs may have
other drawbacks for women, it does offer certain identity resources ruled out by non-
medical treatment approaches. For example, several of the participants in Gammell
and Stoppard's study had made changes in their lives following their diagnosis with
depression. Typically, these changes involved curtailing paid work outside the home
(e.g. switching from full-time to part-time work, taking an extended leave from
employment) or educational activities (dropping courses or changing to a less
demanding academic program). The women described the purpose of these
changes as being to control or reduce stress and they justified making them in terms
of their diagnosis. In this way of accounting for their actions, the women's identity,
or sense of self, as a competent worker or capable student, was not directly challenged. The problem was stress or their illness, rather than their personal
competence (or lack of power to change their lives in other ways). These women
may have drawn connections between particular events or circumstances in their
lives and their depressive experiences, but being diagnosed with depression and prescribed an antidepressant drug by a physician provided an acceptable reason for
making quite major (although not especially empowering) changes in their everyday
lives. Medication may also represent the only form of treatment some women will
consider, because they view the alternatives (e.g. therapy or counselling) as having
little relevance in their own case, a position illustrated in the following excerpt.

> [I]f I had something that brought it [depression] on or something to
> keep it here . . . but like I said there's nothing. I have a really good life with
> my family . . . and no problems . . . so it's it's, there's nothing, not a thing.
> (Gammell and Stoppard 1999: 122)

Concerns raised about use of antidepressant medication to treat women's depressive experiences have focused mainly on medicalization issues. Less attention has

been paid to the actual pharmacological effects of antidepressants. Recent discussions of research on gender and the pharmacology of antidepressants have highlighted several findings with important implications for women's use of these drugs (Hamilton and Jensvold 1995, Weissman and Olfson 1995). First, antidepressants commonly prescribed to women have slower "clearance" rates (time to leave the body) in females than males and therefore greater "bioavailability" in women's bodies. This means that the amount of a drug required to produce an effect will typically be lower for women than men, yet prescribing patterns do not generally reflect awareness of this gender-related difference. Second, the bioavailability of antidepressants is increased when used with oral contraceptives, a combination likely to occur when women of child-bearing age receive treatment for depression. A third finding with relevance to antidepressant use by women is that the active effects of these drugs may be reduced in individuals who are exposed to "chronic stressors such as poverty and victimization" (Hamilton and Jensvold 1995: 22). As discussed earlier (see Chapter 5), poverty and victimization are conditions often characterizing the lives of depressed women.

When gender-related drug effects are ignored, the consequences include increased risk of toxicity and adverse effects ("side-effects") for women who take antidepressants. As Shapiro-Baruch (1995) noted, risks associated with women's use of drugs are further exacerbated when their complaints of side-effects are discounted and their reproductive status (menstrual cycle phase, pregnancy) is not taken into account. With reference to use of antidepressants in the US, Hamilton and Jensvold summarized the conditions which shape prescribing practises in that country in the following way.

> Despite relatively consistent findings, sex/gender-related considerations are rarely recognized as a priority in psychopharmacology research for depression; are not integrated into medical school and residency courses in psychopharmacology or psychiatry; are not integrated in to treatment guidelines; and are not yet highlighted in continuing medical education programs (an exception is the "Advanced Curriculum on Women's Health" meeting sponsored by the American Medical Women's Association).
>
> (Hamilton and Jensvold 1995: 24)

Under such conditions, as Shapiro-Baruch (1995) argues, there is a clear need for closer monitoring of the prescribing practises of professionals.

From the vantage point of the UK, Perkins (1994) has raised similar concerns about the use of ECT (electroconvulsive therapy) with women. Among medically-trained professionals, especially those who work in hospital settings, ECT is likely to be considered the treatment of choice for women who have not responded to drug treatment or who pose a "suicidal risk" (Nairne and Smith 1984). Perkins, a clinical psychologist, provides a first hand account of her treatment with ECT, something which she chose to undergo rather than endure a prolonged period of "severe depression". Her personal experience with ECT prompted her to gather information on how this treatment is administered in practise. Perkins discovered that gender-related effects also play a part in the use of ECT, a key consideration being that the level of electrical current needed to induce a seizure is generally lower in women than men. This is a crucial condition, because avoidance of the memory loss which may follow ECT requires that the minimum amount of electricity be used. However, as Perkins points out, when judged against standards endorsed by the psychiatric profession in the UK, the way ECT is administered in practise often falls short of these guidelines. As women probably form the majority of those who receive ECT, much of the risk associated with this treatment is also borne by women.[6] Perkins argues that such risks can be offset by ensuring that accurate information about ECT is available to women considering this treatment.

Women who choose to use drugs or ECT as a way to overcome their depressive experiences nonetheless may decide at some point to seek alternatives to these treatments. For instance, a woman may become discouraged when the earlier effectiveness of drug treatment is not sustained or because of the discomfort of side-effects (Karp 1993). Some women may also want to combine medication with another form of treatment. The following account, from Gammell and Stoppard's (1999) study, is fairly typical of the reasons women gave for exploring alternatives to drug treatment.

> I felt I couldn't talk to my psychiatrist. You're in five minutes and OK we'll try you on this pill. We'll try you on that pill and there was no counselling . . . so I, Dr. [psychiatrist] said I'll put you in touch with a clinical psychologist and he did, and he put me in touch with a psychologist and that was the best thing that ever happened.
>
> (Gammell and Stoppard 1999: 119)

Alternatives to drugs or ECT include a range of therapy options, but as implied in the above account, the possibilities available are likely to depend on local conditions. For instance, women who live in less-populated areas will have fewer options than those who live in urban centers. Ongoing contact with a professional (e.g. a physician) may enable some women to gain access to services which otherwise would be unavailable to them. Where health services are publicly-funded, family doctors usually act as "gatekeepers" controlling access to other service providers through referral procedures. In places where professionals practice on a fee-for-service basis, a woman's access to treatment alternatives will depend largely on her ability to pay.

Therapy as treatment for women's depressive experiences

One view of therapy is that it represents a less intrusive form of treatment for depression than the more medicalized approaches of drugs or ECT. Although therapy is less physically intrusive than these other treatment modes, it does require a commitment of time and a willingness to share confidences with another person which some women might experience as intrusions into their everyday lives. Therapy involves regular meetings with a person who has usually received some formal training in this way of providing treatment. Apart from wanting to feel better, a woman may seek therapy because it offers a source of emotional support and an opportunity to discuss personal "troubles" with another person, things lacking in her own life. The therapy approaches currently practised reflect a broad range of theoretical perspectives, so that choosing a therapist means that a woman also needs to know something about what is available.

In their overview of treatments for depression in women, McGrath *et al.* (1990: 52–4) list a wide array of therapy modalities, including behavioral, cognitive, inter-personal, psychodynamic and feminist, each of which subsumes several variants. This list by no means exhausts the possibilities. A cursory review of the clinical lit-erature reveals a variety of emerging approaches, including cognitive analytic, narrative, and constructivist, to name a few. Given this diversity, how is a choice to be made among approaches? One strategy might be to consider evidence on the effectiveness of different therapies – which "works" best? This is not an easily answered question, however, as several decades of research and innumerable stud-ies comparing different therapies attest. McGrath *et al.*'s (1990: 50) assessment that "[e]xisting outcome research does not yet answer the question of whether there is an optimal treatment for depressed women" is probably the most reason-able position to take. An answer to the question "which is the best therapy?" also is complicated by the fact that the usefulness of any therapy is likely to depend as much on who the therapist is as it does on client preference.

A broad distinction can be made among approaches to therapy in terms of whether "content" or "process" aspects are emphasized. Some therapies, such as cognitive or behavioral, focus more on content and involve use of specific tech-niques and procedures with clients. Other approaches, such as psychodynamic or humanistic, place relatively greater importance on the process of therapy, empha-sizing the client–therapist relationship. While all therapies have the overarching goal of alleviating a client's depressive experiences, specific goals vary with the par-ticular theoretical model informing the therapy approach (e.g. cognitive therapy focuses on cognitions or beliefs; psychodynamic therapy focuses on unconscious processes). Nevertheless, a feature shared by all approaches is that the individual seeking help – the client – is the focus of the therapist's efforts. Although some approaches involve more than one client (e.g. marital, family, group), therapy is pre-dominantly an individual activity. A client's personal experiences are the starting point for an endeavor circumscribed by the time and place set for meetings with a therapist.

Rather than recommending any particular type of therapy, I am in agreement with the position advocated by Ussher (1991), that choice of therapy should be the client's prerogative. I would modify this position only by adding the caveat that the range, and therefore choice, of therapy available to a woman is likely to be limited by her location and personal finances, and also by her feelings of distress. A woman's ability to choose among treatment options may be hampered by her depressive experiences and the issue of choice also needs to be considered in relation to whether a woman has information about available therapy approaches and what they entail in practise. A common perception is that medication offers a fairly rapid way of overcoming depressive experiences, while therapy may be viewed as a slower treatment mode. These perceptions also are shared by professionals, especially physicians, who are likely to consider antidepressant drugs as a first course of action for any depressed patient. Moreover, because their training is quite specialized, professionals often develop strong commitments to their own profession's particular brand of treatment, while alternatives may be judged in a less favorable light. This means that a woman who is interested in a different treatment approach than is offered by the first professional she sees will need to be fairly assertive in expressing her preferences, something which someone coping with depression may have difficulty doing. Under such conditions, it is not very clear what choice means. Presumably, the more immediate goal of a woman who seeks help in overcoming her depressive experiences is to "feel better" and she is likely to take what is on offer, especially if relief is promised sooner rather than later.

A feminist approach to therapy might be considered by some as the most appropriate choice for women coping with depression. What is meant by a feminist approach to therapy? Some have suggested that putting the words feminist and therapy together is inherently contradictory (Kitzinger and Perkins 1993, Nairne and Smith 1984), because the former is more concerned with changing the structural, material conditions of women's lives, whereas the latter focuses on changes within individual women. Nevertheless, there is now a fairly voluminous literature on feminist approaches to therapy.[7] Does feminist therapy refer to therapeutic interventions carried out by therapists who also are feminist? Alternatively, are feminist therapists "feminists who use therapeutic tools to challenge women's subordination" (Burman 1992: 488)? While some have argued that therapy can never provide a route to achievement of feminist goals (Kitzinger and Perkins 1993), others continue to engage in debate about appropriate directions (models and practises) for the development of feminist approaches to therapy (Brown 1994, Seu and Heenan 1998). In the absence of a clear consensus on the definition of a feminist approach to therapy, one way to proceed is to consider descriptions of feminist therapy in the literature on therapy practise (e.g., McGrath *et al.* 1990 and sources cited in Note 7). Based on this literature, feminist approaches to therapy most often appear to involve an integration of feminist principles with existing therapy approaches. This integration can occur at the level of therapy content, process or both.

With respect to therapy content, feminist approaches draw on existing procedures (e.g. cognitive restructuring techniques) with modifications which take women's experiences into account. Cognitive therapy, for instance, has been adapted to a feminist approach by focusing change efforts on the belief held by some women that they are responsible for meeting the needs of family members, while their own needs should take second place (Hurst and Genest 1995). The process of feminist approaches to therapy also relies on a particular form of client–therapist relationship. During therapy sessions, the therapist typically takes the position of a psychoeducator, a collaborator or colleague rather than expert, someone who shares her knowledge with a client rather than giving directions or advice. The goal of this therapy process is client empowerment (Worell and Remer 1992). A feminist therapist attempts to equalize power in the client-therapist relationship with the aim of "giving" more power to the client (Marecek and Kravetz 1998). By exposing a woman to this form of relationship, a therapist hopes that the client will be better able to recognize the choices available in her own life and to make decisions which are in her own best interests. A concern with power within the client–therapist relationship derives from feminist analyses of the disadvantaged status of women within the broader social-political context. One aim of feminist therapy, therefore, is to counteract the lack of personal power women may experience within their everyday lives.

Whether an emphasis is placed on content or process aspects in feminist approaches to therapy, the assumption is that any improvements or changes experienced by a woman in how she feels or acts will extend beyond the therapy context. While the immediate goal of therapy is helping a woman to feel less depressed, in the longer-term, the goal is changing the conditions which underlie her depressive experiences so she can avoid becoming depressed in the future. When the perspective shifts from individual women to women in general, this longer-term goal can be re-formulated as reducing or preventing altogether the occurrence of depressive experiences among women. Can therapy, feminist or otherwise, contribute to this broader goal and if so how? Or inverting these questions, can strategies having the aim of redressing inequalities and disadvantages faced by women in society also contribute to therapy with individual women who are coping with depressive experiences now?

Exploring links between the personal and the political

Some therapists might be somewhat affronted if their activities were labelled as political. Politics is something occurring within the public arena, not within the privacy of a therapy office, where confidentiality is a paramount ethical consideration. The purpose of therapy usually is perceived to be that of *helping* people, rather than changing the world outside therapy. Politics, moreover, is likely to be seen as something associated with forms of activism or more organized efforts to bring about change in the social world beyond the therapy room. There are links, nonetheless, between therapy and politics. Political activity can have a "therapeutic" impact on the individuals involved as well as on those affected by policy change. Moreover, the work of therapists is never entirely apolitical, because it always takes place within a political context (e.g. therapy may be funded publicly or privately). The connection between therapy and political activity, however, tends to be obscured because different people usually are involved. Feminist therapists may be encouraged, and may encourage their clients, to become involved in political activity outside therapy (Brown and Brodsky 1992), but such activities are likely to be viewed by feminist therapists as being distinct from therapy (Marecek and Kravetz 1998).

The separation between therapy and politics is particularly pronounced when a therapist operates as a private practitioner who is paid fees for her services by clients. This is only one model for delivery of therapy services, however, and feminist therapists with varied professional backgrounds (e.g. counselling, psychiatry, psychology, social work) are employed in a range of settings, including hospitals, clinics, and community-based organizations. In such cases, a therapist is paid a salary by her employer, whether or not she provides individual therapy services. The setting in which a feminist therapist works also will shape and delimit the opportunities she has for political action. A feminist therapist who works in a hospital setting may define her role in terms of advocacy on behalf of clients, helping them to negotiate a service system which often is unresponsive to their needs (Szekely 1993). Those based in community settings may engage in practises which blur the distinction between individual therapy and political activity by combining psychotherapy with social action (Holland 1992). Still further removed from the private practise model are activities aimed at changing the policies governing how therapy services are delivered, so that they become more women-centered or "woman-friendly". Such policy work is likely to be carried out by feminists whose income is not tied directly to provision of therapy.

The notion that political activity is something which only occurs outside the therapy room is also contradicted by the realization that "power", its distribution and purpose, is an inherent part of politics. Power issues arise within interpersonal relationships as well as among social groups in the public arena (Ristock and Pennell 1996). Not only is interpersonal power implicated in the dynamics of the client–therapist relationship, but assumptions about power are embedded within the theoretical approach a therapist draws on for understanding and explaining a client's problems. The theoretical perspectives informing much practise in therapy lead to interpretations of clients' problems as being primarily intrapsychic in nature, rather than pointing to any power disadvantages individual women face because of their social status (e.g. being a single parent living on welfare) or because of visible or cultural attributes (skin color, ethnicity). The tendency of therapy to "psychologise" individuals' difficulties has been criticized as a form of "personalizing the political" by Kitzinger and Perkins (1993). When political issues are reinterpreted as personal matters, opportunities for addressing structural inequalities which limit and diminish many women's lives are removed from consideration.

Power can operate in other ways, in addition to arrangements which control and influence the distribution of material resources within particular social contexts. Power can also function discursively, through language and the words used to label concepts and the symbols used to convey ideas. The theories informing therapy practise also are forms of discourse, sets of ideas used to make sense of clients' problems. For example, some feminist therapists draw on theories about women's psychological specificity which I discussed in Chapter 4. In this case, a therapist might focus on helping a woman understand how her depressive experiences are linked to a relational context within which she is taken for granted, rejected, or physically abused. A different theoretical approach might focus on understanding women's depressive experiences from a perspective in which female psychology is understood as being rooted in the dynamics of the mother–child relationship and a girl's development of femininity through identification with her mother. Theories of this kind may side-step power issues in women's lives, "re-packaging" them as psychological insights, with the purpose of helping women to make sense of their subjective experiences.

Theoretical ideas similar to these have been applied to explain "how certain ideas about women get inside [women's] heads" (Nairne and Smith 1984: 162). From a feminist perspective, it is also important, however, to understand "how the political *becomes* personal" (Heenan 1996: 55, emphasis in original). Such theories may, therefore, make a contribution to understanding why some women express discomfort with the emancipatory project of feminism, preferring instead to see their difficulties as having causes which lie within the individual (Heenan 1996). In sum, although feminist therapy approaches may help some women to overcome their depressive experiences, as Burman (1992: 497) has pointed out, at the same time attention needs to be given "to the real constraints and commitments faced by the client" so as to avoid resorting "to psychologisation of personal problems".

The origins of contemporary feminist approaches to therapy can be traced to "consciousness-raising" (CR) groups, a feature of the women's movement in the 1960s (Greenspan 1993). CR groups involved women meeting together on a regular basis to talk about their personal experiences. Out of these discussions, the recognition emerged that rather than being unique and personal, women shared similar experiences, which in turn could be linked to the patriarchal sociocultural context in which they lived. This identification of the commonalities in experiences threaded through the lives of individual women became encapsulated within the now well-worn phrase "the personal is political". From this understanding has flowed a variety of efforts to improve the conditions of women's everyday lives by revealing and challenging sexist attitudes and discriminatory practises. In recent decades, however, the earlier excitement generated by CR groups has been transmuted into the more professionalized and institutionalized practise of feminist therapy. What once was achieved by informal routes with ordinary women meeting together is now regulated by professional training programs, codes of conduct, and debates on theoretical issues. Kitzinger and Perkins (1993) have characterized this reconfiguration within the domain of feminist therapy of those activities which used to take place in CR groups as illustrating how problems in women's lives, having political roots, have become individualized as personal problems.

Kitzinger and Perkins' (1993) critique of therapy is valuable, because they point out that efforts to address the needs of women coping with feelings of distress should not be pursued to the neglect of the material conditions structuring and regulating the lives of women in general. At the same time, this position need not imply that attention should be shifted entirely from the concerns of individual women to those of the collectivity of women. The way Kitzinger and Perkins conceptualize the position of therapy and politics in relation to each other implies a separation between the personal and the political, one which splits women's experiences from the social reality of their lives. An alternative position is one in which both the personal *and* the political are encompassed within the same framework, something which may be accomplished when the personal and the political are reconceptualized from a material–discursive perspective.

Women overcoming depression: toward a material–discursive framework

A strength of feminist approaches to therapy is the recognition that the problems a woman brings to a therapist are co-constructed by her subjectivity *and* the social context in which she lives. Although conventional approaches to therapy also share a focus on the individual, therapeutic efforts usually are restricted to helping a person adapt better to existing social conditions. A therapist might use procedures to foster changes in a person's thoughts or bodily reactions, but a separation is assumed between the individual and the broader social context. This separation also characterizes empowerment approaches to feminist therapy, however, so long as the issue of "how being granted power in the therapy relationship produces changes in clients' lives in the real world" (Marecek and Kravetz 1998: 23) remains unaddressed. One way to re-think the relationship between the individual and society is to recognize that both material and discursive conditions are implicated, whether analysis begins with the individual or the social context (Ristock and Pennell 1996). Discursive conditions (e.g. discourses of femininity) regulate both individual subjectivity and physical embodiment, as well as shaping structural conditions within society. At the same time, material conditions are always interpreted in terms of the discursive resources available within a particular cultural context. To give one example, Martin (1997) recently proposed that a different metaphor is needed for conceptualizing women's bodies (see Chapter 9). Her suggestion is that a metaphor informed by chaos or complexity theory could lead to development of a view of the female body as a flexible, adaptive, and responsive system, rather than one subject to the vagaries of biochemical processes. A discursive shift of this kind, Martin argues, would also generate more positive self-images for women. Thus, change at the discursive level could have important implications for the subjective and bodily experiences of individual women.

A similar discursive shift is described as occurring among the women whom Schreiber (1996) interviewed about their experiences in overcoming depression. The process involved in these women's recovery from depression was termed "redefining my self" and an important part of this process was identified by Schreiber as "Cluing in".

"Cluing in" was the process in which the woman's consciousness about her self and her world changed, often quite suddenly. The woman's awareness and understanding of her world shifted, so that after "Cluing in", her world was in many ways a different place.

(Schreiber 1996: 484)

For the women in Gammell and Stoppard's (1999) study, for whom overcoming depression involved professional treatment, although varying opinions were expressed about the helpfulness of the treatment they received, some expressed views like the following:

I feel so totally healed and so positive about myself and, oh gosh, it's just like, like on top of the world. Really I just feel like I have a total grip on, on life and, a lot stronger than I used to be . . . Having to go through that, you know, depression, just to just to get where I am is worth it for sure.

(ibid.: 123)

Through her treatment, this woman seemed to have arrived at a new understanding of herself and her situation, a view which apparently was quite inconsistent with her earlier depressive experiences.

Such accounts not only indicate that women who receive conventional treatment *do* overcome their depressive experiences, they also imply that women can recover from depression without the kind of broad-ranging social changes in material conditions which some feminist analyses would suggest are required. Of course, this does not preclude the possibility of individual women also making changes in the conditions of their own lives, and making such changes may be one outcome of their treatment. At the same time, acknowledging that women can overcome their depressive experiences leaves many other issues untouched. Would understanding better how women individually cope with and recover from their depressive experiences help to prevent such experiences among women in general? What contributions can knowledge of this kind make to understanding depression?

One lesson to be learned from women's accounts of overcoming their depressive experiences is that the interpretative dilemmas such accounts seem to pose should be treated as resources for theory development, rather than viewing them as puzzling inconsistencies or mistaken self-delusions. In this endeavor, we need to begin by taking women's accounts seriously, while also recognizing that available theoretical models may be unequal to the task of making sense of what women say about their depressive experiences. An important corollary of this position is that existing theoretical models also are inadequate for understanding what is called depression. In the final chapter, I offer some suggestions on the directions such theoretical explorations might take, linking these proposals to ideas developed in earlier chapters.

Notes

1 As indicated in Chapter 2 (see Note 1), in North America a toll-free telephone service has been established to provide people with information on symptoms of depression for self-diagnostic purposes and on treatment options for depression. A parallel service provides information to medical professionals on prescribing of antidepressant drugs. Apparently, most of the funding for these services has been donated by five major pharmaceutical companies (as reported in the Canadian daily newspaper the *Globe & Mail*, "Phone Line to Aid Depression Sufferers", 4 May 1996, p. A7). Allwood (1996) describes a similar information program in the UK, which is part of the "Defeat Depression" campaign mounted by the Royal Colleges of Psychiatrists and General Practitioners. One aim of this campaign is to increase public awareness about depression.

2 The following description of electroconvulsive treatment (ECT) is provided by McGrath *et al.* (1990: 55):

> A painless form of electric therapy. The patient is prepared by adminis-
> tration of barbiturate anesthesia and injection of a chemical relaxant. An
> electric current is then applied for a fraction of a second through elec-
> trodes placed on the temples, which immediately produces a two-stage
> seizure (tonic and clonic). The usual treatment is bilateral, but unilateral
> stimulation of a nondominant hemisphere [of the brain] has been intro-
> duced in order to shorten the period of memory loss that follows the
> treatment (material in square brackets added).

3 Kate Millett (1970) is usually considered to have coined the phrase "the personal is political", although it is attributed to Carol Hanisch (1971) by Kitzinger and Perkins (1993: 183).

4 The work reported in Scattolon and Stoppard (1999) is based in part on the first author's PhD dissertation (see Scattolon, 1999). The women who participated in this study completed a depression symptom questionnaire following the interview in order to counter the criticism that the women were "not really depressed".

5 Schreiber's (1996) study included women from southern Ontario, a province in central Canada, and from an adjoining area of the US.

6 More women than men are diagnosed with depression, so it seems likely that the major-
ity of those who receive ECT are women. Smith and Richman (1984) analyzed data on ECT use in Canada and found, that among those diagnosed with "depression", pro-
portionately more women than men received this treatment. Women were also more likely than men to receive ECT in other diagnostic categories, so that the overall majority of those receiving this treatment were women.

7 The following is a brief listing of some of this recent literature on feminist therapy: Dutton-Douglas and Walker (1988), Greenspan (1993), Jordan *et al.* (1991), Laidlaw, Malmo and Associates (1990), Worell and Remer (1992) and many articles in the journal *Women & Therapy*.

11

WHY NEW PERSPECTIVES ARE NEEDED FOR UNDERSTANDING DEPRESSION IN WOMEN[1]

In this final chapter, I bring together themes discussed in the preceding chapters to arrive at some conclusions about "depression" in women.[2] As implied by this chapter's title, my conclusions depart considerably from the more familiar path of mainstream approaches to depression. Readers hoping for some definitive statements about depression in women, what causes "it", how it can be treated and cured, why it is more common among women than men, are likely to be disappointed. Instead, I offer some views on directions in which new perspectives for understanding depression in women might be developed. This work is positioned, therefore, within the broader stream of critical psychology (see for example Fox and Prilleltensky 1997, Hollway 1989, Smith *et al.* 1995), while also tracing its roots to feminist critiques of theory and practice in mental health fields (see for example Ballou and Gabalac 1985, Penfold and Walker 1983, Ussher 1991).

The critical aspect of this work is reflected in the assumptions on which it is grounded. These assumptions are inimical to those of positivist approaches to theory and research, still largely dominant within psychology. This dominance persists despite the serious challenges posed to positivist approaches by analyses emanating not only from philosophy of science (Harding 1986, Woolgar 1988) but also from social science and health fields intersecting with psychology (Berger and Luckmann 1966, Csordas 1994, Yardley 1997c). Core themes of these analyses concern the need to acknowledge the role of the knower (or researcher) in the generation of knowledge and the legitimacy of people's accounts of their experiences as a source of knowledge. An issue raised repeatedly by feminists within psychology and other mental health fields is the neglect of women's experiences in the knowledge generated about depression. Within mainstream approaches to depression, the voices which count the most are those of researchers, who assume the role of impartial, objective observers. In contrast, in the present work I have explored the knowledge which emerges when the voices of experts are muted and women's voices, particularly those of women coping with depressive experiences, are given more "air-time". What kind of understanding of depression in women might be developed if inquiry begins with women's experiences rather than being prefigured by experts' theories?

A critical, deconstructive stance to understanding depression was introduced in

Chapter 1, where I identified key issues in feminist and social constructionist critiques of mainstream approaches to research and practise. The focus of Chapter 2, on mainstream approaches to conceptualizing depression, examined the ways in which depression has been defined and how the definition used by a researcher both shapes and limits the knowledge produced. In the chapters in Part II, I explored the implications of feminist and social constructionist perspectives through analysis of several of the theoretical models currently available for explaining depression in women. The focus shifts in the second half of the book (the three chapters in Part III) from the perspective of experts to the standpoint of women where I consider areas which have generally been neglected or ignored in mainstream accounts of depression. My aim throughout has been to foreground women's voices and experiences while simultaneously questioning the criteria used to define positivist research approaches as scientific.

A telling example of how experts' formulations of depression are derived without taking women's experiences into account is discussed by Hamilton (1995) in her analysis of gender-related influences in research on psychotropic drugs. Hamilton notes that the DSM diagnostic category of Major Depressive Disorder (MDD) is assumed to be the prototypical form of depression in research on drug treatments for depression. The MDD category is differentiated from "atypical depressions", forms of depressions with patterns of symptomatology which deviate from diagnostic criteria for MDD. Among women, atypical forms of depression apparently are diagnosed more frequently than MDD, although MDD is the most common type of depression diagnosed in men. As Hamilton (1995: 318) points out, this means that "atypical depressions – predominating even more in females than MDD – are compared to a relative male norm". Hamilton identifies another depressive variant, a mixed anxiety/depression syndrome, as also being common among women but which is not included as a diagnostic category within the DSM.

In drawing attention to these instances of androcentric bias in the DSM, I am not intending to argue for inclusion of atypical forms of depression in this official taxonomy of mental disorders. Instead, what this example illustrates is that the DSM, the cornerstone of mainstream research on depression, apparently excludes an unknown portion of the experiences of women in its formulation of what is called depression. When women's experiences are overlooked in this way, closure of definitional debates (see Chapter 2) will always be premature. The prototypical position held by the MDD diagnosis in research on depression implies that available findings provide only a limited account of depression in women, because the full range of women's depressive experiences remains unexplored.

A critical analysis of positivist approaches to research, which I elaborated in earlier chapters, is not restricted, however, to the issue of how depression is defined. It is part of a more wide-ranging epistemological critique concerning the assumptions underpinning much research, about what can be known and what counts as knowledge. The insistence in positivist research on objective forms of measurement, which ideally can be quantified and expressed in numerical form, operates to exclude subjective aspects of experience, and in particular the linguistically-mediated nature of such experiences, from investigation. An epistemological perspective which embraces subjective experiences and also places especial emphasis on the role of language in shaping meaning has been termed social constructionist (see Chapter 1). When inquiry is based in a social constructionist epistemology this also means acknowledging the impossibility of generating knowledge divorced from the experiences and values of those involved. My own work is grounded in feminist values and my analytic focus on women's experiences reflects this feminist standpoint.

When analyzing mainstream research on depression, the strategy I have adopted is to identify what is missing or taken for granted in experts' accounts when the experiences of women are either disregarded or reframed according to mainstream constructs. In the three chapters in Part III, I explored understanding of depression in women from the perspective of women's experiences, rather than from that of experts who adopt a position as dispassionate, objective observers. Beginning inquiry about depression in women from the vantage point of women's experiences enables subjectivity to be explored while also attending to embodied aspects of women's experiences. Women's bodies both express and symbolize gender, while simultaneously being the means of performing gendered activities. I find it difficult to imagine how women's depressive experiences can be understood apart from the material reality of their embodiment, although theories developed within psychology generally produce disembodied accounts of depression in women.

In mainstream research, gender is typically conceptualized as an individual characteristic based primarily on sex of assignment. As many feminist theorists have noted, however, the compass of gender extends well beyond this individualistic (and individualizing) concept to include the gendered division of social labor and also symbolic aspects of gender within the discursive domain of language and social interaction. The gendered division of labor is embedded and maintained within society by structural conditions and social institutions which create and control allocation of material resources along gendered lines. These gendered arrangements are buttressed by prevailing discursive conditions, including cultural discourses which both constitute and regulate widely shared notions about femininity.

One strategy for exploring the contributions of material and discursive conditions to women's depressive experiences is through analysis of women's accounts using qualitative methods. A particular advantage of this strategy is that women's voices become "audible" rather than being "silenced" by the more usually dominant interpretations of experts. Although use of qualitative research methods does not inevitably imply an epistemological perspective which is social constructionist, inquiry conducted within a "qualitative paradigm" has features which makes it particularly compatible with the goals of researchers who work from a feminist standpoint (Henwood and Pidgeon 1995). I have chosen to emphasize qualitative methods, not because I believe other methods (quantitative, for example) are less useful, but because of my feminist-informed conviction that women's accounts have validity in their own right as a source of knowledge.

The chapters in Part III address women's experiences at different phases of the life span, from adolescence to old age. In each case, I attempt to place understanding of depression in the context of the lived experiences of women, experiences which simultaneously are subjective and embodied. When inquiry is freed from the restrictions of positivist assumptions and notions of objectivity are expanded to include the subjectivities of both knowers (researchers) and research participants (women as "subjects"), new ways of understanding depression in women become possible. The analyses developed in the chapters in Part III illustrate how women's depressive experiences are constituted in relation to the material and discursive conditions shaping their lived experiences. From this material–discursive perspective, depression in women is not conceived as something originating primarily within individual women, best treated one woman at a time. Instead, depressive experiences are understood within a framework encompassing both material aspects of women's lives (including their embodiment) and the discursive conditions which shape their lived experiences. Several strands of these material and discursive themes can be discerned when analysis begins with women's accounts.

Material themes

A theme emerging repeatedly in women's accounts is the close links between their experiences and their embodiment. These links are most clearly apparent in women's concerns about bodily appearance, a preoccupation with body image, marking the experiences of women across the lifespan. Among young women, for instance, appearance concerns take center stage motivated by the perceived rewards of peer acceptance. These rewards include the possibilities for "having a life", one characterized by cultural landmarks punctuating a conventional middleclass lifestyle. In later years, appearance concerns loom large as women age and their bodies lose their youthful contours and coloring, to be supplanted by sagging flesh, wrinkled skin and gray hair. For older women, a concern to avoid "looking their age" by retaining some vestiges of a youthful appearance underlies efforts to mask physical signs of aging. As more obvious consequences of living in an aging body become harder to conceal, women then face the reality of their public invisibility. The accounts of women at different life stages, therefore, reveal the centrality of the body's appearance both to women's sense of self and to the scope of possibilities in their everyday lives.

A second theme present in women's accounts reflects their experiences of living within a body which menstruates, a reproductive body which begins to bleed in early adolescence and ceases to bleed in midlife. For young women menstruation both signals reproductive possibilities and poses challenges in managing the monthly blood flow so that their menstrual status is hidden from others. At younger ages, failure of a period to arrive when expected might indicate pregnancy (planned or otherwise), whereas absence of menstruation in later years may be a forerunner of menopause and the ending of a woman's menstrual life. Although older women may experience the end of their monthly periods with relief, the body makes it presence felt in other ways as joints become creaky and senses less acute. Women's accounts reflect the reality of their embodiment as they talk about their experiences as individuals who live within a female body.

A third way in which a material theme is expressed in women's accounts concerns practises of femininity, the domain of gendered activities culturally defined as the prerogative of women. Chief among these activities is the caring work performed by women for their children and other family members. Although giving birth to a child confers the status of mother on a woman, it also signals the advent of years of childcare responsibilities. Obscured in the romantic dream of marriage and motherhood is the reality that caring work involves physical labor both drawing upon and draining the energies of a woman's material body. The euphemism housework, moreover, masks the never-ending stream of unpaid caring work which women perform as a "labor of love" in service of their families. The material bodies of women are the means for ensuring a nurturing home environment for those who live there. As most women now combine unpaid work in the home with paid employment, juggling the time demands of family, home and job, time management becomes an important skill for metering the body's finite material resources.

Discursive themes

Like all people, women derive and create meaning in their lives through language and when giving accounts of their experiences, they draw on the meanings which language makes available to them. These discursive resources form part of the sociocultural backdrop to their everyday lives and include shared ideas about what it means to be and act as a woman. They also encompass narratives anchored by "story-lines" and "guideposts" which provide the cultural scaffolding for constructing life as a woman. In earlier chapters, I used the term discourses of femininity to denote the set of discursive resources which have women as their focus. These discourses operate through largely unconscious or taken for granted assumptions shared by people living within the same sociocultural context. One avenue for exploring discourses of femininity is provided by analysis of the language used by women in their accounts.

In the chapters in Part III, where I include excerpts from women's accounts, regardless of the specific locations of the lives of the women involved, three main discursive themes seem to crosscut their accounts. These three themes reflect different facets of what it means to be a woman in western culture at this point in history. The first theme concerns the importance of maintaining an attractive appearance. The second focuses on what it means to be a good woman and particularly how to be a good mother. The third theme is one in which a woman's value is linked to her social contribution. Although here I separate these themes for discussion purposes, they are closely intertwined and women may draw on several themes at the same time in constructing their accounts. I am not suggesting that these are the only discursive themes which could be gleaned from an analysis of women's accounts, but they seem to have particular relevance for understanding women's depressive experiences within the material–discursive perspective developed here.

The attractive appearance theme emerges in women's accounts at all ages, from teenage concerns about breast size and body shape to older women's worries about wrinkles and gray hair. For younger women, having an appearance which others, particularly men, find attractive is an overriding concern. These preoccupations with cosmetic aspects of appearance intermesh closely with the cultural imperatives of a romantic discourse which position young women as "Cinderellas" awaiting a prince (handsome or otherwise) to rescue them from a life of drudgery. In young women's accounts, having an attractive appearance becomes a critical precursor for "having a life". In older women's accounts, the focus shifts to anxieties arising from their struggles to maintain an attractive appearance. In this case, the imagined audience broadens beyond men to younger people in general, as reflected in older women's fears of appearing "ugly" to others and of their encroaching public invisibility. The theme of visibility is one that more generally undergirds women's preoccupations with appearance to include not only a concern with attracting male attention but also with diverting others' attention from their bodies and bodily functions. A woman's visibility is important for both gaining and blocking her access to valued social resources. Women's accounts therefore reflect in various ways the idea that their bodily appearance represents an important measure of their worth and that failure in this arena is to risk losing social value.

While a woman's appearance may represent a route for gaining social value, the qualities defining the good woman are more elusive. Central to cultural definitions of femininity are caring and concern for others, empathy and compassion. The unselfish, selfless character of the good woman is associated most closely in women's accounts with the figure of the good mother. In becoming a mother, a woman is presented with renewed resources for establishing a feminine identity through the opportunities having a child affords for demonstrating that she is a good mother. For a woman to be considered a good mother, her children's needs should take precedence over her own and she must attend to these needs in a manner reflecting her loving concern. A woman's feelings on the birth of her baby are likely to be interpreted as signs of her feminine nature and her ability to mother, so that bonding with the newborn takes on particular significance. In the current era, an intensive form of mothering is usually identified with the cultural figure of the good mother. At the same time, good mothering does not always result in a good child, yet the logic of intensive mothering dictates that mothers will be blamed for their children's failings. Becoming a mother emerges in women's accounts as the primary (and perhaps sole?) route for ensuring a feminine identify. When a woman becomes a mother this status can never be taken away (although a child might leave or die) and a side-benefit is the social recognition which accrues to those who can speak from this identity position.

So long as a woman has the potential to bear a child, becoming a mother remains a possibility. Once a woman's menstrual life is over, however, pregnancy is ruled out (except by intrusive artificial means) and she faces the task of constructing an identity which is compatible with her post-menopausal body. Discursively, this task is made difficult by pervasive ageist discourses in which greater social privilege is accorded to being young/er than to being old/er. The absence of positive meanings from which to construct a sense of self as an older woman is reinforced by cultural definitions of the female body in which sexual attractiveness to men and reproductive potential are central elements. Older women's lives are viewed culturally as being devoid of meaningful purpose, a viewpoint which is difficult for women to resist with the discursive resources available to them. Women may contest their positioning within an ageist frame, but the discursive options are limited to nonreproductive aspects of femininity emphasizing the caring and relational qualities ascribed to the good woman. Older women who disregard or in some way violate these tenets of femininity risk discursive attacks on their identity through labels such as "gossip", "hag" or "witch", which further undermine their ability to be perceived as legitimate social participants.

Material–discursive conditions and depression in women

Discourses of femininity do more than reflect beliefs about women. They also shape the contours of women's everyday lives and regulate how women explain and understand their lived experiences. Because researchers are part of the same language community as the women they study, knowledge produced about women more often than not reflects discourses of femininity, while also reinforcing the dualist assumptions inherent in mainstream approaches. In contrast, when knowledge is grounded in women's accounts, both material and discursive themes reveal the central position held by the female body, an entity which is both corporeal *and* culturally constructed. As a material entity, a woman's body provides a means for engaging in practises of femininity, activities deemed properly the responsibility of women. At the same time, a woman's body is a site of cultural meaning and her outward appearance provides a canvas upon which her identity as an appropriately feminine woman is constructed. Thus, the lived experiences of women are always both embodied and social, material and discursive.

An understanding of women's depressive experiences, therefore, needs to begin from a position which embraces both material and discursive dimensions to address how lived experiences arise in the dialectic created by both being and having a female body (Yardley 1996, 1997b: 16). Among other things, this implies acknowledging that the body is simultaneously a physical and symbolic artifact (Lock 1993: 373), both a bio-physical organism and a site of cultural meaning systems and discursive practises (Bordo 1993, Csordas 1994, Furman 1997). Women's bodies have surely been the focus of mainstream theories of depression, but only as material entities explicable within the confines of biomedical theory. This limited perspective on materiality not only excludes the cultural dimensions of women's embodiment, it also precludes consideration of the impact of social structural conditions on the embodied possibilities of women's everyday lives. These material possibilities are shaped by the requirements of family life (e.g. spending quality time with children, caring for sick family members) as well as the consequences of public policies predicated on gendered assumptions (e.g. lack of childcare services, unequal pay for work of equivalent social value). Although the private sphere of home and family is often conceived as being separate from the public world of social policy and commerce, decisions made within the public sphere have impacts that are as real and material in their consequences for women's lives as the biological processes of their bodies.

The material conditions of women's lives cannot, therefore, be considered in isolation from the discursive conditions which shape conceptions of femininity and what it means to be a woman. Discourses of femininity provide a template against which both women and men measure womanly accomplishments, whether in terms of the attractiveness (and sexiness) of a particular woman's appearance, her performance of wifely responsibilities, or the dispositions of her children. For instance, the work many women carry out in preparing meals for family members is usually interpreted as an expression of their caring and concern (Bella 1992), a connection underpinned by the cultural linkage between food and love (Bordo 1993). As women also know, however, preparing meals is much more than providing fuel for the human body. It also involves the work of planning meals, buying needed items, preparing and cooking food, and cleaning and clearing away cooking utensils. Burnt toast or a recipe which fails to live up to expectations, moreover, may not only mean disgruntled family members and disappointed guests, such experiences also undermine a woman's identity as a good woman.[3]

A more persistent source of threat to a woman's sense of self is the material body and the many ways in which it may fail to conform to culturally-constructed images of the ideal female shape. Although women may deride such apparently superficial concerns, they are not immune from the all too real consequences of these discursive constructions. Younger women daily negotiate peer evaluations of their bodily appearance and social worth. Older women confront the image they reflect in the social mirror of belittling and dismissive reactions of younger people. With changes in women's bodies, whether in concert with menstrual life, pregnancy or aging, the body draws attention to its existence in particular ways, not only altering a woman's identity but also transforming her social world (Yardley 1997b: 12). These are just some examples of the myriad ways in which women are caught between the socially constructed imperatives of cultural discourses of femininity and the limits imposed by material conditions, which include their physical embodiment. One consequence of a life lived at the intersection between what is culturally expected and what is materially feasible is the set of subjective and embodied experiences which are called depression.

Such material–discursive contradictions are exacerbated by the fiction of the autonomous individual, able to solve personal problems in a self-sufficient, independent manner without expecting (or receiving) help from others (Kitzinger 1992,

Stearns 1993). Culturally-preferred modes of personal problem-solving tend to be individualized, self-focused and inward-turning. This pattern has been linked to broader historical and cultural shifts in predominant styles of emotional expressivity. The emotional style characterizing social interaction is now less expressive and more self-contained than was the case in the past (Stearns 1994). These more introspective and self-focused strategies also parallel in some respects the subjective and embodied aspects of depressive experiences. Within this broader framework, feelings of hopelessness and helplessness, depressed mood, social withdrawal, fatigue, and inability to engage in everyday activities, experiences called symptoms of depression, can be understood as responses to dilemmas grounded in discourses of femininity, female embodiment and social structural conditions. Thus, explaining depression in women involves understanding how depressive experiences are culturally produced through practises and discourses of femininity, rather than the current preoccupation with causal factors (whether biological, psychological, or social) of a disorder located within individual women. Depressive experiences in women can be understood as consequences of processes which are both material and discursive, outcomes of women's efforts to live up to socially constructed notions of femininity, which rest in turn on material requirements involving the female body.

Women's depressive experiences and discourses of depression

Attempts to understand women's depressive experiences also are shaped discursively. Accounts of depression in women are currently dominated by two main discursive narratives (or story-lines) providing explanations of why a woman might become depressed. I discussed these in Chapter 8 as the "women's bodies" and "women's lives" explanations for depression in women. At this point, no alternative accounts of women's depressive experiences are readily available, so that when women talk about their depressive experiences, they are likely draw on some form of women's bodies or women's lives approach, or perhaps a combination of the two. In a similar fashion, women draw on the cultural resources represented by discourses of femininity in constructing a sense of self (or identity). Alternative discursive frames, such as those generated by feminists, are easily drowned out, swamped by the torrent of cultural materials (TV programs, magazines, movies etc.) which position women within prevailing discourses of femininity.

Discourses of depression also position women in particular ways. For instance, if a woman attempts to make sense of her depressive experiences in terms of a women's bodies discourse, her account will be framed by a medicalized perspective which positions her as a prospective patient in relation to a professional who will provide treatment for a disorder within her body's biochemistry. Women who draw on a women's lives discourse, although less likely to be positioned as patients, lack a subject position from which to articulate their depressive experiences. In the absence of a legitimacy bestowed by professional help-providers, women who

213

frame understanding of their depressive experiences within a women's lives narrative are left with the sole option of getting on with life as best as they are can within the limits of the material resources available to them. These and other issues were discussed in Chapter 10, where I explored the scope of contemporary responses to women's depressive experiences, ranging from the personal to the political.

Discourses of depression also have implications extending beyond individual women and those from whom they seek help. When a perspective such as the women's bodies explanation for depression is widely disseminated, there is general awareness within society of this way of accounting for women's depressive experiences. This means that a depressed woman who seeks support from others (spouse, friends) is quite likely to have her depressive experiences interpreted within the framework provided by the women's bodies narrative. Within this frame, there is no shortage of explanatory options, regardless of a woman's age. The menstrual cycle, pregnancy, childbirth, menopause, and the post-menopausal body spring readily to mind, well-rehearsed explanations for depression in women aired frequently in the various media. These possibilities, moreover, do not exhaust the scope of biomedical and other mainstream approaches and their promotion of decontextualized understandings of depression in women by ignoring the range of material and discursive conditions constituting and regulating women's lives.

In the course of this book, I have explored some material–discursive directions for understanding depression in women. The analyses outlined in earlier chapters are intended to contest prevailing discourses of depression in women through development of alternative discourses based in feminist and social constructionist critiques of the dominant approaches to explaining depression in women. From a feminist standpoint, my goal has been to validate women's depressive experiences, while also raising questions about how such experiences are explained and understood. A social constructionist perspective provides the epistemological grounding and also informs the critique of mainstream positivist approaches to research on depression.

In bringing feminist standpoint and social constructionist perspectives to bear in analzsing women's accounts my intent has been to "disrupt dominant discourses" while also seeking "alternative truths" (cf. Ristock and Pennell 1996). Although I have argued here that a material–discursive approach to understanding depression provides a better fit with women's accounts than currently dominant discourses, I make no special claims about the truth status of the analyses I present. Nonetheless, alternative discourses on depression can serve as a stimulus to change by offering women more affirming and less-stigmatizing ways to understand their depressive experiences. Analyses grounded in women's accounts of their lived experiences also provide one avenue for persuading researchers and professionals of the relevance such knowledge might have for their own endeavors. At this juncture, I believe inquiry from a perspective encompassing both material and discursive dimensions of women's lived experiences has the most to offer in the search for understandings of depression which are emancipatory, while also fostering women's well-being.

Notes

1 This chapter's title is the same as the one I chose for a recent article (see Stoppard 1999).

2 The word "depression" is placed in inverted commas here to signify its socially constructed character. For stylistic reasons, however, I have not used this convention elsewhere in this chapter. Absence of inverted commas is not intended to imply a realist interpretation of the word depression (or derivatives such as depressed, depressive, etc).

3 Although these examples may seem farfetched to some readers, a case in which a woman attempted suicide after burning toast was cited by Peter McLean (1976: 63), a Canadian clinical psychologist who has published extensively in the field of depression and its treatment.

REFERENCES

Abramson, L.Y., Seligman, M.E.P., and Teasdale, J. (1978) Learned helplessness in humans: Critique and reformulation. *Journal of Abnormal Psychology*, 87, 49–74.

Alexander, J., Berrow, D., Domitrovich, L., Donnelly, M., and McLean, C. (eds) (1986) *Women and aging: An anthology by women*, Corvallis, OR: Calyx Books.

Allwood, R. (1996) "I have depression, don't I?": Discourses of help and self-help books. In E. Burman, G. Aitken, P. Alldred, R. Allwood, T. Billington, B. Goldberg, A.J. Gordo Lopez, C. Heenan, D. Marks, and S. Warner *Psychology discourse practice: From regulation to resistance* (pp. 17–36), London: Taylor & Francis.

American Psychiatric Association (1980) *Diagnostic and statistical manual of mental disorders: DSM-III*, Washington, DC: American Psychiatric Association.

—— (1994) *Diagnostic and statistical manual of mental disorders: DSM-IV*, Washington, DC: American Psychiatric Association.

Aneshensel, C.S. (1992) Social stress: Theory and research. *Annual Review of Sociology*, 18, 15–38.

Antonuccio, D.O, Danton, W.G., and DeNelsky, G.Y. (1995) Psychotherapy versus medication for depression: Challenging the conventional wisdom with data. *Professional Psychology*, 26, 574–85.

Ashton, H. (1991) Psychotropic-drug prescribing for women. *British Journal of Psychiatry*, 158 (suppl.10), 30–5.

Avis, N.E., Kaufert, P.A., Lock, M., McKinlay, S.M., and Vass, K. (1993) The evolution of menopausal symptoms. In H.G. Burger (ed.) *The menopause* (pp. 17–32), London: Baillière Tindall.

Ballou, M., and Gabalac, N.W. (1985) *A feminist position on mental health*, Springfield, IL: C.C. Thomas.

Banister, P., Burman, E., Parker, I., Taylor, M., and Tindall, C. (1994) *Qualitative methods in psychology: A research guide*, Buckingham: Open University Press.

Banyard, V.L. and Graham-Bermann, S.A. (1993) Can women cope? A gender analysis of theories of coping with stress. *Psychology of Women Quarterly*, 17, 303–18.

Baum, C., Kennedy, D.L., Knapp, D.E., Juergens, J.P., and Faich, G.A. (1988) Prescription drug use in 1984 and changes over time. *Medical Care*, 26, 105–14.

Bebbington, P. (1996) The origins of sex-differences in depressive disorder – bridging the gap. *International Review of Psychiatry*, 8, 295–332.

Beck, A.T. (1991) Cognitive therapy: A 30-year retrospective. *American Psychologist*, 46, 368–75.

—— (1996) Beyond belief: A theory of modes, personality, and psychopathology. In P.M. Salkovskis (ed.) *Frontiers of cognitive therapy* (pp. 1–25), New York: Guilford.

216

Beck, A.T., Epstein, N., Harrison, R.P., and Emory, G. (1983) *Development of the Sociotropy–Autonomy Scale: A measure of personality factors in psychopathology*. Unpublished manuscript, Center for Cognitive Therapy, University of Pennsylvania Medical School, Philadelphia.

Beck, A.T., Rush, A.J., Shaw, B.F., and Emery, G. (1979) *Cognitive therapy of depression*, New York: Guilford.

Beck, A.T. and Steer, R.A. (1987) *Manual for the revised Beck Depression Inventory*. San Antonio, TX: Psychological Corporation.

Beck, A.T., Steer, R.A., and Garbin, M.G. (1988) Psychometric properties of the Beck Depression Inventory: Twenty-five years of evaluation. *Clinical Psychology Review*, 8, 77–100.

Beitchman, J.H., Zucker, K.J., Hood, J.E., DaCosta, G.A., Akman, D., and Cassavia, E. (1992) A review of the long-term effects of child sexual abuse. *Child Abuse and Neglect*, 16, 101–18.

Bell, S. (1987) Premenstrual syndrome and the medicalization of menopause: A sociological perspective. In B.Ginsburg and B.F.Carter (eds) *Premenstrual syndrome: Ethical and legal implications in a biomedical perspective* (pp. 151–73), New York: Plenum.

Bella, L. (1992) *The Christmas imperative: Leisure, family and women's work*, Halifax, Nova Scotia: Fernwood Publishing.

Belle, D. (1990) Poverty and women's mental health. *American Psychologist*, 45, 385–9.

Belliveau, J.M. (1998) *An evaluation of psychosocial models of depression with low-income women*. Unpublished doctoral dissertation, psychology department, University of New Brunswick, Canada.

Bem, S.L. (1974) The measurement of psychological androgyny. *Journal of Consulting and Clinical Psychology*, 42, 155–62.

Berger, P.L., and Luckmann, T. (1966) *The social construction of reality*, Garden City, NY: Doubleday.

Blatt, S.J., D'Afflitti, J.P., and Quinlan, D.M. (1976) Experiences of depression in normal young adults. *Journal of Abnormal Psychology*, 95, 383–9.

Blatt, S.J., Quinlan, D.M., Chevron, E.S., McDonald, C., and Zuroff, D.C. (1982) Dependency and self-criticism: Psychological dimensions of depression. *Journal of Consulting and Clinical Psychology*, 50, 113–24.

Blatt, S.J., and Zuroff, D.C. (1992) Interpersonal relatedness and self-definition: Two prototypes for depression. *Clinical Psychology Review*, 12, 527–62.

Blaxter, M. (1993) Why do victims blame themselves? In A. Radley (ed.) *Worlds of illness: Biographical and cultural perspectives on health and illness* (pp. 124–42), London: Routledge.

Bordo, S. (1993) *Unbearable weight: Feminism, western culture and the body*, Berkeley, CA: University of California Press.

Boulton, M.G. (1983) *On being a mother*, London: Tavistock.

Bourdieu, P., and Wacquant, L.J.D. (1992) *An invitation to reflexive sociology*, Chicago: Chicago University Press.

Bourne, P., McCoy, L., and Smith, D. (1998) Girls and schooling: Their own critique. *Resources for Feminist Research*, 26 (1/2), 55–68.

Brandt, J. (1998, May) *The balancing act: Being faithful to a theoretical position while maintaining the voice of the participants*. Paper presented at the 15th annual Qualitative Analysis Conference, Toronto, Canada.

Breggin, P.R. (1991) *Toxic psychiatry*, New York: St Martin's Press.

Brotman, S. (1998) The incidence of poverty among seniors in Canada: Exploring the impact of gender, ethnicity and race. *Canadian Journal on Aging*, 17(2), 166–85.

Broverman, I.K., Vogel, S.R., Broverman, D.M., Clarkson, F.E., and Rosenkrantz, P.S. (1972) Sex-role stereotypes: A current appraisal. *Journal of Social Issues*, 28, 59–78.

Brown, G.W. (1989) Life events and measurement. In G.W. Brown and T.O. Harris (eds) *Life events and illness* (pp. 3–45), London: Unwin Hyman.

Brown, G.W., Andrews B., Bifulco A. and Veiel H. (1990) Self-esteem and depression. I. Measurement issues and prediction of onset. *Social Psychiatry and Psychiatric Epidemiology*, 25, 200–9.

Brown, G.W., and Harris, T.O. (1978) *Social origins of depression: A study of psychiatric disorder in women*, London: Tavistock.

—— (1989) Depression. In G.W. Brown and T.O. Harris (eds) *Life events and illness* (pp. 49–93), London: Unwin Hyman.

Brown, L.S. (1994) *Subversive dialogues: Theory in feminist therapy*, New York: Basic.

Brown, L.S. and Brodsky, A.M. (1992) The future of feminist therapy. *Psychotherapy*, 29, 51–7.

Burman, E. (1992) Identification and power in feminist therapy: A reflexive history of a discourse analysis. *Women's Studies International Forum*, 15, 487–98.

Burr, V. (1995) *An introduction to social constructionism*, London: Routledge.

Busfield, J. (1996) *Men, women and madness*, London: Macmillan Press.

Butler, J. (1990) *Gender trouble: Feminism and the subversion of identity*, New York: Routledge

Calasanti, T.M., and Zajicek, A.M. (1993) A socialist-feminist approach to aging: Embracing diversity. *Journal of Aging Studies*, 7, 117–31.

Caplan, P.J. (1989) *Don't blame mother: Mending the mother–daughter relationship*, New York: Harper and Row

—— (1995) *They say you're crazy: How the world's most powerful psychiatrists decide who's normal*, Reading, MA: Addison-Wesley.

Caplan, P.J., McCurdy-Myers, J., and Gans, M. (1992) Should "premenstrual syndrome" be called a psychiatric abnormality? *Feminism & Psychology*, 2, 27–44.

Cappeliez, P. (1993) Depression in elderly persons: Prevalence, predictors and psychological intervention. In P. Cappeliez and R.J. Flynn (eds) *Depression and the social environment: Research and intervention with neglected populations* (pp. 332–68), Montreal and Kingston: McGill-Queen's University Press.

Champion, L.A., and Goodall, G.M. (1994) Social support and mental health: Positive and negative aspects. In D. Tantum and M. Birchwood (eds) *Seminars in psychology and the social sciences* (pp. 238–59), London: Gaskell.

Champion, L.A., and Power, M.J. (1995) Social and cognitive approaches to depression: Towards a new synthesis. *British Journal of Clinical Psychology*, 34, 485–503.

Chesler, P. (1972) *Women and madness*, New York: Avon.

Chodorow, N. (1978) *The reproduction of mothering*, Berkeley, CA: University of California Press.

Cicchetti, D., and Toth, S.L. (1998) The development of depression in children and adolescents. *American Psychologist*, 53, 221–41.

Clark, D.A., and Steer, R.A. (1996) Empirical status of the cognitive model of anxiety and depression. In P.M. Salkovskis (ed.) *Frontiers of cognitive therapy* (pp. 75–96), New York: Guilford.

Clark, D.A., Steer, R.A., Beck, A.T., and Ross, L. (1995) Psychometric characteristics of revised sociotropy–autonomy scales in college students. *Behavior Research & Therapy*, 33, 325–34.

Cohen, M.G. (1997) What women should know about economic fundamentalism. *Atlantis: A Women's Studies Journal*, 21(2), 4–15.

Cole, E. (1994) Over the hill we go: Women at menopause. In M.P. Mirkin (ed.) *Women in context: Toward a feminist reconstruction of psychotherapy* (pp. 310–29), New York: Guilford.

Copper, B. (1986) Voices: On becoming old women. In J. Alexander, D. Berrow, L. Domitrovich, M. Donnelly, and C. McLean (eds) *Women and aging: An anthology by women* (pp. 47–57), Corvallis, OR: Calyx Books.

Coyle, J.M. (ed.) (1997) *Handbook on women and aging*, Westport, CT: Greenwood Press.

Coyne, J.C. (1994) Self-reported distress: Analog or ersatz depression? *Psychological Bulletin*, 116, 29–45.

Coyne, J.C., and Downey, G. (1991) Social factors in psychopathology. *Annual Review of Psychology*, 42, 401–25.

Coyne, J.C., and Whiffen, V.E. (1995) Issues in personality as diathesis for depression: The case of Sociotropy–Dependency and Autonomy–Self-criticism. *Psychological Bulletin*, 111, 358–78.

Croghan, R. (1991) First-time mothers' accounts of inequality in the division of labor. *Feminism & Psychology*, 1, 221–46.

Csordas, T.J. (ed.) (1994) *Embodiment and experience: The existential ground for culture and self*, Cambridge: Cambridge University Press.

Culbertson, F.M. (1997) Depression and gender: An international review. *American Psychologist*, 52, 25–31.

Cutler, S., and Nolen-Hoeksema, S. (1991) Accounting for sex differences in depression through female victimization: Childhood sexual abuse. *Sex Roles*, 24, 425–38.

Daly, J. (1995) Caught in the web: The social construction of menopause as disease. *Journal of Reproductive and Infant Psychology*, 13, 115–26.

Day, A.T. (1991) *Remarkable survivors: Insights into successful aging among women*, Washington, DC: Urban Institute Press.

Denton, F.T., Feaver, C.H., and Spencer, B.G. (1998) The future population of Canada, its age distribution and dependency relations. *Canadian Journal of Aging*, 17, 83–109.

Dickson, G.L. (1991) Menopause – Language, meaning and subjectivity; a feminist post-structuralist analysis. In A.V. Voda and R. Conover (eds) *Proceedings of the Eight Conference of the Society for Menstrual Cycle Research, 1989* (pp. 112–25), Society for Menstrual Cycle Research.

Doyal, L. (1995) *What makes women sick? Gender and the political economy of health*. New Brunswick, NJ: Rutgers University Press.

Dutton-Douglas, M.A. and Walker, L.E.A. (eds) (1988) *Feminist psychotherapies: Integration of therapeutic and feminist systems*, Norwood, NJ: Ablex.

Eagan, A. (1985) The selling of premenstrual syndrome: Who profits from making PMS "the disease of the 1980s"? In S. Laws, V. Hey and A. Eagan (eds) *Seeing red: The politics of premenstrual tension* (pp. 65–79), London: Hutchinson.

Engel, G.L. (1977) The need for a new medical model: A challenge for biomedicine. *Science*, 196, 129–36.

Epstein, S. (1994) Integration of the cognitive and the psychodynamic unconscious. *American Psychologist*, 49, 709–24.

Erikson, E.H. (1968) *Identity: Youth and crisis*, New York: Norton.

Eyre, L. (1991) Gender relations in the classroom: A fresh look at coeducation. In J.S. Gaskell and A.T. McLaren (eds) *Women and education* (pp. 193–219), Calgary, Alberta: Detselig.

Fasick, F.A. (1994) On the "invention" of adolescence. *Journal of Early Adolescence*, 14, 6–23.

Figert, A.E. (1996) *Women and the ownership of PMS: The structuring of a psychiatric disorder*, Hawthorne, NY: Aldine de Gruyter.

Findlay, D.A., and Miller, L.J. (1994) Through medical eyes: The medicalization of women's bodies and women's lives. In B.S. Bolaria and H.D. Dickinson (eds) *Health, illness and health care in Canada* (2e) (pp. 276–306), Toronto: Harcourt Brace Canada.

Formanek, R. (1987) Depression and the older woman. In R. Formanek and A. Gurian (eds) *Women and depression: A lifespan perspective* (pp. 272–81), New York: Springer Publishing.

Fox, B. (1998) Motherhood, changing relationships and the reproduction of gender inequality. In S. Abbey and A. O'Reilly (eds) *Redefining motherhood: Changing identities and patterns* (pp. 159–74), Toronto: Second Story Press.

Fox, D., and Prilleltensky, I. (1997) *Critical psychology: An introduction*, London: Sage.

Freud, S. (1917/1964) Mourning and melancholia. In *Collected Works* (Vol. 14, pp. 243–58). London: Hogarth Press.

Friedan, B. (1963) *The feminine mystique*, New York: Dell.

Furman, F.K. (1997) *Facing the mirror: Older women and beauty shop culture*, New York: Routledge.

Gallant, S.J., and Derry, P.S. (1995) Menarche, menstruation, and menopause: Psychosocial research and future directions. In A.L. Stanton and S.J. Gallant (eds) *Psychology and women's health: Progress and challenges in research and application* (pp. 199–259), Washington, DC: American Psychological Association.

Gammell, D.J. (1996) *Women's experiences of depression: A qualitative analysis*. Unpublished paper, University of New Brunswick, Canada.

Gammell, D.J. and Stoppard, J.M. (1999) Women's experiences of treatment of depression: Medicalization or empowerment? *Canadian Psychology*, 40, 112–28.

Gannon, L. (1993) Menopausal symptoms as consequences of dysrhythmia. *Journal of Behavioral Medicine*, 16, 387–402.

—— (1999) *Women and aging: Transcending the myths*, London: Routledge.

Gee, E.M., and Kimball, M.M. (1987) *Women and aging*, Toronto: Butterworths.

Gergen, M.M. (1990) Finished at 40: Women's development within the patriarchy. *Psychology of Women Quarterly*, 14, 471–93.

Gibson, D. (1996) Broken down by age and gender: "The problem of old women" redefined. *Gender & Society*, 10, 433–48.

Gilligan, C. (1982) *In a different voice*, Cambridge, MA: Harvard University Press.

Ginn, J., and Arber, S. (1995) "Only connect": Gender relations and ageing. In S. Arber and J. Ginn (eds) *Connecting gender and ageing: A sociological approach* (pp. 1–14), Buckingham: Open University.

Graham, H. (1993) *Hardships and health in women's lives*, Hemel Hempstead: Harvester Wheatsheaf.

Gratch, L.V., Bassett, M.E., and Attra, S.L. (1995) The effects of gender and ethnicity on self-silencing and depression. *Psychology of Women Quarterly*, 19, 509–15.

Greenspan, M. (1993) *A new approach to women and therapy* (2e), Blue Ridge Summit, PA: McGraw-Hill.

Griffin, C. (1993) *Representations of youth: The study of youth and adolescence in Britain and America*, Cambridge: Polity Press.

Hamilton, J.A. (1995) Sex and gender as critical variables in psychotropic drug research. In C.V. Willies, P.P. Rieker, M.M. Kramer, and B.S. Brown (eds) *Mental health, racism, and sexism* (pp. 297–349), Pittsburgh: University of Pittsburgh Press.

Hamilton, J.A., and Jensvold, M. (1992) Personality, psychopathology and depressions in women. In L.S. Brown and M. Ballou (eds) *Personality and psychopathology: Feminist reappraisals* (pp. 116–43), New York: Guilford.

—— (1995) Sex and gender as critical variables in feminist psychopharmacology research and pharmacology. *Women & Therapy*, 16, 9–30.

Hanisch, C. (1971) The personal is political. In J. Aget (ed.) *The radical therapist*, New York: Ballantine.

Harding, S. (1986) *The science question in feminism*, Ithaca, NY: Cornell University Press.

—— (1995) "Strong objectivity": A response to the new objectivity question. *Synthese*, 104, 331–49.

Harrison, L. (1997) "It's a nice day for a white wedding": The debutante ball and constructions of femininity. *Feminism & Psychology*, 7, 495–516.

Hays, S. (1996) *The cultural contradictions of motherhood*, New Haven: Yale University Press.

Healey, S. (1986) Growing to be an old woman: Aging and ageism. In J. Alexander, D. Berrow, L. Domitrovich, M. Donnelly, and C. McLean (eds) *Women and aging: An anthology by women* (pp. 58–62), Corvallis, OR: Calyx Books.

Heenan, C. (1996) Feminist therapy and its discontents. In E. Burman, G. Aitken, P. Alldred, R. Allwood, T. Billington, B. Goldberg, A.J. Gordo Lopez, C. Heenan, D. Marks, and S. Warner *Psychology discourse practice: From regulation to resistance* (pp. 55–71), London: Taylor & Francis.

Henwood, K., and Pidgeon, N. (1995) Remaking the link: Qualitative research and feminist standpoint theory. *Feminism & Psychology*, 5, 7–30.

Holland, S. (1992) From social abuse to social action: A neighbourhood psychotherapy and social action project for women. In J.M. Ussher and P. Nicolson (eds) *Gender issues in clinical psychology* (pp. 68–77), London: Routledge.

Hollway W. (1989) *Subjectivity and method in psychology: Gender, meaning and science*. London: Sage.

Hughes, I. (1997) Can you keep from crying by considering things? Some arguments against cognitive therapy for depression. *Clinical Psychology Forum*, No. 104, June.

Hunt, K. (1994) A "cure for all ills"? Constructions of menopause and the chequered fortunes of hormone replacement therapy. In S. Wilkinson and C. Kitzinger (eds) *Women and health: Feminist perspectives* (pp. 141–65), London: Taylor & Francis.

Hunter, M., and O'Dea, I. (1997) Menopause: Bodily changes and multiple meanings. In J.M. Ussher (ed.) *Body talk: The material and discursive regulation of sexuality, madness and reproduction* (pp. 199–222), London: Routledge.

Hurst, S.A. and Genest, M. (1995) Cognitive-behavioral therapy with a feminist orientation: A perspective for therapy with depressed women. *Canadian Psychology*, 36, 236–57.

Ianni, F.A.J. and Orr, M.T. (1996) Dropping out. In J.A. Graber, J. Brooks-Gunn and A.C. Petersen (eds) *Transitions through adolescence: Interpersonal domains and context* (pp. 285–321), Mahweh, NJ: Erlbaum.

Jack, D.C. (1991) *Silencing the self: Women and depression*, Cambridge, MA: Harvard University Press.

—— (1996, August) *Silencing the self: Theory and new findings*. Paper presented at the meeting of the American Psychological Association, Toronto.

Jack, D.C., and Dill, D. (1992) The Silencing the Self Scale: Schemas of intimacy associated with depression in women. *Psychology of Women Quarterly*, 16, 97–106.

Johnstone, L. (1993) Psychiatry: Are we allowed to disagree? *Clinical Psychology Forum*, No. 56, June.

Jones, J. (1994) Embodied meaning: Menopause and the change of life. In M.M. Olson (ed.) *Women's health and social work: Feminist perspectives* (pp. 43–65), Binghamton, NY: Haworth Press.

Jordan, J.V., Kaplan, A.G., Miller, J.B., Stiver, I.P, and Surrey. J.L. (1991) *Women's growth in connection: Writings from the Stone Center*, New York: Guilford.

Kantrowitz, R.E., and Ballou, M. (1992) A feminist critique of cognitive–behavioral therapy. In L.S. Brown and M. Ballou (eds) *Personality and psychopathology: Feminist reappraisals* (pp. 70–87), New York: Guilford.

Kaplan, A.G. (1991) The "self-in-relation": Implications for depression in women. In J.V. Jordan, A.G. Kaplan, J.B. Miller, I.P Stiver, and J.L. Surrey (eds) *Women's growth in connection: Writings from the Stone Center* (pp. 206–22), New York: Guilford.

Karp, D.A. (1993) Taking anti-depressant medications: Resistance, trial commitment, conversion, disenchantment. *Qualitative Sociology*, 16, 337–59.

Katona, C.L.E. (1994) *Depression in old age*, Chichester, UK: Wiley.

Kaufert, P.A. (1994) Menopause and depression: A sociological perspective. In G. Berg and M. Hammar (eds) *The modern management of menopause* (pp. 161–8), London: Parthenon.

Kaufert, P.A., Gilbert, P., and Tate, R. (1992) The Manitoba project: A re-examination of the link between menopause and depression. *Maturitas*, 14, 143–55.

Kendall-Tackett, C., and Marshall, R. (1998) Sexual victimization of children: Incest and child sexual abuse. In R.K. Bergen (ed.) *Issues in intimate violence* (pp. 47–63), Thousand Oaks, CA: Sage.

Kennedy, G.J. (1996) The epidemiology of late-life depression. In G.J. Kennedy (ed.) *Suicide and depression in late life: Critical issues in treatment, research and public policy* (pp. 23–37), New York: Wiley.

Kessler, R.C. (1997) The effects of stressful life events on depression. *Annual Review of Psychology*, 48, 191–214.

Kimball, M.M. (1994) The worlds we live in: Gender similarities and differences. *Canadian Psychology*, 35, 388–404.

Kimball, M.M. (1995) *Feminist visions of gender similarities and differences*, Binghamton, NY: Haworth Press.

Kissling, E.A. (1996) Bleeding out loud: Communication about menstruation. *Feminism & Psychology*, 6, 481–504.

Kitzinger, C. (1992) The individual self concept: A critical analysis of social-constructionist writing on individualism. In G.M. Breakwell (ed.) *Social psychology of identity and the self concept* (pp.221–50), London: Surrey University Press/Academic Press.

Kitzinger, C. and Perkins, R. (1993) *Changing our minds: Lesbian feminism and psychology*, New York: New York University Press.

Koss, M.P., Goodman, L.A., Browne, A., Fitzgerald, L.F., Keita, G.P., and Russo, N.F. (1994) *No safe haven: Male violence against women at home, at work, and in the community*. Washington, DC: American Psychological Association.

Laidlaw, T.A., Malmo, C., and Associates. (1990) *Healing voices: Feminist approaches to therapy with women*, San Francisco: Jossey-Bass.

Larkin, J. (1997) *Sexual Harassment: High school girls speak out*, Toronto: Second Story Press.

Latour, B. (1987) *Science in action*, Cambridge, MA: Harvard University Press.

Leadbeater, B.J., Blatt, S.J., and Quinlan, D.M. (1995) Gender-linked vulnerabilities to depressive symptoms, stress, and problem behaviors in adolescents. *Journal of Research on Adolescence*, 5, 1–29.

Leadbeater, B.J.R., and Way, N. (1996) Introduction. In B.J.R. Leadbeater and N.Way (eds) *Urban girls: Resisting stereotypes, creating identities* (pp. 1–14), New York: New York University Press.

Lee, J. (1994) Menarche and the (hetero)sexualization of the female body. *Gender & Society*, 8, 343–62.

—— (1997) Never innocent: Breasted experiences in women's bodily narratives of puberty. *Feminism & Psychology*, 7, 453–74.

Lee, J., and Sasser-Coen, J. (1996) *Blood stories: Menarche and the politics of the female body in contemporary U.S. society*, New York: Routledge.

Lerner, H.G. (1987) Female depression: Self sacrifice and self betrayal in relationships. In R. Formanek and A. Gurian (eds) *Women and depression: A lifespan perspective* (pp. 200–21), New York: Springer.

Lewis, S.E. (1995) A search for meaning: Making sense of depression. *Journal of Mental Health*, 4, 369–82.

—— (1997, June) *Constructions of identity, subjectivity, and depression in women.* Paper presented at the 58th Annual Convention of the Canadian Psychological Association, Toronto.

Lewis, S.E. and Nicolson, P. (1998) Talking about early motherhood: Recognising loss and reconstructing depression. *Journal of Reproductive and Infant Psychology*, 16, 177–97.

Link, B., and Dohrenwend, B.P. (1980) Formulation of hypotheses about the true prevalence of demoralization in the United States. In B.P. Dohrenwend, B.S. Dohrenwend, M.S. Gould, B.Link, R. Neugebauer, and R. Wunsch-Hitzig (eds) *Mental illness in the United States: Epidemiological estimates* (pp. 114–32), New York: Praeger.

Lock, M. (1993) *Encounters with aging: Mythologies of menopause in Japan and North America*, Berkeley, CA: University of California Press.

—— (1998) Anomalous ageing: Managing the postmenopausal body. *Body & Society*, 4, 35–61.

Lorber, J. (1994) *Paradoxes of gender*, New Haven: Yale University Press.

Lovering, K.M. (1995) The bleeding body: Adolescents talk about menstruation. In S. Wilkinson and C. Kitzinger (eds) *Feminism and discourse: Psychological perspectives* (pp. 10–31), London: Sage.

Lupton, D. (1996) Constructing the menopausal body: The discourses on hormone replacement therapy. *Body & Society*, 2, 91–7.

Lyddon, W.J. (1995) Cognitive therapy and theories of knowing: A social constructionist view. *Journal of Counselling & Development*, 73, 579–85.

Malson, H. (1998) *The thin woman: Feminism, post-structuralism and the social psychology of anorexia nervosa*, London: Routledge.

Malson, H., and Ussher, J.M. (1996a) Bloody women: A discourse analysis of amenorrhea as a symptom of anorexia nervosa. *Feminism & Psychology*, 6, 505–21.

—— (1996b) Body poly-texts: Discourses of the anorexic body. *Journal of Community & Applied Social Psychology*, 6, 267–80.

Marecek, J. and Kravetz, D. (1998) Power and agency in feminist therapy. In I B. Seu and M.C. Heenan (eds) *Feminism and psychotherapy: Reflections on contemporary theories and practices* (pp. 13–29), London: Sage.

Marcia, J. (1980) Identity in adolescence. In J. Adelson (ed.) *Handbook of adolescent psychology* (pp. 159–87), New York: Wiley.

Markens, S. (1996) The problematic of "experience": A political and cultural critique of PMS. *Gender & Society*, 10, 42–58.

Martin, E. (1987) *The woman in the body: A cultural analysis of reproduction* Boston: Beacon Press.

—— (1997) The woman in the menopausal body. In P.A. Komesaroff, P. Rothfield, and J. Daly (eds) *Reinterpreting menopause: Cultural and philosophical issues* (pp. 239–54), New York: Routledge.

Matthews, S.H. (1979) *The social world of old women: Management of self-identity*, Beverly Hills: Sage.

McFarlane, J., and Williams, T.M. (1994) Placing premenstrual syndrome in perspective. *Psychology of Women Quarterly*, 18, 339–73.

McGrath, E., Keita, G.P., Strickland, B.R., and Russo, N.F. (1990) *Women and depression: Risk factors and treatment issues*, Washington, DC: American Psychological Association.

McKinlay, J.B., McKinlay, S.M., and Brambilla, D.J. (1987) The relative contributions of endocrine changes and social circumstances to depression in mid-aged women. *Journal of Health and Social Behavior*, 28, 345–63.

McKinlay, S.M., Brambilla, D.J., and Posner, J. (1992) The normal menopause transition. *Maturitas*, 14, 103–16.

McLaren, A.T. and Vanderbijl, A. (1998) Teenage girls making sense of mothering: What has (relational) equality got to do with it? In S. Abbey and A. O'Reilly (eds) *Redefining motherhood: Changing identities and patterns* (pp. 127–44), Toronto: Second Story Press.

McLean, P. (1976) Therapeutic decision-making in the behavioral treatment of depression. In P.O. Davidson (ed.) *Behavioral management of anxiety, depression and pain* (pp. 54–90), New York: Brunner/Mazel.

McMahon, M. (1995) *Engendering motherhood: Identity and self-transformation in women's lives*, New York: Guilford.

—— (1998) Between exile and home. In In S. Abbey and A. O'Reilly (eds) *Redefining motherhood: Changing identities and patterns* (pp. 187–200), Toronto: Second Story Press.

McQuaide, S. (1998a) Opening spaces for alternative images and narratives of midlife women. *Clinical Social Work Journal*, 26(1), 39–53.

—— (1998b) Women at midlife. *Social Work*, 43(1), 21–31.

McReynolds, P. (1989) Diagnosis and clinical assessment: Current status and major issues. *Annual Review of Psychology*, 40, 83–108.

Merritt-Gray, M., and Wuest, J. (1995) Counteracting abuse and breaking free: The process of leaving revealed through women's voices. *Health Care for Women International*, 16, 399–412.

Miedema, B., and Stoppard, J.M. (1994) "I just needed a rest": Women's experiences of psychiatric hospitalization. *Feminism & Psychology*, 4, 251–60.

Miller, J.B. (1986) *Toward a new psychology of women* (2e), Boston: Beacon Press.

Miller, L.J. (1997) Underdog strategies: Negotiating power from the underside. Unpublished paper, Department of Sociology, University of Calgary, Alberta, Canada.

Millett, K. (1970) *Sexual politics*, Garden City, NY: Doubleday.

Mirowsky, J. (1996) Age and the gender gap in depression. *Journal of Health and Social Behavior*, 37, 362–80.

Mischel, W. (1973) Toward a cognitive social learning theory reconceptualization of personality. *Psychological Review*, 80, 252–83.

Mohide, E.A., and Streiner, D.L. (1993) Depression in caregivers of impaired family members. In P. Cappeliex and R.J. Flynn (eds) *Depression and the social environment: Research and intervention with neglected populations* (pp. 289–331), Montreal and Kingston: McGill-Queen's University Press.

Moore, S.M. (1995) Girls' understanding and social constructions of menarche. *Journal of Adolescence*, 18, 87–104.

Munroe, S.M. and McQuaid, J.R. (1994) Measuring life stress and assessing its impact on mental health. In W.R. Avison and I.H. Gotlib (eds) *Stress and mental health: Contemporary issues and prospects for the future* (pp. 43–73). New York: Plenum.

Nairne, K. and Smith, G. (1984) *Dealing with depression*, London: The Women's Press.

Nicolson, P. (1986) Developing a feminist approach to depression following childbirth. In S. Wilkinson (ed.) *Feminist social psychology: Developing theory and practice* (pp. 135–49), Milton Keynes: Open University Press.

—— (1992) Explanations of post-natal depression: Structuring knowledge of female psychology. *Research on Language and Social Interaction*, 25, 75–96.

—— (1995) Feminism and psychology. In J.A. Smith, R. Harré, and L. Van Langenhove (eds) *Rethinking psychology* (pp. 122–42), London: Sage.

—— (1998) *Post-natal depression: Psychology, science, and the transition to motherhood*, London: Routledge.

Nolen-Hoeksema, S. (1987) Sex differences in unipolar depression: Evidence and theory. *Psychological Bulletin*, 101, 259–82.

—— (1990) *Sex differences in depression*, Stanford, CA: Stanford University Press.

Nolen-Hoeksema, S., and Girgus, J. (1994) The emergence of gender differences in depression during adolescence. *Psychological Bulletin*, 115, 424–43.

Nylund, D., and Ceske, K. (1997) Voices of political resistance: Young women's co-research on anti-depression. In C. Smith and D. Nylund (eds) *Narrative therapies with children and adolescents* (pp. 356–81), New York: Guilford.

Oakley, A. (1986) Beyond the yellow wallpaper. In A. Oakley *Telling the truth about Jerusalem* (pp. 131–48), Oxford: Blackwell.

Ogden, J. (1997) The rhetoric and reality of psychosocial theories of health. *Journal of Health Psychology*, 2, 21–9.

Oinas, E. (1998) Medicalization by whom? Accounts of menstruation conveyed by young women and medical experts in medical advisory columns. *Sociology of Health & Illness*, 20, 52–70.

Olfson, M.D., and Klerman, G.L. (1993) Trends in prescription of antidepressants by office-based psychiatrists. *American Journal of Psychiatry*, 150, 571–7.

Parker, I., Georgaca, E., Harper, D., McLaughlin, T., and Stowell-Smith, M. (1995) *Deconstructing psychopathology*, London: Sage.

Parlee, M.B. (1992) On PMS and psychiatric abnormality. *Feminism & Psychology*, 2, 105–8.

Paykel, E.S. (1991) Depression in women. *British Journal of Psychiatry*, 10, 22–9.

Penfold, P.S., and Walker, G.A. (1983) *Women and the psychiatric paradox*, Montreal: Eden Press.

Perkins, R. (1994) Choosing ECT. *Feminism & Psychology*, 4, 623–7.

Petersen, A.C., Compas, B.E., Brooks-Gunn, J., Stemmler, M., Ey, S., and Grant, K.E. (1993) Depression in adolescence. *American Psychologist*, 48, 155–68.

Phares, E.J. (1984) *Introduction to personality* (2e), Glenview, IL: Scott, Foresman.

Phoenix, A., Woollett, A., and Lloyd, E. (eds) (1991) *Motherhood: Meanings, practices and ideologies*, London: Sage.

Pipher, M. (1994) *Reviving Ophelia: Saving the selves of adolescent girls*, New York: Ballantine.

Polkinghorne, D.E. (1992) Postmodern epistemology in practice. In S. Kvale (ed.) *Psychology and postmodernism* (pp. 146–65), London: Sage.

Pollock, K. (1988) On the nature of social stress: Production of a modern mythology. *Social Science and Medicine*, 26, 381–92.

Popay, J. (1992) "My health is all right, but I'm just tired all the time": Women's experience of ill health. In H. Roberts (ed.) *Women's health matters* (pp. 99–120), London: Routledge.

Radloff, L.S. (1977) The CES-D scale: A self-report depression scale for research in the general population. *Journal of Applied Psychological Measurement*, 1, 385–401.

Raston, C. (1998, March) *Employment in Britain*, London: The Foreign and Commonwealth Office.

Regier, D.A., Narrow, W.E., Rae, D.S., Manderscheid, R.W., Locke, B.Z., and Goodwin, F.K. (1993) The de facto US mental and addictive disorders service system. Epidemiological catchment area prospective 1-year prevalence rates of disorders and services. *Archives of General Psychiatry*, 50, 85–94.

Renshaw, D.C. (1994) Beacons, breasts, symbols, sex and cancer. *Theoretical Medicine*, 15, 349–60.

Richardson, J.T.E. (ed.) (1996) *Handbook of qualitative research methods for psychology and the social sciences*, Leicester: BPS Books.

Riger, S. (1992) Epistemological debates: Feminist voices. *American Psychologist*, 47, 730–40.

Ristock, J.L. and Pennell, J. (1996) *Community research as empowerment: Feminist links, postmodern interruptions*, Toronto: Oxford University Press.

Robins, C.J., Ladd, J., Welkowitz, J., Blaney, P.H., Diaz, R., and Kutcher, G. (1994) Personal style inventory: Preliminary validation studies of new measures of sociotropy and autonomy. *Journal of Psychopathology and Behavioral Assessment*, 16, 277–300.

Ross, C.A., and Pam, A. (1995) *Pseudoscience in biological psychiatry: Blaming the body*, New York: Wiley.

Ross, C.E., and Mirowsky, J. (1988) Child care and emotional adjustment to wives' employment. *Journal of Health and Social Behavior*, 29, 127–38.

Rostosky, S.S., and Travis, C.B. (1996) Menopause research and the dominance of the biomedical model 1984–1994. *Psychology of Women Quarterly*, 20, 285–312.

Rothfield, P. (1997) Menopausal embodiment. In P.A. Komesaroff, P. Rothfield, and J. Daly (eds) *Reinterpreting menopause: Cultural and philosophical issues* (pp. 32–53), New York: Routledge.

Rude, S.S., and Burnham, B.L. (1995) Connectedness and neediness: Factors of the DEQ and SAS dependency scales. *Cognitive Therapy & Research*, 19, 323–40.

Russell, D. (1995) *Women, madness and medicine*, Cambridge: Polity Press.

Scattolon, Y. (1999) *Perceptions of Depression and Coping with Depressive Experiences among Rural Women in New Brunswick*. Unpublished Doctoral Dissertation, University of New Brunswick, Fredericton, Canada.

Scattolon, Y. and Stoppard, J.M. (1999) "Getting on with Life": Women's experiences and ways of coping with depression. *Canadian Psychology*, 40, 205–19.

Schneider, L.S. (1996) Biological commonalities among aging, depression, and suicidal behavior. In G.J. Kennedy (ed.) *Suicide and depression in late life: Critical issues in treatment, research and public policy* (pp. 39–50), New York: Wiley.

Schreiber, R. (1996) (Re)defining my self: Women's process of recovery from depression. *Qualitative Health Research*, 6, 469–91.

Selye, H. (1956) *The stress of life*. New York: McGraw-Hill.

Seu, I.B. and Heenan, M.C. (1998) *Feminism and psychotherapy: Reflections on contemporary theories and practices*, London: Sage.

Shapiro-Baruch, A. (1995) The dismissal of female clients' reports of medication side effects: A first hand account. *Women & Therapy*, 16, 113–27.

Slife, B.D., and Williams, R.N. (1997) Toward a theoretical psychology. *American Psychologist*, 52, 117–29.

Smith, D.E. (1987) *The everyday world as problematic: A feminist sociology*, Toronto: University of Toronto Press.

—— (1990) The statistics on women and mental illness: The relations of ruling they conceal. In D.E. Smith *The conceptual practices of power: A feminist sociology of knowledge* (pp. 107–38), Toronto: University of Toronto Press.

Smith, J.A., Harré, R., and Van Langenhove, L. (1995) *Rethinking psychology*, London: Sage.

Smith, W. and Richman, A. (1984). Electroconvulsive therapy: A Canadian perspective. *Canadian Journal of Psychiatry*, 29, 693–9.

Stanton, A.L., and Danoff-Burg, S. (1995) Selected issues in women's reproductive health: Psychological perspectives. In A.L. Stanton and S.J. Gallant (eds) *Psychology and women's health: Progress and challenges in research and application* (pp. 261–305), Washington, DC: American Psychological Association.

Stark-Adamec, C., Stoppard, J.M., Pyke, S.W., Baruss, I., and Arlett, C. (1986, March) *Sex and gender differences in mental health morbidity*, report prepared for the Mental Health Division, Health and Welfare Canada, Ottawa.

Stearns, C.Z. (1993) Sadness. In M. Lewis and J.M. Haviland (eds) *Handbook of emotions* (pp. 547–61), New York: Guilford.

Stearns, P.N. (1994) *American cool: Constructing a twentieth century emotional style*, New York: New York University Press.

Stiles, W.B. (1993) Quality control in qualitative research. *Clinical Psychology Review*, 13, 593–618.

Stoppard, J.M. (1989) An evaluation of the adequacy of cognitive/behavioral theories for understanding depression in women. *Canadian Psychology*, 30, 39–47.

—— (1993) Gender, psychosocial factors and depression. In P. Cappeliez and R.J. Flynn (eds) *Depression and the social environment: Research and intervention with neglected populations* (pp. 121–49), Montreal and Kingston: McGill-Queen's University Press.

—— (1997) Women's bodies, women's lives and depression: Towards a reconciliation of material and discursive accounts. In J.M. Ussher (ed.) *Body talk: The material and discursive regulation of sexuality, madness and reproduction* (pp. 10–32), London: Routledge.

—— (1999) Why new perspectives are needed for understanding depression in women. *Canadian Psychology*, 40, 79–90.

Surrey, J.L. (1991) The "self-in-relation": A theory of women's development. In J.V. Jordan, A.G. Kaplan, J.B. Miller, I.P Stiver, and J.L. Surrey (eds) *Women's growth in connection: Writings from the Stone Center* (pp. 51–66), New York: Guilford.

Swann, C.J., and Ussher, J.M. (1995) A discourse analytic approach to women's experience of premenstrual syndrome. *Journal of Mental Health*, 4, 359–67.

Szekely, E.A. (1988) *Never too thin*, Toronto: Women's Press.

—— (1993, February) *Can feminist therapy be practiced in a medical-hospital setting?* Paper presented at a conference on Eating Disorders and Body Image: Can Feminist and Medical Approaches Work Together?, The Toronto Hospital, Toronto, Canada.

Taylor, V. (1996) *Rock-a-by baby: Feminism, self-help and postpartum depression*, New York: Routledge.

Thompson, J.M. (1995) Silencing the self: Depressive symptomatology and close relationships. *Psychology of Women Quarterly*, 19, 337–53.

Thorne, B. (1993). *Gender play: Girls and boys in school*, New Brunswick, NJ: Rutgers University Press.

Tizard, B. (1991) Employed mothers and the care of young children. In A. Phoenix, A. Woollett, and E. Lloyd (eds) *Motherhood: Meanings, practices and ideologies* (pp. 178–94), London: Sage.

Tolman, D.L. (1994) Doing desire: Adolescent girls' struggles for/with sexuality. *Gender & Society*, 8, 324–42.

Tolman, D. L., and Debold, E. (1994) Conflicts of body and image: Female adolescents, desire, and the no-body body. In P. Fallon, M. Katzman, and S. Wooley (eds) *Feminist perspectives on eating disorders* (pp. 301–17), New York: Guilford.

Trickett, P.K., and Putnam, F.W. (1993) Impact of child sexual abuse on females: Toward a developmental psychobiological integration, *Psychological Science*, 4, 81–7.

Turner, R.J., and Roszell, P. (1994) Psychosocial resources and the stress process. In W.R. Avison and I.H. Gotlib (eds) *Stress and mental health: Contemporary issues and prospects for the future* (pp. 179–210). New York: Plenum.

Umberson, D., Chen, M.U., House, J.S., Hopkins, K., and Slaten, E. (1996) The effect of social relationships on psychological well-being: Are men and women really so different? *American Sociological Review*, 61, 837–57.

United Nations Development Program [UNDP] (1995) *Human Development Report*. New York: Oxford University Press.

Ussher, J.M. (1989) *The psychology of the female body*, London: Routledge.

—— (1991) *Women's madness: Misogyny or mental illness?*, Hemel Hempstead: Harvester Wheatsheaf.

—— (1992) Science sexing psychology. In J.M. Ussher and P. Nicolson (eds) *Gender issues in clinical psychology* (pp. 39–67), London: Routledge.

—— (1997a) *Body talk: The material and discursive regulation of sexuality, madness and reproduction*, London: Routledge.

—— (1997b) *Fantasies of femininity: Reframing the boundaries of sex*, London: Penguin.

van den Hoonaard, D.K. (November,1996) On her own: Older women's experiences of widowhood. In proceedings of an inter-disciplinary research conference: *Research into healthy aging: Challenges in changing times* (pp. 284–97), Halifax, Nova Scotia, Canada.

Van Langenhove, L. (1995) The theoretical foundations of experimental psychology and its alternatives. In J.A. Smith, R. Harré, and L. Van Langenhove (eds) *Rethinking psychology* (pp.10–23), London: Sage.

Wade, T.C. and Wade, D.K. (1995) Biopsychiatric attacks on women: An aberration or a predictable outcome of biopolitics? *Women & Therapy*, 16, 143–61.

Walker, A. (1995) Theory and methodology in premenstrual syndrome research. *Social Science and Medicine*, 41, 793–800.

Walker, A.E. (1997) *The menstrual cycle*, London: Routledge.

Walters, V. (1993) Stress, anxiety and depression: Women's accounts of their health problems. *Social Science and Medicine*, 36, 393–402.

Weaver, J.J. and Ussher, J.M. (1997) How motherhood changes life – a discourse analytic study with mothers of young children. *Journal of Reproductive and Infant Psychology*, 15, 51–68.

Weissman, M.M., Bland, R., Joyce, P.R., Newman, S., Wells J.E., and Wittchen, H. (1993) Sex differences in rates of depression: Cross-national perspectives. *Journal of Affective Disorders*, 29, 77–84.

Weissman, M.M., and Klerman, G. (1977) Sex differences and the epidemiology of depression. *Archives of General Psychiatry*, 34, 98–111.

—— (1987) Gender and depression. In R. Formanek and A. Gurian (eds) *Women and depression: A lifespan perspective* (pp. 3–15), New York: Springer.

Weissman, M.M., and Olfson, M. (1995) Depression in women: Implications for health care research. *Science*, 269, 799–801.

Wetherell, M. (1995) Romantic discourse and feminist analysis: Interrogating investment, power and desire. In S. Wilkinson and C. Kitzinger (eds) *Feminism and discourse: Psychological perspectives* (pp. 128–44), London: Sage.

Whiffen, V.E. (1992) Is post partum depression a distinct diagnosis? *Clinical Psychology Review*, 12, 485–508.

Whiffen, V.E., and Clark, S.E. (1997) Does victimization account for sex differences in depressive symptoms? *British Journal of Clinical Psychology*, 36, 185–93.

Whitley, B.E. (1985) Sex-role orientation and psychological well-being: Two meta-analyses. *Sex Roles*, 12, 207–25.

Whitley, B.E., and Gridley, B.E. (1993) Sex-role orientation, self-esteem, and depression: A latent-variables analysis. *Personality and Social Psychology Bulletin*, 19, 363–9.

Wilkinson, S. (1988) The role of reflexivity in feminist psychology. *Women's Studies International Forum*, 11, 493–502.

Wilson, G. (1995) "I'm the eyes and she's the arms": Changes in gender roles in advanced old age. In S. Arber and J. Ginn (eds) *Connecting gender and ageing: A sociological approach* (pp. 98–113), Buckingham: Open University.

Wolf, N. (1991) *The beauty myth: How images of beauty are used against women*, New York: Morrow.

Wood, L., and Rennie, H. (1994). Formulating rape: The discursive construction of victims and villains. *Discourse & Society*, 5, 125–48.

Woolgar, S. (1988) *Science: The very idea*, London: Tavistock.

Woollett, A. (1991) Having children: Accounts of childless women and women with reproductive problems. In A. Phoenix, A. Woollett, and E. Lloyd (eds) *Motherhood: Meanings, practices and ideologies* (pp. 47–65), London: Sage.

Woollett, A. and Marshall, H. (1997) Discourses of pregnancy and childbirth. In L. Yardley (ed.) *Material discourses of health and illness* (pp. 176–98), London: Routledge.

Worell, J. and Remer, P. (1992) *Feminist perspectives in therapy: An empowerment model for women*, Chichester, UK: Wiley.

Worthman, C.M. (1995) Hormones, sex, and gender. *Annual Review of Anthropology*, 24, 593–616.

Yardley, L. (1996) Reconciling discursive and materialist perspectives on health and illness: A reconstruction of the biopsychosocial approach. *Theory and Psychology*, 6, 485–508.

—— (1997a) Introducing discursive methods. In L. Yardley (ed.) *Material discourses of health and illness* (pp. 25–49), London: Routledge.

—— (1997b) Introducing material–discursive approaches to health and illness. In L. Yardley (ed.) *Material discourses of health and illness* (pp. 1–24), London: Routledge.

—— (1997c) *Material discourses of health and illness*, London: Routledge.

—— (1997d) Reconstructing the body-concept: Review essay. *British Journal of Psychology*, 88, 709–13.

Zelizer, V.A. (1985) *Pricing the priceless child: The changing social welfare of children*, New York: Basic.

AUTHOR INDEX

SUBJECT INDEX